STRATEGY & TACTICS OF THE
GREAT GENERALS AND THEIR BATTLES

STRATEGY & TACTICS OF THE

GREAT GENERALS AND THEIR BATTLES

FOREWORD BY GENERAL OMAR BRADLEY
EDITED BY BRIGADIER PETER YOUNG

BISON BOOKS CORP

Published by Bison Books Corp, 17 Sherwood Place,
Greenwich CT 06830 USA

Copyright © 1984 Bison Books Corp.

ISBN 0 86124 195 9
Printed in Hong Kong

CONTENTS

FOREWORD BY GENERAL OMAR N. BRADLEY

At a time in history when the impact of technology and the machine threatens to overwhelm the role of the individual, it is well to be reminded of the unique importance of man, in particular of the lone leader, acting solely on the basis of his courage, intelligence, and imagination, who by his action or example affects the course of the world. *The Victors* provides a vivid picture of 16 military leaders and the battles in which they won crucial victories. These men, all of whom lived within the past two centuries, are sterling examples of the power of leadership and the individual in a world too often neglectful of their roles.

This book describes major battles in six great conflicts, from the Napoleonic wars through the Korean war, and shows how in each of these the actions of a single leader were crucial to its outcome. Readers may not always agree with the author's interpretations, but they will nevertheless come away from these pages with an increased awareness that in the bloody test of warfare the individual remains the key to victory.

The two outstanding leaders of the Napoleonic wars were clearly Napoleon himself and his British opponent, the Duke of Wellington. We see Napoleon at probably his greatest victory – the battle of Austerlitz, where he cleverly destroyed a larger allied force in a remarkable display of brilliance and audacity. He demonstrated at once his skill both as a planner and as a leader who exercised firm and knowledgeable control of events once the battle was joined. At Waterloo, where Wellington defeated him in a decisive contest, the British commander emerges clearly as a wise, experienced soldier with the ability to improvise and the tact and personal flexibility to work with a frustrating combination of allies.

From the age of Napoleon, we move forward to the American Civil War, that great, bloody conflict that split the nation and created and destroyed military reputations with cruel finality. The three commanders discussed here are interesting contrasts: Grant, the silent, dogged, crushing campaigner; Meade, the controversial, careful architect of victory; and Lee, the brilliant commander who aroused excitement and adoration more, perhaps, than any other military leader of the war. Our view of Grant is the Grant of Vicksburg, perhaps his most brilliant victory, where the Union general's persistence, courage, and singleness of purpose, more than anything else, determined the outcome of the battle. For Meade, of course, Gettysburg is the obvious

battle. The author recounts Meade's skillful check of Lee's advance; his careful, almost methodical stemming of the Confederate tide; and finally his controversial failure to destroy Lee and his army. Lee himself was probably at his best at Chancellorsville, where his keen ability to divine his foe's intentions, his magnificent command presence and his clear tactical excellence determined the outcome of the fight. The author here pays equal tribute to Jackson at Chancellorsville, and the reader may judge for himself where lies the greater merit.

A few years later, the figure of General von Moltke emerges as a decisive player in the Franco-Prussian war, specifically at the crucial battle of Sedan. Moltke, of course, is famous more as a planner than as a commander, and at Sedan he displayed his keenness, flexibility, imagination and ability to improvise. He demonstrated a different form of leadership than most of the others described in this book, and his brilliance is thus even more outstanding.

World War I provides the opportunity to examine four major commanders, all Europeans and all involved in critical actions. Field Marshal von Hindenburg was the German commander at the battle of Tannenburg, a victory that crushed forever the military hopes of Czarist Russia. Although the author of this account slights Hindenburg's contribution in favor of the important role of General Ludendorff, Hindenburg really deserves primary credit: he held command responsibility, approved all actions and on occasion even had to steady Ludendorff's nerve. All in all, it is a fascinating battle.

Three desperate contests on the western front complete our look at World War I. At the first battle of the Marne, the French General Joffre skillfully halted the onrushing German offensive. While the author of this account gives equal credit for the victory to General Galliéni, Joffre must receive substantial praise for conceiving and carrying out the strategy that transformed humiliating French defeats into a great strategic victory. Two years later, at Verdun, General Pétain displayed stubborn determination to resist repeated German onslaughts. By careful use of limited resources, he halted the enemy, restored French morale, and saved a cause that seemed hopelessly endangered. Finally, the crucial 'Black Day' in August 1918 sealed the fate of the German army and provided Field Marshal Haig with his greatest triumph. Criticized for the oppressively heavy casualties British troops had suffered earlier, Haig here demonstrated the will, imagination and fortitude without which victory would have been impossible. His singleminded concentration on the enemy's weaknesses rather than his own demonstrated an attribute of military leadership too often forgotten in less favorable appraisals.

World War II is represented by five victorious commanders. The first, General Guderian, developed the combined arms-mobile warfare tactics that brought rapid success to German arms in the early stages of the war. The battle of the Meuse shows him to have been an innovative, brilliant and daring leader, the foremost practitioner of *blitzkrieg* in the German army. His compatriot, General Rommel, was almost equally a master of this new form of slashing warfare. A bold and flexible commander, he demonstrated at Tobruk his skill and imagination, resourceful qualities later to be dimmed in the tragic final days of his life. His opponent in one of the war's decisive battles was the British General Montgomery. At El Alamein, Montgomery's careful skill and detailed precision took the measure of the more flamboyant Rommel. Controversial though this victory was, it was Montgomery nonetheless who demonstrated what the historian of this battle calls the 'self-confidence, determination and rapport with the ranks to elicit the dogged, unremitting effort that eventually resulted in the British victory.'

The single American representative of World War II — General George Patton — was a brilliant, aggressive, hot-tempered and overwhelming commander. Above all, he was controversial. The description here of his role in the Battle of the Bulge clearly shows his mastery not only of the armored forces that gave him fame, but also of the combined tank, infantry, artillery, air and support units that together won this superb victory.

The final World War II leader on display is the impressive Soviet commander, Marshal Zhukov. Zhukov — who organized and commanded massive armies, threw them into battle with careful staff work and preparations and combined the elements of modern armored warfare to win great battles like the one described here at Berlin — was ruthless in his sacrifice of life to achieve his ends. In this he may be typical of Soviet leadership, but there is no denying his place among the great victors of World War II.

The last commander discussed in these pages is the American General MacArthur. He appears here, not in his role as an architect of victory in the Pacific during World War II, but rather in the dramatic Korean setting of the landing at Inchon. While critics will probably always argue over the merits of this bold coup, it epitomized a courageous leader who combined skill, self-assurance, imagination and determination to win a battle unparalleled for drama and effect.

The 16 leaders thus described exemplify the characteristics of leadership and command so necessary for military success. The battles that gave them fame are equally illustrative of combat at its fiercest. Together these victors and their triumphs offer a fascinating view of the art of war.

OMAR N. BRADLEY
General of the Army

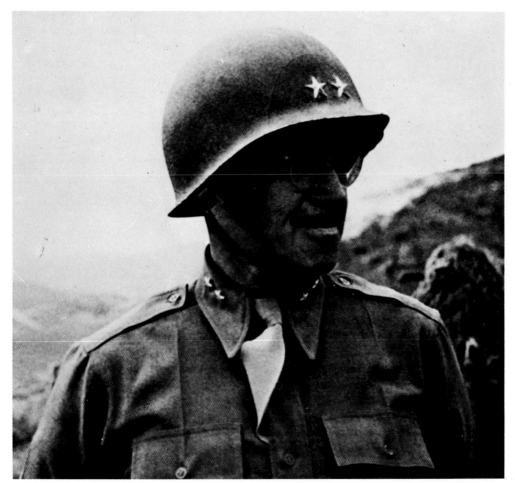

General of the Army Omar Nelson Bradley, one of America's most distinguished soldiers. During World War II he served as a corps commander in Sicily and North Africa before moving to Britain to join the preparations for the invasion of France. After commanding First US Army at D-Day he led 12th Army Group until the end of the war in Europe. After World War II he was Chief of Staff of the US Army and was appointed Chairman of the Joint Chiefs of Staff in 1949. He was promoted to the rank of five-star general in 1950.

INTRODUCTION

After the disgraceful rout at Castlebar (27 August 1798) the Duke of Ormonde, the commander of the Kilkenny Militia, remarked that the British would have done better had there been no generals present. It was not the first nor the last occasion upon which such a thought occurred to a British colonel. No doubt that is true of other armies as well. How, for example, would the 7th Cavalry have got on had General Custer not been present at the Little Big Horn? (26 June 1876). Perhaps they would have stayed on their horses, and carved their way out. It was said of Inkerman (5 November 1854) that it was a soldiers' battle fought in a fog, the implication being that the generals, unable to see what was going on, could not influence the battle one way or the other. They could bring up reinforcements, but they could not tell what they were doing. Perhaps things had been much the same at Auerstadt (14 October 1806), when the Prussians, 63,000 strong, encountered a French corps (26,000) in a fog. They ought to have won, but unfortunately for them the French commander, Marshal Louis-Nicolas Davout was practically blind anyway: to him the 'fog of war' was no worse than usual and so he was able to sort things out very satisfactorily.

This 'fog of war' is a very real thing, and it is the general's job to pierce it, to answer the plaintive cry of his staff officers: 'What the hell is going on now?' Wellington had this gift, that is, the imagination to divine what was happening on 'the other side of the hill' as he put it, whether it was Soult, Massena or Napoleon himself that he had to deal with.

The other thing which every general is up against is what Clausewitz called *friction de guerre*, and which may be translated as 'grit in the works.' It can never be altogether eradicated, there will always be valiant busybodies with a genius for misunderstanding their orders, even though accidents can to some extent be avoided by foresight and by training.

What qualities would you look for if it fell to your lot to sit on a selection board charged with the promotion of general officers? Had you been one of Barras' colleagues would you have sent the young Bonaparte to Italy in 1796? Had Abraham Lincoln sought your advice would you have spoken up for Meade, or Reynolds or who. (There was not that much talent in the Army of the Potomac!) Would you have advised Winston S Churchill to send Montgomery to try conclusions with Rommel? Even with hindsight it is hard to say whether good decisions were made in these three cases. Bonaparte was to supplant the benefactors, who had given him a fair wind, and was to plunge Europe into wars of unprecedented violence. Meade, for all his good qualities, hardly ranks with the great captains of all time — the infamous Sherman, who does not figure in these pages, was, and it gives me no pleasure to say so, a much better general. As for the Montgomery problem it is difficult to see how, given the same quantity of reinforcements, and weapons, Auchinleck, who was after all an excellent tactician, could have failed to destroy the Afrika Korps. He might even

have followed up victory with a relentless pursuit.

The victors paraded in these pages are 16 in number and the victories chosen to illustrate their talents fall in the 145 year period from 1805 to 1950. Some of them lived to a great age, and some did not. It is said that 'All they that take the sword shall perish with the sword' (St Matthew's gospel). This lot did not. Patton was the victim of a traffic accident and Rommel was compelled, by Hitler's agents, to take poison. The rest, it seems, died in their beds.

Other things being equal it is thought that a good young general is more likely to be useful than a good old one. Who can say? When Napoleon and Wellington, both born in 1769, met at Waterloo the one was stout and sick, the other young and brisk. Of the rest only Rommel, one of the youngest of all those under discussion, was seriously hampered by ill health during his campaigning days.

Needless to say some of these generals were more successful than others. Zhukov, who was only 48 when he took Berlin, alone of the 16 began his military career as a private soldier; from a brave NCO in the Czarist Army he became 'the general who never lost a battle.' Wellington and Moltke could certainly claim the same distinction, while Napoleon and Lee, for all their talents could not. Indeed had Napoleon been the servant of the French government instead of the Emperor one may doubt whether he would have been employed after 1812. The Moscow campaign, Leipzig and Waterloo were disasters that few reputations could have survived — except that of a Head of State!

Wellington would stand high in the list of the world's great generals, if only because he did not allow himself to be hypnotized by Napoleon's reputation, but — with a rather indifferent army — meted out to the Emperor the same treatment he had so often meted out to his marshals. 'Ça peut être une bataille d'Espagne' said General Reille before the fight began. How right he proved. Napoleon proved no better able than Massena or Soult to solve the problems set by the defensive tactics which Wellington had perfected in the Peninsula. Moltke, one feels, would have approved of Wellington's ideas for not only did they both excel in the fields of staff work and logistics, but Moltke was 'the first to realize the great defensive power of modern firearms, and . . . inferred from it that an enveloping attack had become more formidable than the attempt to pierce an enemy's front' (Henry Spencer Wilkinson). Moltke's work is represented here by Sedan, but Königgratz (1866) was no less a masterpiece. He was an extraordinary man — scholar, traveller, strategist and linguist. He was so taciturn that he was said to be 'silent in seven languages.' His tall, spare figure, his tanned old face, his marvellous discretion all contributed to the legend of the 'man of gold,' the ideal character whom all admired, and who had no enemies. It is not given to many generals to make such an impression upon their contemporaries!

Robert E Lee enjoyed a rather similar reputation in the Confederate States' Army. It is true that he did not have a record of unbroken success to compare with those of Wellington or Moltke. Lee's ill-equipped armies were always outnumbered. In 1861 he was offered the command of all federal forces, and only rejected it because his own state, Virginia, seemed about to secede. The war between the States might have been brief indeed had Robert E Lee been Mr Lincoln's general. It is an interesting speculation.

Meade was a good officer, loyal and strict, and as the victory of Gettysburg deserves respect but he can scarcely be awarded a place among the great captains of all time. Nor can Ulysses S Grant, who, though he picked up his trade as he went along, was never more than a 'good, plain cook.' Hindenburg, too, has no serious claim to be considered one of the great captains. In fact, he merely supplied the backbone and personality for his chief of staff. Ludendorff had the brains and Hindenburg had the nerve, and at Tannenberg Hoffman provided the plan.

Joffre, though scarcely a thunderbolt of war, must take much of the credit for his one great victory, the Marne. He displayed throughout a monumental *phlegme*. He strained every nerve to see that the line did not break. Saddled with a fool for an ally – Sir John French – he managed by sheer force of personality to shame him into cooperation at the vital moment. Above all he proved ruthless in sacking the numerous generals who failed. He had determined and intelligent support from Messimy, the Minister for War, and from General Galliéni, the Governor of Paris, and one could say that the victory of the Marne was won by a triumvirate. Still let us not rob this phlegmatic Frenchman of his one great triumph. To his British allies, Joffre, with his monumental calm seemed very far from their idea of the volatile, unpredictable Gallic warrior. Somehow the conditions of 1914 demanded a Joffre. Who else of the French generals of 1914 could have survived the stresses and strains of the Battle of the Marne? It is not easy to supply a name. By 1940 his staff officer, Gamelin, had attained his rank. The little man was not the one to wield his master's sword. He had forgotten that an army must be prepared to take the offensive!

Haig is a very much underrated officer. His career commands but little interest these days. But is this fair? He had distinguished himself in the Sudan and in the Boer War and was a thoroughly well-trained officer, who had held appointments of the first importance. It is damning him with faint praise to say that he was a much better general than French, whom he succeeded, and in fact the worst things one can say of him is that – in an infantry/artillery war – he was a cavalryman, brought up to a very different style of fighting, and that he was incapable of talking to the soldiers in the 'matey' sort of way that Montgomery used to do in World War II – Haig had been properly brought up. The Somme and Passchendaele were at best Pyrrhic victories, but the same cannot be said of the great series of battles in which, between 8 August and 11 November 1918, his armies pressed forward and broke the Hindenburg Line. Haig was the first of the Allied leaders to sense that the war could be won in 1918. In an order issued to his armies in the third week of August, he said that the situation had changed decisively, and that the time had come to press the enemy everywhere with the utmost energy. At this time Foch, no pessimist, was hoping for victory in

1919, while the British government was planning to make a final effort in 1920. Those who think of Haig as a butcher will do well to consider how many thousands of lives were saved by bringing the war to a swifter conclusion. After the war Haig devoted himself tirelessly to the cause of his old soldiers, uniting the various organizations for ex-service men into the British Legion, the largest benevolent organization ever created in Great Britain. His early death at 67 was evidently due to overwork. Although he did not appeal to the men in the way that Marlborough, Roberts, Wellington or Montgomery did, his veterans turned out in their thousands to line the route of his funeral procession.

MacArthur and Patton, Montgomery, Rommel and Zhukov all distinguished themselves in World War I. MacArthur collected a truly astonishing collection of medals in 1918, but, given the choice, the young Rommel, whose *Infanterie Greift An* (*Infantry Attacks!*) is still a classic, was the man one would choose to serve with! His flair for minor tactics was simply phenomenal. Rommel's personality was such that he was admired by the Eighth Army almost as much as by the Afrika Korps. In 1940 Guderian, with his 'get-a-move-on' attitude had shown the same flair for leadership. It came naturally. MacArthur, Patton and Montgomery all built themselves up as 'characters' in a way that was quite deliberate. Distasteful though it may seem it was no doubt a sensible exercise in Public Relations. Omar Bradley and 'Lightning Joe' Collins were more fortunate. The Press Corps took to them and no doubt to their surprise and amusement they found the title 'GI's general' conferred upon them. Nobody worked harder on his own image than Viscount Montgomery of Alamein – so much so that it is difficult to tell the substance from the shadow. He was well-served by his Chief of Staff, de Guingand, and by Sir Miles Dempsey, the commander, from Normandy to the Baltic, of the British Second Army – a man who was not in search of laurels and left no memoirs! If many an officer, British as well as Allied, found Montgomery abrasive and egocentric, he did not lack for a following of those who welcomed his firm hand on the wheel and were prepared to take him at his own valuation. The fact is that he *did* have good ideas in the field of planning, training and morale. The present writer commanded a unit in three of his campaigns. When Montgomery was in command the British soldier simply did not believe that he could be beaten. If that is not a pearl of great pride I know nothing. Success is what counts in war. Men who must stake their lives in battle do not like to think that they may be throwing them away in vain. After all, with the exception of Arnhem, Montgomery's plans worked pretty well.

We live, we are often told, in an age when the young – those of military age– are devoted to drink, drugs, vandalism and violence. From their ranks may rise an alcoholic hooligan with just sufficient talent to steer one or other of the great powers to the conquest of the world: a world so ravaged as to be a prize that no sensible person would wish to win. World War II has had its critics, but I am glad that it fell to my lot to go through that one, rather than the nuclear holocaust we are promised for next time. Who will be the Victors then?

Peter Young.

NAPOLEON AT AUSTERLITZ 1805

Marshal Louis-Alexandre Berthier, Napoleon's Chief of Staff, described Austerlitz as 'the Emperor Napoleon's most famous victory.' It was certainly one of the Emperor's most impressive achievements. On 2 December 1805, deep inside hostile territory between the Moravian towns of Brünn and Olmütz, he inflicted a catastrophic defeat on a numerically superior Allied army. It was certainly not his first victory, nor was it to be his last. The campaign and battle of Austerlitz must, however, rank among the most remarkable episodes of a dazzling career.

The 2 December was a fitting date for victory. Only a year before Austerlitz, on 2 December 1804, Napoleon had crowned himself Emperor of the French in the Cathedral of Notre Dame. This in itself was no mean feat, representing as it did the culmination of a rise from obscure origins to undisputed eminence within the state. Born at Ajaccio in Corsica in 1769, Napoleon Bonaparte was commissioned into the French artillery in 1785. The turmoils which followed the revolution, and his distinguished performance at the siege of Toulon in 1793, facilitated his speedy promotion, and 1796 saw him set the seal on his rising military reputation in the brilliant Italian campaign. His subsequent adventures in Egypt brought him few laurels, but his failure in the East did not prevent him from returning to France and replacing the Directory with the Consulate. The aspiring general became First Consul and, in the summer of 1802, with fresh victories over the Austrians to his credit, he was voted Consul for life.

Napoleon spent 1801–03 in the reorganization and revival of France. Fruitful though these efforts were, they brought him domestic but not international stability. War between Britain and France flared up once more in May 1803; the British blockaded French ports and began to seize French colonies, while Napoleon responded by closing European ports to British trade and assembling a formidable army of invasion on the channel coast. Britain naturally sought continental allies, and attracted Russia and Austria, followed by Sweden and Naples, into an anti-French league, the Third Coalition. Prussia remained neutral, but Spain, Bavaria and Württemberg adhered to France. The Coalition's war plan was complex. The Austrian Archduke Charles commanded a powerful Austro-Russian force in northern Italy, and a smaller Austrian army under the Archduke John was stationed in the Tyrol. Further north, the Archduke Ferdinand, under the tutelage of his Chief of Staff, General Mack, threatened Bavaria. From the northeast came the doughty warriors of Holy Russia. One army under General Levin Bennigsen approached Prussia, while another, led by the plump and avuncular General Mikhail Ilarionovich Kutuzov, marched toward the Upper Danube to join with Ferdinand. Between these two great columns tramped a third under General Buxhöwden, who was to support Bennigsen before moving south to join Kutuzov. Away to the north an improbable association of Russians and Swedes was, with British assistance, to advance from Stralsund to Hanover, and on the southern flank an Anglo-Russian force was to appear in northern Italy.

An ambitious plan like this, filling the map of Europe with converging forces, would have been difficult enough to execute if slick staff work and wholehearted cooperation had been features of the alliance. As things were, the scheme was flawed from its inception by convoluted command arrangements and serious inter-Allied misunderstandings. Among the latter was the failure to appreciate that the Austrian and Russian calendars differed by 10 days, an oversight which was to have unfortunate consequences.

While the Allied projects took shape, the bulk of the French army was concentrated around Boulogne on the channel coast in preparation for a descent on England. By mid-August 1805 this operation seemed less practicable than ever, and Napoleon realized that the inability of the French and Spanish fleets to keep the British out of the channel rendered a crossing impossible. Moreover, the situation in Central Europe grew more ominous day by day. The Emperor therefore decided to shelve his plans for an invasion of England, and to march eastward with all possible speed, falling upon Ferdinand and Mack before going on to deal with the advancing Russians.

Napoleon's plan was nothing if not bold. Speed and secrecy were its prerequisites, but it was no easy task to move an army of over 200,000 men across the face of Europe. That the scheme was at all feasible was a tribute to Napoleon's achievements during his army's stay at Boulogne. The stormy years which followed the Revolution had witnessed the expansion of the French army and the removal of social barriers to promotion. However, until 1803–04 there had been a marked tendency for soldiers to identify more strongly with their division, or with the particular army in which they served, than with the French army as a whole. The Boulogne camp, whatever its real strategic purpose – and there were those who suspected that Napoleon was never entirely serious about the British invasion plan – played a vitally important role in training and unifying the army. It also aided the Emperor's own efforts to consolidate his hold on the army, and to participate in lavish ceremonies which seemed to turn even staunch republicans into devoted supporters of the Empire.

The Austerlitz campaign was to involve about 200,000 French soldiers, just under half the total strength of the *Grande Armée*. The force comprised the Imperial Guard, the Reserve Cavalry and seven corps. Each of the latter consisted of two or more infantry divisions with attached cavalry, artillery and engineers. There was, though, no standard corps organization, and these formations varied in size between Nicolas Jean de Dieu Soult's huge IV Corps with its 41,000 men and the tiny VII Corps of Pierre François Charles Augereau with a mere 15,000. Corps were normally commanded by marshals, a rank reintroduced by Napoleon in 1804. Most of the marshals were astonishingly young; Charles Augereau and Jean-Baptiste Jules Bernadotte however were over 40 years of age. The corps was an essential ingredient of the 1805 plan and, indeed, an indispensable instrument of Napoleonic strategy generally. A corps was self-contained and flexible, and yet used to operating as a cohesive body. Providing that its staff work was sound, an army composed of corps could march divided – easing the pressure on roads and provisioning facilities – but could unite on the battlefield.

If the hard training carried out at the camp of Boulogne had imparted a high gloss to the fighting units and formations of the *Grande Armée*, the same period had witnessed the final development of Imperial Headquarters into the form which, with minor alterations, it was to retain for the next decade. The most important of its three branches was Napoleon's own *Maison*, 'the cabinet of genius,' in which he formulated his detailed plans. Marshal Louis Alexandre Berthier, Napoleon's Chief of Staff until 1814, headed the General Staff of the *Grande Armée*, which dealt with more routine matters of administration. Finally, the General Commissary of Army Stores supervised the acquisition and distribution of stores and supplies of all sorts. The pivot of this entire apparatus was the Emperor himself. His boundless energy and retentive brain dominated Imperial Headquarters, and through it the army as a whole. Although the simple green undress uniform of a colonel of the *Chasseurs à Cheval* of his Guard which the Emperor habitually wore could not conceal his growing corpulence, he was capable of spending hours in the saddle and remaining fresh throughout a 14-hour working day. He lived simply when in the field, spending the night in whatever quarters were available or in his well-equipped coach. His elevation to Imperial honors had little effect upon his campaigning habits; he remained a field commander of almost republican simplicity.

On 27 August Napoleon unleashed the *Grande Armée*. The seven corps, Reserve Cavalry and Imperial Guard scythed through France and the Rhineland, each corps marching on its own axis to finish up on a 70-mile front between Ulm and Ingolstadt on the Danube. Ferdinand and Mack, around Ulm, wrangled over strategy until it was almost too late. The Archduke got away with some cavalry on the night of 14—15 October, but Mack capitulated, with about 24,000 men, on the 20th.

Napoleon's sudden irruption into the Upper Danube brought the Allied war machine grinding to a halt. Kutuzov had been making for Ulm and had reached Braunau on the

Above: General Prince Mikhail Ilarionovich Golenishev-Kutuzov was the formal commander of Austro-Russian armies in 1805. He was regarded as the grand old man of the Russian forces.

Right: Napoleon enters Vienna after the Austrians declared the city open on 12 November 1805.

Far right top: Nicolas Jean-de-Dieu Soult, who was appointed Marshal of the Empire on 19 May 1804.

Far right: Joachim Murat, another of Napoleon's Marshals. His prompt action secured the Vienna bridge without loss of life.

Inn by 23 October. His junction with Mack had been impeded by the rigors of the march as well as the calendar problem; now it would never take place. The French advance was resumed on the 25th, but Kutuzov avoided encirclement and made a successful fighting retreat, crossing the Danube at Krems on 8 November. Four days later the French bluffed their way across the Danube and entered Vienna. On 13 November Joachim Murat, leading the pursuit with his cavalry, was duped into accepting an armistice, and by the time this had been repudiated by an enraged Napoleon Kutuzov had slipped away, although his rearguards fought a brisk action at Shöngraben on the 16th. Three days later the old general and his exhausted force joined Czar Alexander I and the main Russian army near Olmütz. The French reached Brünn on the same day, but the *Grande Armée*, a gruelling campaign of marching and fighting behind it, was so footsore that Napoleon was forced to suspend active operations four days later.

The first phase of Napoleon's daring and dramatic campaign had gone remarkably well. He had marched undetected to the Danube, and gobbled up the luckless Mack. The second phase, his pursuit of Kutuzov, had been rather less satisfactory, although it had brought him the prestigious plum of Vienna. Now opened the third phase, which seemed fraught with peril for the French. In the south, the Archdukes John and Charles were concentrated with a powerful army around Marburg, watched by part of Auguste Frédéric Louis Viesse Marmont's corps. The main Austro-Russian army was at Olmütz, growing stronger by the day as reinforcements tramped in from the East. A force under Ferdinand was approaching Iglau, northwest of Brünn, and threatened the French rear. The Allies might have lost Vienna, but they enjoyed unobstructed communications with Russia and Silesia, and their growing forces threatened the French from three sides. Napoleon, on the other hand, was deep in hostile territory, and at the end of a tenuous line of communications, faced by powerful adversaries eager to revenge the setbacks of the earlier part of the campaign.

Napoleon's response to this seemingly depressing strategic situation was as characteristic as it was brilliant. He shunned the safest course of action, retreat, and decided instead to shatter the Allied threat by defeating its strongest element, the army concentrated around Olmütz. The execution of this plan depended upon an elaborate deception scheme. While Marmont, with instructions to avoid a pitched battle at all costs, stood off the Archdukes in the south, the Guard, Soult, Jean Lannes and three cavalry divisions, concentrated at Brünn, with a hussar brigade forward at Wischau on the Olmütz road. Once the Allies had been lured forward to snap up the forces at Brünn, Louis Nicolas Davout would be summoned from Vienna and Jean-Baptiste Bernadotte from Iglau. This would give Napoleon some 75,000 men as opposed to the 88,000 of the Allied central force. The moves of Bernadotte and Davout had to be accomplished in total secrecy, for if the Allies knew of their arrival around Brünn there was every chance that they would decline to attack — and an Allied attack on his supposedly weak forces was exactly what Napoleon hoped to induce. He expected the Allies to attempt to outflank him from the south; when they did this he planned to launch his own counterattack, stabbing, in the classic pattern of double envelopment, at both flanks of the Allied force.

The plan was perilously finely balanced. It depended upon the Allied commanders taking the bait, and relied upon the Emperor's ability to concentrate rapidly before his enemies realized what was afoot. If the Allies attacked too early – or, indeed, declined to attack at all – then the plan would fail and the ominous strategic situation could only worsen as winter progressed. However, as events were to show, Napoleon had gauged the mood of his opponents precisely. Friction between the Austrians and Russians had worsened; the Russians now professed contempt for the battered remnants of the Austrian army, blaming the reverses of the autumn upon Austrian cowardice or stupidity. Kutuzov remained in nominal command of the Allied army, but real power was in the hands of the young Czar and his coterie of elegant and ambitious advisers. There was general support for a counteroffensive which would teach the upstart Bonaparte a lesson he would never forget, a policy which commended itself not only to the Russians but also to the Emperor Francis of Austria, a

fugitive from his own capital, and to his Chief of Staff, the able but pedantic Major General Weyrother. Wiser heads in the Allied councils recommended caution, but Alexander, lured on by extravagent reports of French demoralization, was eager to bring Napoleon to battle.

On 27–28 November the Allies moved westward from Olmütz, driving in the French outpost line. Napoleon, informed of the move on the afternoon of the 28th, rode forward to see the state of affairs for himself. He now began the delicate process of concentrating his forces east of Brünn, while at the same time giving the Allies the impression that he was afraid of giving battle. General Anne Jean Marie René Savary had been sent on a diplomatic mission to Allied headquarters on the 28th, ostensibly to negotiate but in reality to measure Allied feelings and to convey the impression that Napoleon wished to avoid battle. On the following day Napoleon received a visit from Count Dolgoruki and, although the latter was eventually sent off with a flea in his ear, the incident simply confirmed the Allied leaders in their conviction that they were dealing with a beaten man.

On 29 November both armies slid into position between Brünn and Olmütz. The ground taken up by the French was already familiar to Napoleon. Eight days before he had pointed to a stubby hill, the Santon, and informed his entourage that a battle would take place in that area. Indeed, his engineers and gunners had begun preparing the region for defense almost immediately. Just south of the Santon ran the straight, tree-lined road linking Olmütz with Brünn, where it turned south to Vienna. The so-called Mountains of Moravia, heavily-wooded hills, lay to the northwest, while about five miles southeast of the Santon stood the village of Austerlitz, a cluster of houses around the chateau of Prince Kaunitz. Two miles west of this the ground rose onto the Pratzen plateau. The village of Pratzen lay between the high points of the Pratzeberg and the Staré Vinohrady, in the neck of a small valley on the plateau's western edge. A mile or so west of Pratzen the Goldbach

Top left: Louis-Nicolas Davout was in command of III Corps at Austerlitz.

Left: A Napoleonic War cartoon showing Napoleon playing leapfrog with the nations of Europe.

Right: Napoleon painted by the official court painter, Jacques Louis David.

stream wended its muddy way through the villages of Puntowitz, Kobelnitz, Zokolnitz and Telnitz. At Puntowitz the Goldbach was joined by the Bosenitz stream, which ran through Jirschikowitz before going under the Brünn–Olmütz road a few hundred yards from the Santon. The valley of the Goldbach was boggy, and south of Telnitz, where it joined the Littawa, were a number of shallow fish ponds, covered by a thick layer of ice.

Several details of the ground had brought themselves forcefully to Napoleon's attention. Firstly, the Santon, rising sharply above the surrounding countryside, formed a solid pivot for the French left. It dominated the road, and was of equal value as a defensive buttress or as a spring-board for an advance. Secondly, the soggy valley of the Goldbach, with its miserable villages, had some potential as a temporary defensive line, and at its northern end it formed a useful concentration area, for it was 'dead ground' to observers on the Pratzen. Finally, the Pratzen itself domi-nated the center of the position. It was not as steep as is sometimes supposed; its western and northeastern slopes were easily passable to troops of all arms, but its south-eastern edge, falling away to the valley of the Littawa, was much more precipitous.

On the afternoon of 1 December, Napoleon, his familiar figure muffled up in a singed gray riding coat, established himself on the Zurlan hill, south of the main road, between the Goldbach and Bosenitz streams. Much of his army had already moved into position. Lannes' V Corps, containing the infantry divisions of Suchet and Caffarelli as well as a light cavalry division, held the Santon sector, with a formidable battery on the hill itself. Behind the V Corps were the Imperial Guard and Oudinot's Grenadier Division, in the area of the Zurlan. Bernadotte's I Corps, fresh – if that is quite the right word – from its march from Iglau, stood slightly west of the Zurlan, screened from observation.

The valley of the Goldbach itself was thinly held by the widely extended IV Corps of Soult, whose left was linked to the concentration in the northern sector by Murat's cavalry in Schlapanitz. The villages of Telnitz and Zokolnitz, the latter with its castle and walled game park, were garrisoned by Legrand's division of the IV Corps. Soult's overextension was, to a degree, intentional, being an element of Napo-leon's plan for inducing the Allies to attack his right. In part, however, it reflected the disturbing fact that Davout's III Corps, on the march from Vienna, had not yet arrived. Its leading division did not stumble into Gros-Raigern, south of Telnitz, until after dark, after an exhausting march of 76 miles in 46 hours.

The late arrival of Davout led to a modification of the original plan. Napoleon had hoped to persuade the Allies to attack his weak right-center, in the area of Zokolnitz and Kobelnitz, and then to strike them with his concen-trated forces in the north, along the axis of the main road, and with Davout's corps in the south. By nightfall on the 1st it had become clear to the Emperor that this would not do. Davout's men were simply too tired to participate in a vigorous offensive, and in any case it appeared that the ponderous Allied army was itself edging to the south, extending itself over the ground across which Davout was to have attacked. The two-pronged assault was therefore replaced by an oblique attack, spearheaded by the divisions of Vandamme and Saint-Hilaire (IV Corps), which were to thrust eastward onto the Pratzen once the Allied mass had ground its way onto the plateau's southwestern edge. In the north, Lannes was to hold the Santon, while Bernadotte deployed between Puntowitz and Jirschikowitz in prepara-tion for an assault on Bläswitz. On the southern flank, Legrand's men were to do their best to hold the line of the Goldbach until Davout came up in support. The Guard and Oudinot's Grenadiers were to be held in reserve.

Napoleon's orders went out at about 2000 hours, and the Emperor then dined on his favorite dish of potatoes and onions fried in oil, in the relative comfort of an improvised hut on the Zurlan. He chatted with a small group of senior officers, and snatched some sleep before General Savary awoke him at midnight with the news that the Allies had just entered Telnitz, and were clearly present in great strength on the southern end of the Pratzen. Napoleon

Left: Napoleon and his marshals before the battle on 2 December 1805, from a painting by Carle Vernet.

SITUATION 0900 HRS, 2 DECEMBER, 1805

FRENCH | AUSTRO-RUSSIAN

INFANTRY

CAVALRY

1400 HRS, NAPOLEON'S RIGHT WHEEL (SUPPORTED BY SOULT AND DAVOUT)

BATTLE ENDS, 1700 HRS

© Richard Natkiel, 1981

rode south to see for himself and, after a muddy scramble with a Cossack patrol in the valley of the Goldbach, he established that the Allied advance seemed to have stopped. As he walked back to the Zurlan through the bivouacs of the Guard he was recognized by a grenadier who twisted a wisp of straw into a torch to light the Emperor's way. The man's comrades followed suit, and Napoleon returned to his humble quarters in a blaze of light. Back on the Zurlan, he made some final modifications to his plan to allow for the fact that the Allies had slipped further south than he had originally anticipated. Soult's attack was shifted slightly southward, and Bernadotte's I Corps, although still in reserve, was moved behind Soult's left-hand division, that of Vandamme. Murat's role now assumed greater importance, for the infantry strength of the northern sector had decreased, and Murat's cavalry would have to prevent the French left and center from drifting apart. As the final adjustments to his dispositions took place, in the freezing predawn of 2 December, Napoleon managed to get a little more sleep.

Slumber was the last thing in the minds of most of the Allied commanders. During the night the Allied army swung clumsily forward onto the Pratzen in a plan designed to pulverize the French right and bundle Napoleon back against the mountains of Moravia. This grand design was largely the work of Weyrother, who had expounded it, in somniferous detail, to senior commanders in Kutuzov's headquarters at Krenowitz at about midnight. The attack was to be carried out by a number of mixed columns. On the southern flank, the Austrian Lieutenant General Kienmayer was to screen the left of Lieutenant General Doctorov's 13,500 Russian infantrymen, who were to cross the Goldbach at Telnitz before swinging north. On Doctorov's right the columns of Generals Andrault Langeron and Przbyswski aimed for the country between Telnitz and Zokolnitz, and for the latter village itself. The three southerly columns were to operate under the far from eagle eye of the Russian General Buxhöwden, who seems to have spent much of the time trying to keep the cold at bay by consuming alcohol. North of Buxhöwden's force marched 24,000 infantry under Generals Kollowrath and Miloradovitch, making for the Goldbach around Kobelnitz. Prince John of Liechtenstein's cavalry were to deploy in the area of Bläswitz to link the Allied center to its

General Rapp brings news of the success of the main attack to Napoleon, during the Battle of Austerlitz.

right wing, the detachment of Prince Bagration. Bagration was under orders to cover the main road until the assault was seen to go in; he was then to assist by attacking up the road. The only formation left in reserve was the newly arrived Russian Imperial Guard, posted behind Bläswitz to support Bagration and Liechtenstein.

Weyrother's scheme had many attractions. Nevertheless, it contained an almost equal number of flaws. Firstly there was an unshakable assumption – partly the result of Napoleon's deception – that the French were morally paralyzed and would not interfere with the descent from the Pratzen and the crossing of the Goldbach. Secondly, the final details of the project were produced only after some of the columns had already started to move. Orders had to be translated and sent out in the darkness to a massive army on the march. The Allied columns bore no resemblance to French corps; they were extemporized formations, cobbled together in haste and often led by officers whose knowledge of the master plan was somewhat sketchy. It is small wonder that there was confusion in the Allied ranks long before the first shot echoed over the marshes of the Goldbach.

Napoleon had issued his customary prebattle proclamation to his troops on the previous night and, despite their chilly bivouacs, his men were in good heart as they stood to arms before first light. They might have been less confident had they known how heavily the numerical balance was tilted against them. Of the 73,000 or so French troops in the area only about 60,000 were fit to fight, while about 85,000 Austrians and Russians were already on the move, and further Allied reinforcements were expected.

Few battles start neatly, and Austerlitz was no exception. At about 0700 hours Kienmayer's force entered Telnitz, and fighting flared up around the village as both Doctorov and Davout fed in more troops. The Russians took the village, and Przbyswski's men stormed Zokolnitz, a mile to the north. Smoke, therefore, already lay thick in the valley of the Goldbach when Napoleon, munching a hasty breakfast, summoned his corps commanders to a final

briefing on the Zurlan. The news from Telnitz confirmed that the Allied attack was developing as expected, and Napoleon sent his marshals back to their commands after only a few words. Soult, however, he kept the longest. 'I beg Your Majesty to hold me back no longer,' urged the anxious marshal. 'I have 20,000 men to set in motion.' 'How long will it take you to climb the Pratzen?' asked Napoleon. 'Less than 20 minutes, Sire,' replied Soult. 'In that case,' concluded the Emperor, 'we will wait for another quarter of an hour.'

Soult's men had been issued with a triple ration of brandy and, fortified by almost half a pint of raw spirit each, as well as by their commander's oratory, they were ready for anything. At about 0900 hours the divisions of Vandamme and Saint-Hilaire advanced, bursting from the mist into bright sunlight halfway through their ascent. Saint-Hilaire seized Pratzen and the Pratzeberg, and Vandamme, after a brush with an off-course Allied detachment, secured the Staré Vinohrady. It was now only 0930 hours, and the keys of the Pratzen were in French hands. On the southern end of the battlefield, in the smoky chaos of Zokolnitz and Telnitz, the Allied attack had lost momentum in the face of a staunch defense.

It was in the north that events were taking a crucial turn. The pugnacious Bagration, dissatisfied with the role allotted to him by the Weyrother plan, decided to move forward on his own initiative, and at about 1000 hours he collided with Lannes north of Bläswitz. The leading elements of Liechtenstein's cavalry, who had found themselves well to the south of their proper position and had ridden through several advancing columns to get there, gave some support to Bagration's left, while to Bagration's left rear the Russian Guard stamped its immaculate way toward Bläswitz.

Although by midmorning Napoleon had the satisfaction of knowing that his opponents' plan had gone badly awry, his own was not proceeding as he might have wished. Bagration's determined attack gave Lannes all he could cope with, and although the southern flank was holding up much better than had been expected, the Emperor was now becoming preoccupied with the fate of his center. Vandamme and Saint-Hilaire had indeed established themselves on the Pratzen, but they soon found themselves vying for the tenancy of this vital feature with the forces of Kollowrath and Miloradovitch, which had fallen victim to numerous delays and were consequently still on the Pratzen. After a period of very fierce fighting, Saint-Hilaire's men managed to win secure possession of the southern crest of the plateau, beating off spirited counterattacks from Kollowrath and from a brigade of Langeron's column which had swung north to help. Vandamme was more fortunate, and established himself around the Staré Vinohrady with relative ease.

Until the Pratzen was secured Napoleon remained at his command post on the Zurlan, receiving information from couriers, watching the progress of the fighting and sending off gallopers with orders. At about 1130 hours, with the Staré Vinohrady firmly in French hands, he rode forward onto the plateau, followed by his entire reserve – the Guard, Oudinot's Grenadiers and the I Corps. He seemed to have won the battle in the center, and the fighting along the

Above: The scene at the battle showing Napoleon's view over the valley, based on a drawing of an eye witness.

Left: The charge of the Mamelukes at Austerlitz. The Mamelukes were an elite cavalry force first raised in 1803, and part of the Imperial Guard Cavalry.

Far left top: General Prince Peter Bagration, who was in command of 13,000 troops positioned east of the Goldbach Heights during the battle.

Goldbach in the south crashed on in stalemate. In the north those dogged rivals, Lannes and Bagration, were locked in a bitter struggle which swayed to and fro between Bläswitz and Bosenitz. It was not until early afternoon that Bagration was at last pushed back, and even then he retired in his customary resolute style. The fighting in the north had been much fiercer than Napoleon had anticipated. Moreover, both Lannes and Murat had suffered numerous casualties and were in no condition to mount a vigorous attack.

However disappointed Napoleon might have been by the lack of progress on his left, he at least had the satisfaction of knowing that he retained the Guard, Bernadotte and Oudinot – the latter soon to be sent off to the south – in reserve under his hand. The only reserve formation now left in the hands of the Allied commanders was the Russian Imperial Guard, under the swarthy and savage Grand Duke Constantine. He had approached Bläswitz toward mid-morning, but discovered, to his surprise and chagrin, that the village was held by the French. In response to an appeal from his Imperial brother, wandering like an unhappy wraith among the wreckage of the Allied center, he dispatched a battalion to help Kollowrath and Miloradovich on the Pratzen. He then took up position about a mile southeast of Bläswitz, and sent forward the Preobrazhensky and Semenovsky Regiments, supported by the Guard Cuirassiers. This attack, delivered with commendable determination, broke two of Vandamme's regiments. Thus

Napoleon in defeat on the *Bellerophon* taking him to St Helena.

it was that no sooner had Napoleon ridden onto the Staré Vinohrady than a crowd of fugitives ran past him, rather sheepishly shouting *'Vive L'Empereur'* as they did so.

Napoleon at once ordered Marshal Bessières to support Vandamme with his own Guard. Bessières' first attack failed, and Constantine fed his remaining regiments into the fighting. Bessières renewed his efforts, and Bernadotte sent D'Erlon's division of the I Corps to assist. The Russian Guard fought manfully but was at last driven back, with heavy losses in men and guns. The defeat of the Russian Guard removed the threat to the French center, and extinguished the only Allied reserve. Nevertheless, although Napoleon was now in a dominant position, his oblique attack on the Allied right had not worked, and any French victory would be inconclusive. Napoleon was not content to accept this. He decided to carry out a great right wheel by his forces on the Pratzen, with the intention of cutting off Buxhöwden's force at the southern end of the battlefield.

The move was under way shortly after 1400 hours. The infantry of Vandamme and Saint-Hilaire, with powerful support, struck southwest from the Pratzen, and the Guard followed them. Friant chose just this moment to push his division of the III Corps into a counterattack, and the stolid Russian infantry around Zokolnitz were overwhelmed and their commander, Przbyswski, was captured. Kienmayer and Doctorov, further south, disengaged the remnants of their columns with very considerable skill, although many of their men were, inevitably, cut off. Buxhöwden and his

staff got away over the Littawa somewhat in advance of their retreating forces, but as Vandamme's men secured Aujest, escape for much of Buxhöwden's command became impossible. Some Allied soldiers tried to escape across the frozen ponds of Satschan and Menitz, and a number were drowned when the ice broke. However, subsequent French claims that 20,000 Allies perished in the ponds were wildly exaggerated.

Napoleon had again moved to a position from which he could observe the decisive sector of the battlefield. As Soult's men descended from the Pratzen he had established himself at the chapel of St Anthony, on the southern slopes overlooking Aujest. From this vantage point he watched the partial encirclement of the Allied left, and urged on his commanders, replacing one of them, General Boyé, whose dragoons had not produced satisfactory results.

The battle was over by 1700 hours. Most of the French spent the night on the battlefield, while the debris of the Allied armies lurched away to the east. Bagration, Liechtenstein and Constantine brought their survivors off in good order, but the remainder of the Allied force presented a sorry spectacle as it shuffled back through the sleet. Allied casualties totalled some 27,000 men — roughly one-third of those engaged. French losses were much smaller, something under 10,000 men, many of whom were wounded.

The Emperors of Austria and Russia, the latter dazed by a day of wandering about the field with only a few companions, met at Czeitsch on the road to Hungary at noon on 3 December. Although fresh troops were at hand, neither monarch had the stomach for more fighting, and the Russians resumed their retreat while Joseph made terms with the victors. He met Napoleon on the afternoon of the 4th. The latter had prepared for the occasion by donning a clean shirt — his first for a week. The meeting was a success; an armistice was agreed upon, and the Russians subsequently undertook to leave Austria as quickly as possible.

Contemporaries were well aware of the momentous nature of Austerlitz. News of the battle broke the heart of William Pitt, the British Prime Minister; he died soon afterward. The Coalition was shattered. Austria made a humiliating peace, losing great tracts of territory and over two million subjects. Napoleon was less successful with Russia, for the Czar repudiated a tentative agreement in September 1806. Prussia, cowed by the presence of the triumphant *Grande Armée* on its southern borders, concluded a unilateral treaty with France in return for the Kingdom of Hanover. Not only was Prussia thereby brought within the French sphere of influence, but she also became an object of contempt and suspicion to her former allies.

The slopes of the Pratzen still bore their grisly harvest of unburied dead when military experts began to dissect Napoleon's victory. The Russians and Austrians found it convenient to blame their column commanders for incompetence or worse, but many officers appreciated that their armies had attempted to execute a plan for which they were simply not prepared. The Weyrother project, admirable though it looked on paper, did not commend itself to execution by an Allied force whose staff work was decidedly patchy. However, whatever was wrong with the Allied army on 2 December was not the fault of its junior ranks. It would be hard to match the desperate courage of the

T

Napoleon meets Francis I, the Austrian emperor, after the battle.

of the
city d
Water
remai
still o
reput;
  Wa
battle.
in the
young
missio
a rem;
none c
critica
The Di
'a dam
ever sa
It has k
victory
unente
deserve
French
this ir
poigna
stagger
  Wel
Waterl
betwee
sieges ;
fought
had em
of India
their gl
too eas
was, to
belief tl
was to
convict
  After
employ
appoint
1808 tl
recently
opportu
mand o
at Roliç
senior o
escape
Vimiero
of the r
of their
'I, at lea
and at
with his
columns
could n
lessons

men of the Galicia, Azov and Narva Regiments around Kobelnitz, or the staunch valor of the Croats and Hungarians of Kienmayer's detachment. The Allied army was not so much outfought as outgeneralled, and for this nobody was more responsible than Napoleon himself.

It is hard to cut through the myth and propaganda surrounding Napoleon's role at Austerlitz. His supporters, naturally enough, regarded the battle as a master stroke of sublime brilliance, whereas some historians have suggested that Napoleon was dangerously overextended, and was saved from catastrophe only by the blunders of the Allies. The truth lies somewhere between these extremes. It is, in any case, dangerous to consider the battle of Austerlitz outside the context of the campaign; Napoleon himself wrote that 'the victory of Austerlitz was only the natural outcome of the Moravian plan of campaign. In an art as difficult as that of war, the system of a campaign often reveals the plan of battle.' Napoleon's 1805 campaign was indeed bold to the point of rashness, but it represented one of the few viable strategic courses open to him. To have waited for the Allies to link up in Germany and threaten France, while the British blockade strangled French industry, was a recipe for disaster. It was far better to catch the Allies off guard and defeat them in the critical theater of operations. Moreover, Napoleon had to hand an instrument forged in the crucible of revolutionary France, tempered in the wars of the Revolution and polished at the Boulogne camp. He knew exactly what it was capable of, and was able to undertake a strategic deployment which would have confounded a less maneuverable force.

Once in Moravia, Napoleon succeeded in imposing his own will on his opponents. The fact that the Allies were disunited and overconfident does not detract from this achievement. Just as a fencer judges the ability of his opponent in the first few seconds of a bout, so Napoleon took the measure of the Allied commanders and correctly deduced that they could be persuaded to lunge at him if he seemed to drop his guard. His own riposte – the original double envelopment scheme – was planned on exactly this basis.

History is full of generals who have shown themselves adept at planning battles. Capable of bringing their armies onto the battlefield and setting them in motion according to a sound policy, they have nevertheless often failed to respond to the fluid circumstances of battle or to answer the challenge of imponderables. Napoleon's conduct at Austerlitz vividly demonstrates his ability to fight as well as to plan a battle. He made two modifications to his original plan, reshaping it to fit changing circumstances. Finally, when part of his plan went wrong, he was able to improvise and execute an alternative which rendered his victory conclusive. Although the battle did not follow the course he had anticipated, he remained firmly in control, meeting eventualities as they arose. Historians may quibble about which battle may justly be termed Napoleon's finest. But on 2 December 1805, in the aptly-named Battle of the Three Emperors, Napoleon established himself as the military colossus of his age. The Allied generals underestimated him on the eve of Austerlitz. It was a mistake nobody would make again.

The Duke of Wellington before the battle.

fleeting opportunity. He had a good grasp of the problems of supply and transport, an attentive eye for discipline and morale, and was familiar with the perils of alliance warfare. Yet something was lacking. His exploits, remarkable and significant though they were, remained peripheral. The Spanish ulcer had debilitated Napoleon, but it was the fighting in Russia, Germany and Northern France that had broken him. Moreover, Wellington had rarely faced an opponent whose forte was independent command. Napoleon's marshals were, with a few exceptions, more capable as subordinates than as commanders in their own right. Had Europe remained at peace from 1814 onward, Wellington would probably be remembered as a competent and workmanlike general, whose capabilities were never fully tested against a first-rate opponent in a major battle.

Be this as it may, there can be no doubt that Wellington successfully made the transition from soldier to diplomat in 1814–15. The Paris post grew somewhat uncomfortable as Louis' subjects grew increasingly nostalgic for the exiled Emperor. Wellington was reluctant to relinquish the post lest it should seem that he was being driven from France by the threat of violence. He was also markedly unenthusiastic about the possibility of becoming commander in chief in America. On Christmas Eve 1814, however, peace was signed between Britain and the United States at Ghent, and with this the specter of the American command receded. A more congenial appointment fell vacant when Lord Castlereagh, British representative at the Congress of Vienna, was forced to return to England for the opening of Parliament. Wellington took his place, and joined the squabbling Allies in their efforts to redraw the map of Europe in the aftermath of the defeat of France.

The Duke was immersed in his labors at Vienna when, on 7 March, he received word that Napoleon had left the island of Elba for an unknown destination. The wily Prince Metternich astutely observed that he would make straight for Paris, and indeed this is what he did. Louis XVIII's government collapsed like a house of cards; most of his army went over to Napoleon without firing a shot. The representatives of the powers at Vienna, united at last by this threat to the very security they were striving to create, had already declared their steadfast opposition to Napoleon. Wellington was offered an ill-defined advisory post by the Czar, but declined, declaring later that he would prefer to carry a musket. He was instead given command of the right wing of the Allied armies – a force of British, German and Dutch-Belgian troops in the Low Countries. A Prussian army, under the veteran Marshal Blücher, with whom Wellington enjoyed friendly relations undiminished by mutual incomprehension, was on the Duke's left flank. An Austrian force was concentrating in the Black Forest, and more Austrians threatened the South of France while a Russian army marched ponderously toward the central Rhine.

Wellington arrived in Brussels early on the morning of 5 April, and took command of the Anglo-Dutch force, hitherto in the hands of the Prince of Orange. The problems which immediately confronted him placed no less of a strain on his abilities as a diplomat than had the negotiations in Vienna. The British portion of his force, initially some 14,000 men, was of uncertain quality, and included a number of inexperienced and poorly trained units. Yet if this caused Wellington dismay, the state of his Dutch-Belgian allies was even more alarming. Many Dutch-Belgian officers – including the Minister of War – had fought for Napoleon and were pro-French. Political considerations forced Wellington to employ the Prince of Orange and the young Prince Frederick of the Netherlands in senior command appointments, despite their lack of experience. This in turn offended some of Wellington's British subordinates, notably the valiant and profane Sir Thomas Picton. The training, equipment and staff work of the Dutch-Belgians left much to be desired, and the frontier fortresses had scarcely improved since Wellington's visit the previous summer.

The Duke at once set to work reorganizing this heterogeneous force into an army. He made strenuous attempts to obtain more British troops, particularly veteran infantry, and many Peninsular battalions were on their way back from America. He reduced the number of companies in his King's German Legion battalions and used the surplus officers and noncommissioned officers to strengthen Hanoverian militia battalions. Wellington realized that his army was of decidedly patchy quality, and strove to weld it together by ensuring that, wherever possible, good units were intermingled with bad or inexperienced ones. His I Corps, under the Prince of Orange, contained two British and two Dutch-Belgian divisions, and Lord Hill's II Corps was composed of two British divisions, a Dutch-Belgian division and a Dutch-Belgian brigade. The latter two formations were, nominally at least, commanded by Prince Frederick of the Netherlands. Two British divisions, the Brunswick Corps and a Nassau contingent, formed the Duke's reserve. The Earl of Uxbridge commanded the British and Hanoverian cavalry, eight brigades in all, to which were added three Dutch-Belgian brigades. Wellington mixed Englishman and foreigner, veteran and recruit in all the British infantry divisions, except the 1st Division. Sir Charles Alten's 3rd Division, for example, contained an inexperienced British brigade, a veteran brigade of the King's German Legion, and a regular Hanoverian brigade.

Wellington's energetic efforts to create order out of chaos were, ironically, mirrored by those of his opponent. Although war had not yet been formally declared, Napoleon was well aware that if his regime was to survive he must defeat the Allied armies in detail, before their combined offensive was ready. He therefore turned his fierce energy onto the problem of raising men and providing them with arms and equipment. A defensive strategy was out of the question. Napoleon had to attack, and the Low Countries and the multinational force they contained were the most obvious target. Not only were the armies of Wellington and Blücher the most immediate threat to France, but the Low Countries also contained a strong Bonapartist faction. If Napoleon struck fast, he had every chance of jamming the complex Allied war machine and exploiting the military and political divisions which bedevilled Wellington in the early summer of 1815.

Wellington and Blücher had every hope of launching their own offensive without French interference, but were nevertheless aware that Napoleon might try to preempt their attack. A conference at Tirlemont on 3 May estab-

Marshal Michel Ney, Prince of the Moskowa.

lished an interarmy boundary and laid down certain general principles: liaison staffs were exchanged and arrangements made for the passage of intelligence between the armies. The two commanders seem to have agreed to take the Roman Road from Bavay to Maastricht as the line of demarcation, and to concentrate the bulk of their forces on the front from Ghent to Namur. Each army would support the other if attacked, and tentative arrangements were made for a Prussian concentration at Sombreffe and an Anglo-Dutch concentration at Nivelles. Vague though many details of the conference are, the meeting was nevertheless of prime importance: it cemented the excellent personal understanding between Wellington and Blücher, and established the principle of mutual assistance upon which the campaign was to turn.

By the end of May the Prussian army was deployed with two of its corps forward at Charleroi and Ciney, a third close at hand just north of Namur and the fourth in reserve near Liège. Just across the Roman Road from the Prussian I Corps at Charleroi was the Anglo-Dutch I Corps, deployed in the area Mons-Genappe-Enghien. The II Corps lay to its west, in the area Leuze-Alost-Renaix, while the Reserve Corps was billeted around Brussels. Uxbridge's cavalry occupied a narrow pocket between the corps, in the valley of the Dender. Both armies were fairly widely dispersed in order to make the best use of the billeting facilities available.

By early June it was apparent that something was happening behind the French frontier, though it was far from easy to say what it was. Napoleon, aided by French sympathizers in the Netherlands, had a reasonably clear picture of his enemy's dispositions while Wellington had little reliable intelligence. Napoleon still hoped to defeat the Allies in detail; he planned to throw his main weight onto the boundary between the two armies, hoping that each would fall back on its own lines of communication.

As he partook of his customary early breakfast in Brussels

on the morning of 15 June, Wellington can have entertained few worries for the immediate future. He had every confidence in Blücher, and could concentrate his entire force on either flank within 48 hours. Much less time than that would be needed to deploy the bulk of his army to meet any threat within his area of responsibility. If the French attacked Blücher, the Duke would concentrate at Nivelles; if, on the other hand, the blow fell on Wellington, the Prussians would march on Sombreffe. As the Duke enjoyed his tea and toast, the possibility of a French offensive was probably not uppermost in his mind. All being well, he hoped that Blücher and he would mount their own attack before the French were ready.

This satisfactory state of affairs did not survive the day. In midafternoon Wellington heard that the Prussian I Corps had been sharply attacked early that morning. This disturbing news was therefore rather old by the time it reached Brussels, indicating that the flow of intelligence between the armies was by no means as smooth as it should have been. Furthermore, the information was vague, giving the Duke no idea of the strength or extent of the French attack. Wellington, in default of more precise intelligence, did what he could on the facts available, and late in the afternoon orders went out for divisions to concentrate at their assembly points. The Duke's first fear seems to have been for his right, and he was thinking in terms of a concentration at Nivelles to meet a French thrust through Mons.

On the night of the 15th Wellington attended the Duchess of Richmond's ball. This was by no means as irresponsible as it might appear. Cancelling the ball would have encouraged the pro-French element in Brussels, and it was no bad thing for the Duke to have a number of his senior officers about him at a crucial time. More news — and news of a decidedly gloomy nature — arrived while Wellington was actually at the ball. He first heard that the Prussian advance guard had been driven back by the French at Fleurus — only a few miles from Blücher's planned concentration point at Sombreffe. Then, during supper, he heard from the Prince of Orange that French scouts had reached Quatre Bras, an important junction on the main route between the armies. The Dutch-Belgian commander at Quatre Bras had, on his own initiative, decided to hold the crossroads rather than march to his concentration point at Nivelles. Nevertheless, the situation was delicate: the main weight of the French offensive seemed likely to fall on the interarmy boundary, rather than on the Anglo-Dutch right where Wellington had expected it. 'Napoleon has humbugged me, by God!' said Wellington to his host. 'He has gained 24 hours' march on me.' 'What do you intend doing?' the Duke of Richmond asked. 'I have ordered the army to concentrate at Quatre Bras,' replied Wellington, 'but we shall not stop him there, and so I must fight him *here*,' and a thumb-nail jabbed at the map, indicating a ridge across the Brussels-Charleroi road, just south of the village of Waterloo.

The Duke's reserve left Brussels at dawn on the 16th, with orders to march to the road junction at Mont Saint Jean. Wellington himself rode forward later, and by midmorning had arrived at Quatre Bras. So long as this crossroads remained in his hands, he enjoyed good lateral communications with the Prussian concentration point at Sombreffe, eight miles to the east along the Nivelles-Namur road. Wellington reached the junction to find it securely held by General Perponcher's Dutch-Belgian division. He ordered his reserve forward from Mont Saint Jean, dispatched officers to bring up those units ordered to concentrate at Nivelles, and sent a message to Blücher with details – some of them unintentionally false – of his army's dispositions.

These steps taken, Wellington crossed the Roman Road, and met Blücher at a windmill near the village of Brye. The Prussian told him that three of his corps were now concentrated in front of Sombreffe, holding a forward slope dotted with small villages. This position was certainly not to the Duke's taste; he feared that the Prussians would be 'damnably mauled' if they fought there. Wellington then outlined his own plan for a concentration at Quatre Bras, and added that he thought it quite likely that the French would attack him there. He declined a suggestion made by General Graf von Gneisenau, Blücher's Chief of Staff, that he should reinforce the Prussians, but eventually agreed to move all available troops from Quatre Bras to Sombreffe, always provided that he was not attacked in the meantime.

By the time the Duke returned to Quatre Bras, the situation there had taken a turn for the worse. The French were clearly about to launch an attack, and when it came many of the Dutch-Belgians recalled an urgent appointment elsewhere and slid off to the rear. Fortunately for the Duke, his

Left: Marshal Soult restrains
Napoleon from making a last
desperate attack during the battle.

Below: The French cuirassiers
charge the British squares by Felix
Philippoteaux, painted in 1874.

The battle of Waterloo from 11 am to 3 pm, 18 June

0   MILE   ¼   ½

MONT ST JEAN

Wellington
72,000 men

Lambert
de Ghigney

Tripp
Mont St Jean farm

Brunswick
Merlen
Somerset   Ponsonby
W. Halkett
Sir L. Cole   Vincke
Pack
Best
P i c t o n
Arentshildt
Kruse
Reserve Corps   Kempt
Saxe-
Sir H. Clinton   **I Corps**
Kielmansegge   Ompteda   Bylandt   Perponc
Dörnberg
95th   Sandpit
Adam   C. Halkett
Du Plat (K.G.L.)   Grant   LA HAYE   C   B
(K.G.L.)   Baring   SAINTE
II Corps   Maitland   (K.G.L.)   B   B   B
Cooke
Hill   Marcognet
Byng
Donzelot   Quiot (Allix)   D'Erlon
13 Hussars   Mil

HOUGOUMONT   Delort   St

Macdonnel   Domon
Subervie
A   Simmer
Piré   A   Bachelu
Prince Jérôme   Foy
R e i l l e   Jannin
D'hurbal   II Corps   G   u   a   r   d
K e l l e r m a n   Lhéritier
I m p e r i a l
Guyot   Guards Corps
Young Guard
Napoleon   Middle Guard
68,600 men   Old Guard

ROSSOMME

	ALLIES	FRENCH
INFANTRY	▬▬▬	▬▬▬
CAVALRY	▲▲▲▲▲	△△△△△
ARTILLERY	╫╫╫╫╫	╫╫╫╫╫
SKIRMISHERS		

(A) FRENCH ATTACK ON HOUGOUMONT, 11.30 AM
(B) D'ERLON'S ATTACK, 1.30 PM
(C) PONSONBY'S CHARGE, 2 PM

© Richard Natkiel, 1981

Right: The charge of the Life Guards ended the second phase of the battle. It repelled d'Erlon's attack but it also laid low 2500 Allied horsemen.

Vivian (K.G.L.)

Prussian IV Corps (Bülow with 36,000 men) approaching from Wavre

PAPELOTTE

TER LA HAYE

FRISCHERMONT

Jacquinot

uettes

The French dispositions at the battle of Waterloo at 10 am, 18 June

▭▬▭ INFANTRY   △△△ CAVALRY

To Brussels

BRAINE L'ALLEUD

MONT ST JEAN

Wellington

Part III Corps

III Corps (Kellermann)

HOUGOUMONT

II Corps (Reille)

PAPELOTTE   TER LA HAYE   OHAIN

I Corps (D'Erlon)

FRISCHERMONT

Part III Corps

IV Corps (Milhaud)

Imperial Guard

LASNE

Imperial Guard

To Nivelles

Napoleon

V Corps

ROSSOMME   PLANCENOIT

MAISON DU ROI

© Richard Natkiel, 1981

0   MILE   1
0   KILOMETERS   1½

Flanking march of the Prussian Army on 18 June

To Brussels

Lasne

LA BAVETTE   III Corps

BAS WAVRE   Blücher

I Corps   POINT DU JOUR   WAVRE

WATERLOO   GENVAL   FROIDMONT   N. CABARET   BIERGES   AISEMONT   II Corps from midday

I Corps from 2pm

IV Corps   DION-LE-MONT   IV Corps from 4 am

OHAIN   II Corps   LIMALE

MONT ST JEAN   LASNE   ST LAMBERT

BRAINE L'ALLEUD   Wellington   FRISCHERMONT   L'AUZELLE

PAPELOTTE

HOUGOUMONT   LA HAYE STE   COUTOURE   NEUF SART

LA BELLE ALLIANCE

Napoleon   MARANSART   CEROULX   Grouchy from 2pm

PLANCENOIT

MAISON DU ROI   CORBAIS

Dyle

MT ST GUIBERT

© Richard Natkiel, 1981

0   MILES   5
0   KILOMETERS   8

opponent at Quatre Bras was Marshal Michel Ney, who had uncomfortable memories of Wellingtonian positions in Spain, and feared that the slight ridge which screened part of the position might conceal the full strength of the Allied army. Reinforcements, notably Picton's 1st Division, arrived as the day wore on, but it was an anxious time for Wellington, whose position was far more exposed than he would have wished. Nevertheless, he held Quatre Bras throughout a desperate June afternoon, partly by bluff and partly because of the sheer fighting ability of the indomitable 1st Division.

Things had gone less well with Blücher, who had been badly mauled at Ligny, receiving — as the Duke had predicted — 'a damned good hiding.' Napoleon's *corps de réserve* had spent the day fruitlessly marching between the battlefields of Ligny and Quatre Bras, when its appearance on either field would probably have clinched matters. The Prussians were, however, forced to withdraw; the only question was in which direction this retirement would take place. Gneisenau, who believed that Wellington's service in India had made him as devious as any native ruler, felt that the Duke had failed in his promise to support his allies, and suggested that the army should fall back along the best roads available, which led eastward, toward the Prussian base. Blücher had been rolled on by his wounded horse while leading a cavalry charge during the battle, but he had dosed himself with a horrid brew of gin, rhubarb and garlic and was still full of fight. He remembered that Wellington's promise had been conditional upon his not being attacked himself, and he therefore determined to fall back on Wavre, from where he could still support Wellington, or withdraw to the east if necessary.

Wellington had no definite news of the Prussian with-drawal until about 0730 hours on the morning of the 17th. A little later he received a full account from a Prussian staff officer, and told Müffling, his Prussian liaison officer, that he would give battle on the Mont Saint Jean position if Blücher would support him with at least a corps. It was obviously essential for the Duke to conform to Blücher's northerly movement, and, having agreed with Müffling that the French were likely to make a slow start that morning, he ordered his men to breakfast before setting off. By midmorning all units ordered up from Nivelles had arrived, and Wellington began to disengage, feeding troops back down the Brussels road. At about midday he observed with satisfaction, 'Well, there is the last of the infantry gone, and I don't care now.' His forces were all but clear of Quatre Bras by 1400 hours when Napoleon himself appeared at the head of a mass of lancers. The British retirement was accompanied by a violent thunderstorm which added to the miseries of the combatants but also drenched the fields, confining movement to the only metalled road. This prevented French cavalry from outflanking the retreating force, and made it easier for Wellington to accomplish that most difficult of maneuvers, a withdrawal in contact with the enemy. There was a brisk rearguard action in Genappe, but the pursuit had died away long before midnight, as the Duke's army took position in the rainy cornfields below Mont Saint Jean.

Napoleon's principal worry was that the Duke would slip away altogether, depriving him of the benefits of his initial move and the fighting on the 16th. In the early hours of the 18th the Emperor rode along his outpost line and

The view from La Haie Sainte during the last phase of the battle.

saw, with relief, the glow of bivouac fires along the ridge to the north, showing that Wellington intended to offer battle. Napoleon desired nothing more: 'I have them now, these English,' he remarked with pleasure.

Wellington's position lay along a low ridge south of the hamlet of Mont Saint Jean. Although it was by no means as good as many of the reverse slope positions he had used in the Peninsula, it was not without numerous advantages. Most of his force was posted just over the crest line, and could avoid the worst effects of French artillery fire by lying down. The ridge also shielded movements between the flanks of the position, facilitating the deployment of reserves. A strong outpost line garnished the forward slope, and the farms of Papellotte, La Haie Sainte and the Chateau of Hougoumont had been prepared for defense and garrisoned. The Brussels road ran squarely through the position, and it was just to the west of this route that Wellington had posted the bulk of his force. He recognized that the right flank of his position was in the air, and suspected that Napoleon might try to roll him up from the west. To obstruct a really wide outflanking move, strong detachments were posted at Hal and Tubize, about eight miles to the west. This force took no part in the battle, but it offered useful insurance to the Duke's weak right flank.

Satisfactory though the Mont Saint Jean position seemed, Wellington was only prepared to fight in it if he had guaranteed Prussian support. He had some 68,000 men under his hand, and was well aware that Napoleon had over 100,000 troops, who could be employed against either the Anglo-Dutch or the Prussians. In the small hours of the 18th he received word from Blücher that two Prussian corps would move to his support at dawn. Wellington expected them to be making their presence felt by midday, and he was confident of holding Napoleon till then; with the arrival of this message, therefore, his decision to stand and fight became irrevocable.

However great the Duke's apparent confidence at dawn on the 18th, his impassive profile must have concealed certain misgivings. Quatre Bras had confirmed the unreliability of the Dutch-Belgians, who could be expected to perform no better in a major battle. The Duke believed that his position was, ultimately, tenable only with Prussian assistance, but his experiences in Spain, coupled with more recent events, gave ample evidence of the fallibility of allies. Moreover, this was the first time that Wellington had met Napoleon in a pitched battle. Wellington had a poor opinion of the Emperor as a man, calling him 'low and ungentleman-like.' Despite this he felt that Napoleon's presence on a battlefield was worth 40,000 men, and he was by no means unaware of his formidable military record. The Duke had faced French attacks often enough in the Peninsula to know what to expect if Napoleon launched a frontal assault, and probably felt that this was a far less frightening eventuality than a fluid battle of maneuver in which the more supple French army would be likely to excel. Finally, despite the presence of the force at Tubize and Hal, the ugly prospect of a flanking attack cannot have been far from the Duke's mind. Whatever his doubts, Wellington kept most of them to himself, although he did send a discreet letter to a lady in Brussels suggesting that she might care to visit Antwerp. He appears to have made no plans for retirement in the event of a French victory, and when his second in command, Lord Uxbridge,

Wellington encourages the British infantry squares.

asked him what his plans were, the Duke replied that 'Bonaparte has not given me any idea of his projects, and as my plans will depend upon his, how can you expect me to tell you what mine are?' Then he softened for a moment, put his hand on Uxbridge's shoulder, and said: 'There is one thing certain, Uxbridge; that is, that whatever happens you and I will do our duty.'

Napoleon's intentions, founded as they were upon sublime assurance, were simple enough. He proposed to bombard the Anglo-Dutch position, and to use cavalry to force Wellington to disclose his troops; he would then administer the knock-out blow with an infantry assault. Some of those on his staff, memories of the Peninsula fresh in their minds, protested that the task might prove rather more difficult than this. 'Just because you have been beaten by Wellington,' snapped the Emperor, 'you think he's a good general. I tell you, Wellington is a bad general, the English are bad troops, and this affair is nothing more than eating breakfast.' It was to prove a singularly indigestible meal.

The Emperor's conviction that the simple recipe of frontal assault would beat the Anglo-Dutch, coupled with his belief that the Prussians had been so badly hammered at Ligny that they would be intent on escaping and not aiding Wellington, led him to make two important decisions. Firstly, he postponed the main attack from 0900 until 1300 hours, to allow the ground to dry out, permitting his artillery to move more easily off the roads and enhancing the ricochet effect of its fire. Secondly, his orders to Marshal Grouchy, who was following the Prussians, failed to emphasize the importance of preventing a junction between Blücher and Wellington. These decisions were to prove crucial. Time was of the essence, and Napoleon's only hope of victory lay in crushing the Anglo-Belgians before the Prussians could intervene.

Bad Prussian staff work went some way toward compensating for the inaccuracy of Napoleon's appreciation of the condition of Blücher's army. Bülow's corps, which had not been engaged on the 16th, was ordered to lead the advance, although it lay furthest from Wellington's army. Its line of march lay across that of the other two corps — Blücher's remaining corps, under Thielmann, faced Grouchy beyond Wavre — and the resulting confusion meant that there was no possibility of Bülow arriving on the battlefield before 1600 hours. Wellington would therefore have to wait for Prussian help for at least four hours longer than he expected.

The Duke spent the morning putting the finishing touches to his dispositions, and watching the French army as it deployed. He wore a blue frock-coat and a low black cocked hat and, eminently practical as he was, from time to time donned a short cloak to keep off the showers. He rode his favorite charger, Copenhagen, a fact which caused some dismay to the infantry in whose squares he later took refuge, for the horse was a notorious kicker. By midmorning the French were drawn up in parade array, and it was clear that Napoleon had over 70,000 men in the field. The corps of Reille and d'Erlon stood on either side of the Brussels road, with a great battery of 84 guns just to the west of the road. Behind this were Lobau's VI Corps and the Imperial Guard. The cavalry corps of Kellermann and Milhaud, a formidable mass of mounted men, were behind Reille and

General Blücher marching to join Wellington's forces.

d'Erlon ready for the attack.

A fanciful depiction of the British Guards attacking.

The battle began at about 1130 hours with a French attack on Hougoumont. Napoleon, possibly recognizing Wellington's anxiety for his right, intended this as a feint, but its initial repulse so enraged the divisional commander concerned that he renewed the assault, assisted by some troops from a neighboring division. Wellington, giving an early demonstration of his ability to be always on hand at the critical point, sent a battalion forward to counterattack, and supported it with another battalion soon afterward. The fighting at Hougoumont grew from a flicker into a blaze, steadily drawing in more and more troops – about 3500 of Wellington's men and 14,000 French. Not only was the attack a failure as a diversion, for it did not induce Wellington to weaken his center, but the Chateau also remained in British hands all day, providing a serious obstacle to French attacks west of the Brussels road.

The great bombardment began just after 1300 hours. Shortly before his guns opened fire, Napoleon had received the unwelcome news that the leading elements of Bülow's corps had been seen to the east, beyond the Bois de Paris. Undeterred by this, the Emperor assured Soult, his Chief of Staff, that the odds were still in his favor. The bombardment, deprived as it was of a solid target, did relatively little damage, and when d'Erlon's men advanced at about 1330 hours they were warmly received by the Allied artillery and the infantry of Picton's division. Picton was killed leading his men into the French, and his soldiers were soon hard pressed to sustain the weight of d'Erlon's attack. Moreover, on d'Erlon's left a *cuirassier* brigade had already swamped a Hanoverian battalion and now threatened Wellington's center. The Duke, his eye on ·the trouble spot, ordered Uxbridge to take forward Somerset's Household Brigade and Ponsonby's Union Brigade. The British heavy cavalry moved past the German infantry battalions in square west of the Brussels road, swept through the *cuirassiers*, whose horses were blown by their uphill charge, and crashed into d'Erlon's flank. Three of d'Erlon's four divisions were routed, and over 3000 men were captured. However, indiscipline proved the undoing of the British cavalry; elated by success, they surged on to the enemy gun line, where they were sharply counterattacked by fresh cavalry. Barely half of them returned.

The crippling of two fine cavalry brigades was a serious disappointment to Wellington, but it was a small enough price to pay for the laceration of a French corps and the protection of his center. The fighting had also consumed valuable time, for it was not until 1530 hours that Ney ordered forward the next attack. He was repulsed from La Haie Sainte but, seeing transport apparently retreating down the Brussels road, he brought a *cuirassier* brigade to accelerate what he believed to be a withdrawal. Two cavalry divisions followed, more or less on their own initiative, and at about 1600 hours Ney led forward some 5000 horsemen on a 700-yard front between Hougoumont and La Haie Sainte. Receiving a cavalry charge in square was a trying experience for infantry, but as long as they stood firm there was little to fear. Wellington had instructed his gunners to remain at their places until the last possible

General Blücher sends his cavalry into battle in the nick of time.

personal relationship with Blücher was of vital importance, otherwise it seems certain that the Allied armies would have drifted apart on 16–17 June. The Duke's decision to fight on the 18th was dependent upon the promise of Prussian support. It is, therefore, fruitless to criticize Wellington for having been rescued only by the timely arrival of the Prussians. He counted upon Prussian assistance, and had every reason to expect it sooner than it came.

Wellington's selection of the Waterloo position has also been the topic of considerable debate. It was certainly not the classic ridge line of the Peninsula. A general, however, must take the ground in a theater of war as he finds it, and the ridge of Mont Saint Jean was one of the few satisfactory positions blocking the Charleroi-Brussels road. During the battle itself, Wellington never lost his grip, in spite of frequent fluctuations in his fortunes. He showed that rare ability to be always at the right place at the right time; it was his personal intervention which shored up the damaged center after the fall of La Haie Sainte, and his own order which initiated the destruction of the Imperial Guard. The Duke's constant appearance at points of crisis did much for the morale of his troops; he hazarded himself as much as the most lowly private soldier, and the heavy casualties among his staff bear solemn testimony to the risks he ran. His conduct of the campaign was, nevertheless, certainly not flawless. He was, perhaps, a little too complacent shortly before the French offensive. A more serious weakness was his unwillingness to trust his senior subordinates with the secrets of his mind. Had the Duke become a casualty, as well he might, on the morning of the 18th, the Allied army would have lost its brain as well as its soul.

Historians continue to ask themselves questions about Waterloo. Did Napoleon's mistakes, rather than Wellington's skill, determine the course of the battle? Should the Duke have detached the Hal-Tubize force? How would he have fared against the Emperor at his best? These questions, interesting though they may be, must remain mere speculation – while the facts speak for themselves. On 18 July Wellington, at the head of a diverse Anglo-Dutch force, fought to a standstill a confident and enthusiastic army led by a man whose military prowess had dazzled Europe. It was no supine and passive defensive battle, but a conflict in which the defender capitalized upon his enemy's weaknesses as well as his own strengths. Great though the part played by the private soldier was, Waterloo was no mere soldiers' battle, in which victory was extemporized by individual valor. Without Wellington's guiding hand such valor would not have denied the Guard its triumphal march through Brussels. At Waterloo, Wellington's presence was everything. His grateful countrymen nicknamed him the 'Iron Duke,' but they did him less than justice. Wellington's military character was, rather, of the finest spring steel, and never was its strength and resilience better shown than at Waterloo.

Wellington and Blücher meet as victors at Belle Alliance after the battle. Blücher greeted Wellington with the words 'I stink don't I' because he had taken a garlic cure during the battle.

LEE AT CHANCELLORS-VILLE 1863

Great battles and flamboyant generals have long been topics for study. In the evaluation of battles of the Civil War one battle in particular is set apart from the others in this regard. Combined in one engagement are the elements of bold strategy, classic maneuvering, brilliant generals and an army fighting desperately for survival against overwhelmingly superior odds. The details of General Robert E Lee and the Army of Northern Virginia at Chancellorsville are those which are found in best-selling novels or on the silver screen. Yet those were in fact the prime ingredients at Chancellorsville. What emerges in analysis however, is a confrontation of one general prepared to gamble everything in desperately bold aggressiveness against another general floundering in overconfident misinformation and indecisiveness.

Of all Civil War generals none can compare with the mystique and admiration which has surrounded Robert E Lee. Beyond commanding an army, Lee held the love and respect of his soldiers, his fellow countrymen and even his enemies. He was in every respect a gentleman-soldier; a gentleman caught in a struggle of personal beliefs and a strong commitment to his countrymen, Northern and Southern; a soldier sworn to his duty to the Confederacy and his rank.

Robert Edward Lee was born in 1807, son of a Revolutionary War hero who had become governor of Virginia. The surname Lee is associated with others of the highest distinction and is considered one of the foremost family names in Virginia. To complete his education young Lee attended the Military Academy at West Point, graduating second in his class. As a young officer he gained a reputation for resourcefulness and daring during the Mexican War. With the passing of time he continued to climb within the military ranks and even served as the Superintendent of West Point from 1852–55.

When the secession of southern states made war an imminent possibility, Lee was offered command over all Federal troops. However, he refused to commit himself until he learned if his beloved Virginia would also secede and join the Confederate States of America. In later writings Lee referred to this period of decision as the most difficult of his lifetime. While he did not believe in secession, neither did he believe in slavery. Lee was convinced that war was a terrible mistake, but he felt honor bound as a true Virginian to offer his services to the Confederate cause.

During the early months of the Civil War General Lee held a local command in his home state, acting as a military advisor to the Confederate President, Jefferson Davis. In May of 1862, Lee was offered command of the Army of Northern Virginia. Thus began the creation of a legend and powerful mystique, the likes of which have rarely been seen. Lee and his army hold a fascination for students of military history with which perhaps only Rommel and his Afrika Korps can compare.

In spite of this, one grain of doubt remains when considering the reputation Lee acquired through the exploits of his army. Ever present in the shadow of Lee's overwhelming popularity was the influence of another great Confederate commander, General Thomas Jonathan 'Stonewall' Jackson. Robert E Lee has been cited as a brilliant commanding general, yet 'Stonewall' Jackson's role in bringing about that

acclaim cannot be denied and was clearly evident in and essential to the victory at Chancellorsville.

During the months of 1862 after his assumption of command over the Army of Northern Virginia Lee campaigned through his home state, denying the Union hope of capturing the Confederate capital, Richmond. The strategical and tactical abilities of Lee's staff achieved a level which frustrated not only the Union commanders but President Lincoln as well. It caused the Union to doubt its ability to win the war and caused many to fear that the United States

General Robert E Lee, the Commander in Chief of the Confederate Army.

would indeed remain divided.

Lee and the Army of Northern Virginia continued to accumulate victories as Lincoln sifted the ranks in an attempt to find a commander who would be a match for Lee's obvious talents. After General Burnside's fiasco at Fredericksburg in December 1862, when Union forces were thrown against the breastworks of the Confederate defense to be senselessly slaughtered, Lincoln began to search once again for a competent commanding general. The decision was made which brought forward the main Union character in the forthcoming Battle of Chancellorsville, Major General Joseph 'Fighting Joe' Hooker, to assume command of the Army of the Potomac in January 1863.

General Hooker had also gained a reputation in the Mexican War, and in the early days of the Civil War had shown himself to be a hard working, able divisional commander. Unfortunately for himself and the Union army, 'Fighting Joe' had one fatal flaw – overconfidence in himself as a man and as a commander. This led him to believe that his personal evaluation of a given situation was always accurate and never needed revision. His demeanor was considered pompous by his fellow officers, and the troops sniggered at his overindulgences of drink and women. His excesses in the latter category led the troops to give the name 'Hooker' to the prostitutes who followed the army.

The obvious flaws in his character could not completely override the abilities which Hooker did possess. The basis for his campaign at Chancellorsville was extremely creative and based on sound assessments. Had the plan been executed by a competent Union commander of different

General George McClellan by Matthew Brady.

temperament the battle may have provided the Union with its first decisive victory in the Eastern Campaign. Hooker also set forward policies aimed at raising the morale, confidence and readiness of the troops. He instituted a furlough policy and commenced training programs which included mock battles within the brigades. He set about rebuilding the Army of the Potomac, reorganizing the troops into large fighting corps capable of sustaining themselves in battle. He also restructured the Union cavalry in attempts to bring it to a level on a par with its Southern counterpart. Finally, Hooker created the first independent intelligence service for the Army of the Potomac. This service was composed of a network of riders, scouts and spies under Colonel Sharp's command, who gathered information about the enemy and in some cases planted false information to deceive and confuse the Confederate command. Hooker's predecessors, McClellan and Burnside, had always relied on the Pinkerton Agency to supply information. Unfortunately such information was often erroneous or exaggerated. Within weeks of its formation Hooker's intelligence network had given him an accurate knowledge of not only Lee's position but Confederate troop strength and condition. Although Hooker's future as a commander held disaster for himself and the Army of the Potomac, he had instituted changes and procedures which would prove valuable to the long-term welfare of that army.

An introduction to the Battle of Chancellorsville would not be complete without some discussion of the man who had acted for some time as General Lee's right hand, General 'Stonewall' Jackson. In character and bearing Jackson was the epitome of the Southern gentleman and officer. He was a religious man and a devoted husband and father. Jackson began his military career with West Point training, later to become an instructor at the Virginia Military Institute. He was extremely proud of this private academy and believed in the school motto that those who occupied its halls were 'yet to be heard from.' On the day of the Battle of Chancellorsville, in the midst of the assault against the Union right flank, 'Stonewall' Jackson is said to have remarked to one of his staff, 'The Yankees will hear from VMI today!'

As a soldier Jackson had the unique ability to take any plausible plan of action and implement it successfully on the tactical battlefield. With reference to the Battle of Chancellorsville it will be easily recognized that while Lee did indeed conceive the strategy and act as the restraint in the execution of the plan at its most critical moment, Jackson ensured the success of the maneuver which led to ultimate victory.

Those two men, Lee and Jackson, so completely complemented each other that it is impossible to do justice to either without discussing both. Both Lee and Jackson were unusual in the respect, admiration and concern each felt for the simple soldiers under their command. Unlike many generals of that time, neither believed in nor condoned the wasting of precious lives, sent into battle as cannon fodder. The obvious concern Lee and Jackson demonstrated for the individuals under their command was the primary reason that their troops could and would perform miraculous feats on the field of battle. Earlier in the war, during the Valley Campaign, Jackson's troops maneuvered so rapidly on the

General Thomas 'Stonewall' Jackson.

battlefield that they earned the nickname 'foot cavalry.' Such maneuvering was only possible because the men of his command would go without food or rest in obedience to his orders.

There is an incident which bears telling at this point, for not only does it demonstrate the mutual respect between Jackson and his men, but it also holds a consequence which would prove fatal in the Chancellorsville Campaign. Hearing of an advance on the night before the Confederate attack on the Union right flank, Jackson sped to the front leaving his personal belongings and wagons far behind in the rear. In the bitter cold of the night one of Jackson's young aides-de-camp. Lieutenant J P Smith, discovered the general huddled in sleep with neither blanket nor cloak to keep him warm. The lieutenant was appalled by Jackson's condition and insisted that the general take his cape. Jackson refused the offer, but when it seemed that the young lieutenant's feelings had been extremely hurt he accepted the offer, not wishing to appear ungrateful. Jackson dozed again and Lieutenant Smith huddled near the fire and also fell asleep. Sometime during the night Jackson must have awakened to see the lieutenant shivering on the cold ground, for he rose up and without waking the young officer, replaced his cape. In the early morning hours Lieutenant Smith woke to find the general as he had the night before, without coverings, and his cape gently spread over his own form. The irony of the incident lies in the fact that it was on that night that Jackson apparently caught the cold which soon afterward contributed to his death.

For all his sterling qualities, Jackson too had one principal flaw as a commander. Too often he was inclined to pursue the enemy without concern for the total scope of the engagement. As exemplified by the Valley Campaign, he could win the majority of the battles yet lose sight of the true and ultimate objectives. Once again this demonstrates how perfectly well suited were Jackson and Lee, and how their natures achieved a delicate balance of strategy and tactics. Lee understood the total scope of an encounter, while Jackson implemented these objectives.

Lee's Army of Northern Virginia held the field with approximately 60,000 veteran Confederate soldiers. In opposition to his forces, Hooker's Army of the Potomac was some 200,000 strong. The overwhelming difference in manpower was of course crucial to Lee's thinking prior to, during and after the campaign.

Lee had positioned his troops outside Fredericksburg at approximately the same locations where, during the Battle of Fredericksburg, he had dealt General Burnside a staggeringly costly defeat. That defeat had almost completely destroyed the morale of the Union army, causing the soldiers and even President Lincoln to lose confidence in its generals. Although he therefore faced an army of deteriorating morale, Lee also suffered from many handicaps. Most obvious was the outnumbering of his own forces by more than three to one. Perhaps more crucial, however, was the army's poor state of readiness to do battle once again. Much in line with the old quotation 'the spirit was willing but the flesh was weak,' Lee's troops were near the point of exhaustion. Few troops, if any, had had a leave of absence within easy memory. Food and supplies were dwindling, and the splendid uniforms in which many had marched to war had become tattered rags. Both arms and equipment were in short supply, and the troops had to rely heavily on what could be scavenged from successful skirmishes to re-equip themselves. More than a few Confederate officers believed that if the Southern troops were as well supplied and equipped as their Northern counterparts the war would have ended the previous year.

Compounding those disadvantages, Lee's army had been forced to fight one defensive action after another. The initiative had swung into Union hands. Lee was convinced that if he were to have any major success in the future and thus entice foreign support to the Confederate cause, he would have to regain that initiative. In the days prior to the Battle of Chancellorsville Lee and his officers struggled to resolve that dilemma without arriving at any sound course of action.

Jackson and Major General J E B Stuart were in favor of instituting an all-out offensive against the Union forces, but Lee recognized their eagerness as voiced pride in their men and army. It would take more than high morale, pride and confidence to bring about the changes which were so desperately needed. Much to Lee's amazement it was the commander of the Army of the Potomac who gave the necessary aid to the Confederate Army. General Hooker brought the battle to Lee and then handed him the reins of initiative through indecision.

That circumstance was certainly not a part of Hooker's battle plans. After rebuilding Union morale and reorganizing the troops, Hooker's intention was to trap Lee into maintaining his position on the heights above Fredericksburg while the majority of the Army of the Potomac swung in a broad movement which would surround Lee's forces.

To that end, three corps would encircle the heights, two would attack above Fredericksburg, and another two corps would wait in reserve to deliver the final, crushing blow.

Hooker's confidence in his superior numbers and the planned maneuver was so strong that he gave no thought to any outcome other than the destruction of the Confederate forces wherever they chose to give battle, or Lee's full retreat along the road to Richmond. Hooker was convinced that Lee would turn tail and run rather than face the superior odds of the Army of the Potomac. It was a sound and operable plan, if only Hooker had not been so rigid in his predictions of Lee's reactions.

On 27 April General Hooker began his flanking maneuver and the Battle of Chancellorsville was underway. What occurred from that point on must be seen from two perspectives: the daring of Lee and Jackson in attacking the attacker; and Hooker's overconfident bumbling.

The 27–28 April saw the three Union corps swinging wide around the Confederate's left northernmost flank. Confederate cavalry units on that flank reported the enemy movements to General Stuart and by the early morning of 29 April Lee had been informed of the unusual Union activity. The information was somewhat fragmented and Lee pondered over the significance of the maneuver as he watched Major General John Sedgwick cross the Rappahannock River with the Union XI Corps. In spite of the obvious advance of the Union forces, and the threatening posture in which they positioned themselves along his front, Lee could not believe that the main assault would be aimed in that area. Therefore, on the morning of the 29th he dispatched General R H Anderson with part of his division to cover the left flank.

During those morning hours Lee received constant and insistant proddings from his generals, particularly Jackson, to sweep down from the heights and destroy Sedgwick's corps while it attempted to take formation below them. Jackson argued that his units alone could defeat Sedgwick and dispose of any imminent threat to the Confederate Army's position. Lee's wisdom, sense and consideration for the scope of planning came into full display at that time.

His generals felt certain that Hooker's flanking maneuver was merely a ploy to draw defenses away from a major frontal assault but Lee believed otherwise. Lee remembered these savage days of December 1862 when General Burnside threw Union regiments, brigades, divisions and corps against the heights in wholesale slaughter. That fiasco had so sickened and appalled Lee that nothing could convince him that the Union generals intended another such assault. He therefore determined that the forces circling to his north constituted the major threat. Lee held his generals firmly in check while he awaited further information from his

The burning of Baton Rouge, Louisiana in December 1862 was another example of the Union's tactics of total war.

Right: General Hooker's
headquarters at Chancellorsville.

cavalry. Only after discerning the type of maneuver Hooker actually intended would Lee commit himself to action.

By the morning of 30 April Anderson's forces had begun to entrench east of Chancellorsville, to Lee's rear. Reports filtered back to Lee throughout the day that the three Union corps had approached Chancellorsville and were poised to strike against the Confederate rear. Later in the day another Union corps was located and one lone Confederate division was all that stood between the combined strength of four Union corps and the rear of the Confederate army.

On the same day General Hooker arrived at the scene and assumed personal command of his forces. His confidence in his strategy was higher than ever as he received reports of constant rail movements from Fredericksburg along the lines which led to Richmond. Hooker began to believe that Lee had indeed chosen the lesser of two evils and had begun a retreat.

Lee was by then fully aware of Hooker's intent. He realized that if Hooker could pin and encircle the Confederate forces the four Union corps, who alone outnumbered Lee's army, would crush the Army of Northern Virginia between them.

Lee was exploring the feasibility of a retreat, realizing

that while losses would be high they would be acceptable if the army could indeed escape, when Hooker suddenly handed Lee a reprieve. Hooker's self-assuredness in victory had become so strong that he halted his troops for the night. Lee found that fact unbelievable, yet reports continued to arrive confirming the halt. He acted immediately, deciding that if Hooker were willing to give up the initiative he, Lee, was more than happy to accept it.

On the night of 30 April Lee dispatched Major General Lafayette McLaw's division to reinforce General Anderson and made the decision to attack Hooker's forces in the rear. He left one Confederate division to hold the heights and check any assault which Sedgwick's forces might attempt. He sent Jackson with three divisions on a sweep around the Union's right, northern flank, hoping to throw the Union forces of balance with his attack and forcing them on the defensive or into a retreat.

This crucial part of the plan could only succeed because of one man, 'Stonewall' Jackson, for although Lee knew what must be done only Jackson could do it. At that moment of decision Lee shifted the focus of command to Jackson as he shifted the campaign from one of strategy to one of tactics.

Upon reaching Anderson's and McLaw's forces, Jackson quickly assessed the situation and initiated the plans for the counterflanking maneuver. As his troops set out Lee arrived to confer with Jackson. The exact details of that conference remain a mystery, as the generals spoke in strict privacy. Apparently, however, Lee approved of Jackson's plans, yet he questioned the time factor and the ability of Confederate troops to maneuver into a position which would allow for both the surprise and numbers necessary for success. Neither man could forget that the course on which they had set themselves meant the pitting of a small corps of less than six divisions against a force four times that number. The fact remained that they had captured the initiative and although the risks were high each general had supreme confidence in the other's instincts and abilities.

Thus the final battle plan was agreed upon. Lee, with some 20,000 troops, would hold the center, keeping Hooker's attention focused on himself through minor skirmish actions. In that way he could buy the time Jackson needed for the full day's march across the enemy's front. If Hooker recognized the ploy then the results could prove fatal for the Army of Northern Virginia.

The 2 May was a day of anxious anticipation and apprehension; a day which would hold great victory and crushing loss. Early that morning Jackson's phase in the plan of action was implemented. Two factors were essential to the success of his mission. First he had to traverse the area between the fronts of the opposing armies, swing his corps

Major General John Reynolds marches to join Union forces at the Battle of Chancellorsville.

round and position his troops at the weakest point of the Union right flank, all without the Union commander realizing what was happening. Jackson's second major concern, about which he could do little but hope, was that Hooker would refrain from implementing his own offensive against any sector of the Confederate army. The key factors in the complete Confederate plan were so delicately balanced that only with speed, control and a fair measure of luck could it hope to succeed.

Jackson realized that at best it would be midafternoon or early evening before his troops were in a position to carry out Lee's strategy. With General R E Rodes' division in the lead and Fitzhugh Lee's cavalry covering his flank, Jackson set his forces to their task. After a 15-mile march across the front, Jackson found himself between Catherine's Furnace and the Brock Road. It was there that he turned his force to accomplish an outflanking move. It was also just outside Catherine's Furnace that Union troops, noticing the large concentration of Confederate soldiers moving across a clearing, began harassing the ranks with rifle and cannon fire. As Confederate cavalry exposed itself to screen those troops Jackson felt sure that the element of surprise was lost. Union officers did begin sending messages to their corps commanders stating that a Confederate maneuver had been sighted which appeared to be setting upon the Union right flank. Those reports were soon before General Hooker with requests for orders concerning the new developments.

After assessing his position and the information brought to him, Hooker drew two disastrous conclusions. First, he decided that his position and troop strength were so formidable that he would pay little attention to a maneuver which he believed was merely a weak Confederate ploy to draw the focus from Lee's presumed retreat. His second fatal error was a result of the lateness of the evening. He decided not to make any move at that time, but to hold his position and wait for what morning would bring. Little did he realize that it would only bring disaster.

At approximately 1700 hours on 2 May Jackson, believing that his luck could not hold, began positioning his troops in a line along the Union right flank in an area known as 'the Wilderness.' Periodically Union fire power had been brought to bear on his troops around Catherine's Furnace and they had also skirmished with Union pickets in that area. Although communications had been received many of the Union officers were convinced that more was afoot than an effort to shield Lee's retreat. The junior officers

General Hooker's Army marches to Chancellorsville, where they were to adopt a defensive position and dig entrenchments near a road junction outside the city.

in some of those units were immigrants who had fought in European armies who realized the need to maintain contact with the enemy to avoid being taken by surprise. Although they sent messages to their commander demanding some response to the Confederate maneuvers, their demands fell on deaf ears. In all but a few isolated pockets along the lines, Union troops were in a formation which more closely resembled a bivouac than an army facing a formidable enemy.

By 1715 hours a sufficient number of Confederate troops had completed the maneuver to allow Jackson to give the order to attack. Much to his surprise the Union forces were totally unprepared, and the XI Corps was caught completely off guard. General Oliver O Howard, Union commander in that area, had considered 'the Wilderness' of trees, brush, and brambles which lay along his right flank an adequate protection from any enemy assault. However, as the XI Corps was preparing for its evening meal, Jackson's troops attacked. With bugles blaring Confederate troops surged through 'the Wilderness' with such speed and force that few Union units had time to form a resistance to the onslaught.

In the ferocity of the attack, and with complete disregard for their own safety, Confederate troops fell upon the enemy, many literally having their clothing ripped from their bodies as they pushed through the thorny undergrowth. Both Union and Confederate officers were amazed at the soldiers' determination in pushing the assault to its limits, destroying any hope the Union officers might have had in rallying their own forces. One unknown Union officer, after his capture, declared that in their unbelievable charge through 'the Wilderness' Confederate troops descended like demons on the Union camp.

As Southern troops rolled up the Union right flank, darkness and chaos descended on the battlefield. In some isolated areas Union officers managed to form defensive lines, only to have them shattered by routed friendly forces moving as a sea which dragged everything in its path. Some sources go so far as to note that Union officers and noncommissioned officers attempted to keep their men from fleeing by shooting any soldier who broke ranks. This seemed to be the last straw for the Union troops, and the already brittle state of morale was shattered.

The Confederate charge slowly began to lose impetus, not through lack of spirit but through a lack of cohesiveness between the units and their commanders. Although 'the Wilderness' had been the source of surprise it had also caused disruption to the Confederate line all across the front. Jackson and his divisional commanders were faced with the situation of having their troops scattered along an erratic front, confused not only by the events and the increasing darkness, but also through separation from their commanders.

In the pandemonium Confederate units found themselves mixed with other regiments. Both sides fired not on known enemy positions, for there were none, but on the sound of other gunfire. Many incidents are recorded of units accidentally firing on friendly troops out of confusion and fear. It was expressly this type of confusion which would later lead to the greatest Confederate disaster of all.

Throughout the entire day, and even as the events on

the right flank were taking place, Lee's troops skirmished in an attempt to occupy Hooker's attention, particularly with Anderson's division. There are no recorded conversations or written evidence which give any conception of Lee's thoughts during Jackson's maneuver, but it can be speculated that it was with fear and anxiety that he awaited the results.

With the impetus of the Confederate attack slowing down in the deepening twilight, Jackson became impatient, feeling that with slightly more drive he could gain possession of the United States Ford Road, which led directly to the Union army's rear area. The majority of his officers had lost control of their troops, and each felt that some type of consolidation was necessary before pressing on. Rumors were rife among the ranks. Union cavalry had been caught up in the attack and had broken up into small groups attempting to fight their way back to their own lines. These cavalry troops contacted and skirmished briefly with Confederate infantry.

Infantry caught in the open feared the cavalrymen, who could attack without warning. These brief skirmishes and the confusion of the moment only added to the increasing fears of the Confederate soldiers. Jackson himself had become aware of a rumor that Union forces were massing in preparation for a charge down the road from Chancellorsville.

It was at that time that Jackson's impatience overrode his better judgement. Taking his staff and several couriers he set off down the road toward the area where the attack was said to be massing. Having decided that his personal reconnaissance was necessary, he would not heed the warnings of his fellow officers to send a younger, less indis-

General Hooker's forces fight off a Confederate attack on Sunday 3 May 1863. The Union forces were taken by surprise and fought a losing battle for four days.

pensable, person than himself survey the situation. Jackson believed that he could only command properly if he knew exactly what was transpiring.

After travelling a short distance along the road, Jackson's contingent was fired upon by a group of Union soldiers who were trying desperately to rejoin their regiment. The Union troops had also heard rumors and feared that Confederate cavalry, which was supposedly moving along the front, was bearing down on them. Several members of Jackson's group were killed or wounded by the volley and it is believed that it was then that Jackson received a wound in his right hand. The contingent turned and fled back toward Confederate lines.

As the small cavalcade approached the Confederate lines a cry of 'Yankee cavalry' went up from the ranks. The bewildered Confederate soldiers opened fire. Two more of Jackson's party fell dead and the general himself was shot twice more, in the left wrist and between the left elbow and shoulder. Wounded in both arms Jackson was unable to control his mount which bolted into the thick undergrowth. As his horse careered through the brush, Jackson was struck by a low hanging branch which caused him to reel in the saddle. Captain Wilbourn of the Signal Corps, in a valiant effort to save the general from further harm, caught Jackson as he fell to the ground.

Almost immediately General A P Hill and his staff came upon the scene. They sent for the corps surgeon and an ambulance wagon for the general. As Jackson was lifted to a litter, disaster struck once again. Union artillery, guessing at the location of the enemy from the sound of gunshot, opened fire with shell and grape shot. Several more members of both generals' staffs were killed and General Hill himself received a minor wound. Even as Jackson passed his command to Hill, that general was also removed from action, leaving General Rodes the next officer in line.

General Rodes however was not the man to manage such a maneuver nor consolidate the troops, and command passed to General 'Jeb' Stuart who like Jackson was a very daring and resourceful figure.

The assault was now in complete chaos. The Union forces were in uncontrolled retreat and the Confederate troops were attempting to reorganize and establish a front in the darkness. These efforts were difficult enough, yet were compounded by the rumors which circulated about the Union forces and the incident with Jackson and Hill. Stuart did what lay in his power to calm the army, but with little apparent success.

By the end of the first day's fighting both armies were shrouded in gloom. The Union despaired over an attack which had completely routed the right flank and the Confederates were disconsolate over the circumstances which caused the removal of their beloved Jackson. Although Jackson's wounds were not severe, he did lose his left arm. Eight days later, as a result of his weakened condition, the cold which he had caught on the night before the attack worsened into pneumonia, causing his untimely death. The Confederate success was indeed paid for dearly.

With order somewhat restored the Confederate forces continued their attack on 3 May. Many had gone for more than 30 hours without adequate food or rest. They dis-

covered that although the right flank had been routed, for the most part the Union Army was still intact and offering stout resistance. The Union troops were displaying a staunch attitude but the same could not be said for their commanding general. Hooker's spirit and confidence had been totally destroyed on the previous night. He could not believe that the Confederate attack had inflicted such a loss, nor even that such an extraordinary maneuver had been mounted against him. Hooker suddenly doubted his intelligence reports, his army, his plans and, most importantly, his own infallibility. To make matters worse, Hooker's headquarters was hit by a Confederate artillery round early in the day, which knocked the general temporarily unconscious. For the remainder of the day he appeared to be in a daze. His mind apparently clouded, he ordered a full retreat of the army.

The order for retreat came in spite of the fact that nowhere along the line of attack were Confederate forces making any substantial headway. Lee had taken complete command of the army once again, and although he tried all day to cut off the Union forces as they retreated from the battlefield he could not accomplish any tactical advantage. Union forces therefore retreated safely across the Rappahannock River. Although Lee and Stuart made every attempt, they simply were not able to accomplish what each felt Jackson could easily have done.

On 4 May, as the retreat continued, Hooker ordered Sedgwick to attack Major-General Jubal Early's lone division at its position on Marye's Heights. By noon Sedgwick had cracked the Confederate defenses and was headed toward Chancellorsville. With the news of this Union success, and with hopes dwindling of inflicting further losses against Hooker in the main frontal area, Lee turned his attention to the latest assault. To meet the threat Lee shifted his entire army against Sedgwick. In a succession of unsuccessful attacks and skirmishes Lee managed only to hold Sedgwick's advance, inflicting very few casualties, before Sedgwick turned and escaped across the river. Lee changed direction once again, marching back toward Chancellorsville, only to find that Hooker's forces were too far away for the exhausted Confederate troops to give battle.

By 5 May the Chancellorsville Campaign was officially over. Jackson's leadership had resulted in Hooker fleeing the field. Lee was credited with defeating the new commander of the Army of the Potomac, though he did not defeat the army itself. What in fact did he accomplish?

First and foremost, Lee defeated Hooker, throwing the Union command once again into chaos and undermining the morale and confidence of the Union troops in their leaders. He turned back a Union Army three times the troop strength of his own Confederate force and with the aid of a competent staff, primarily Jackson, extinguished Union hopes of a decisive victory at that time. Through continued success the myth of Lee's invincibility was once more confirmed in the minds of the Union rank and file and started to spread to the citizens of the North. Worse yet, President Lincoln and his staff began to believe the legend.

Lee once again proved that he had an uncanny knack for understanding his enemy's strategies. He established

Confederate prisoners marching north after Chancellorsville.

his true mastery over given situations. His ability to command was aided by the great respect paid him by his officers and the trust with which they awaited his judgment of the situation, rather than striking out on their own and acting independently. A key example of that ability was demonstrated in the manner in which he held his generals in check, particularly Jackson, when they wanted desperately to attack Sedgwick's forces in the early days of the battle. In spite of their own individual qualities as commanders and generals, Lee's staff responded to their commanding general, awaiting his orders. The quality of leadership was truly Lee's.

In spite of the fact that Lee saw through Hooker's plan he held off for the right moment and situation and came up with an aggressively daring strategy which would wrest victory from his enemy. This triumph is overshadowed by two definite factors. First is the previously mentioned point that he was a strategist and not a tactician. Second is his relationship with Jackson. In short, Lee was the 'thinker' and Jackson was the 'doer.' This is clearly evident in the manner in which Jackson accomplished the flanking maneuver, and Lee's inability to deliver the final blow to the retreating Union army once Jackson's influence had been removed.

From 3 May onward Lee's forces were lacking in fighting strength and direction. Lee marched to and fro on the battlefield between fronts attempting to trap or defeat some part of the Union forces. Had Jackson been present this would surely have been a success or at least greater damage would have been inflicted upon the Union forces.

Another bitter fact of the engagement was the number of casualties. After the battle Union casualties numbered some 17,000, while Confederate losses were listed at 13,000. Most of the Confederate casualties occurred after Jackson's removal from the field, while Lee was in command. While numerical losses were similar, the percentages of overall troop strength make the figures staggeringly disproportionate.

In combining the losses which Lee would ill afford, the indecisive maneuvering from 3–5 May, the inability to inflict a crucial defeat and the loss of 'Stonewall' Jackson to the Confederate army, Chancellorsville was a very hollow victory. If it were not for Hooker's loss of nerve, Lee would probably have found himself facing defeat.

Yet these points do not indicate that Lee should be denied his title as a great general. He was after all only a man and not the demigod which many believed him to be. It can perhaps even be said that Lee's heart went out of the war with the loss of his trusted aide and confidante, Jackson. Indeed, Jackson's death caused a great cry of mourning to echo throughout the South. A lunatic in a Baltimore asylum is credited with Jackson's most telling epitaph when he said, 'a terrible battle must be raging in heaven when God and his archangels need the services of "Stonewall" Jackson.' There would be no replacement for Jackson in the service of Lee's Army of Northern Virginia.

In the final analysis of General Robert E Lee during his years as the commander of the Army of Northern Virginia it is perhaps sufficient to say, 'Lee was competent, Lee and Jackson were invincible; Lee was a general, Lee and Jackson were a legend.'

GRANT AT VICKSBURG 1863

In the campaign staged by Ulysses S Grant at Vicksburg, a multitude of influences, strategies and events combined to produce a battle unlike any other of the Civil War. In essence the importance of the campaign lay not so much in the defeat of an enemy or the turning of a tide, but in the battle's effects on future events.

With the exception of Robert E Lee, Ulysses Simpson Grant is perhaps the most renowned Civil War general. His success was partly a result of his unusual attitude to war, which is best described by a colleague in the Vicksburg Campaign. A man of kindred spirit, General William Tecumseh Sherman voiced the definition well when he quite simply stated, 'War is hell.'

Grant saw war as a necessity which comes and goes as societies demand. Once the inevitable act of war was undertaken, warfare itself became a job which had to be done. Grant, unlike most of his contemporaries, was not a general in the Civil War for glory and love of country, nor to defeat slavery or uphold the Union. He was a soldier by profession and war was the business and commodity he knew best.

It is with that perspective that the key to Grant's success can be best understood. The objective of war is victory for oneself and defeat for the enemy. To that end one must strive to completely destroy the enemy's ability to fight. Not only must the enemy be initially defeated, but his power to continue the conflict must be eliminated. It was that concept which Grant implemented in his strategies.

For many months the Union searched for a man capable of defeating his Confederate counterparts and bringing victory to the Union. By March 1864 such a man had risen to supreme command of the Union armies and had become known as 'Mr Lincoln's General.' Yet the man, who would become not only a legendary figure of the Civil War but the eighteenth President of the United States, at one time seemed likely to end his career in ignominy.

Ulysses Simpson Grant was born in 1822. He attended the Academy at West Point during the same time period as others who would figure prominently in the Civil War. Unlike Lee, Grant was not academically inclined and he eventually graduated in the bottom half of his class at West Point. He received his initiation into active service during the Mexican War where he was decorated on several occasions for his heroism. Grant also displayed a keen grasp of tactics which earmarked him for a promising military career. Unfortunately, after the war the boredom of the frontier, combined with his inability to cope with alcohol led Grant to resign his commission rather than face court-martial.

In civilian life Grant drifted from one misadventure to another and by the time the Civil War broke out he was completely destitute. With little hope of success in a civilian position, Grant viewed the war as a means of extricating himself from his difficulties. He secured a position with the 21st Illinois Volunteers only with difficulty, as his civilian reputation of failure and drunkenness preceeded him. It was with great reluctance and through sheer necessity that he was given the command.

His primary duty was not only to command but also to drill the new volunteers. In spite of the various problems which beset him, Grant quickly rose to the rank of Brigadier General of the Illinois Military District. In that capacity he became involved in the war in the West along the Mississippi River, generally considered of secondary importance compared to the conflict raging in the East around the two capitals.

Although in his efforts during the later months of 1861 Grant showed tendencies toward indecisiveness, he received national acclaim in February 1862 with the brilliant seizure of Fort Henry and Fort Donelson on the upper tributaries of the Mississippi. In April of the same year Confederate forces made a surprise attack on his position and Grant converted possible disaster into victory in what has become known as the Battle of Shiloh. The following year Grant became an integral force in the campaign which proved to be not only the turning point of the Civil War but the turning point of Grant's career — the Battle of Vicksburg.

It seems curious that the Battle of Vicksburg, and not Gettysburg which has become more legendary, was the true turning point. It is perhaps because Vicksburg was a true military campaign rather than the simple confrontation of two armies. However it was Vicksburg's location which gave it its major importance. Located on the eastern bank of the Mississippi, on a sharp bend in the river, Vicksburg was a natural fortification and control point. No ship could travel the narrow passage without passing under the guns of the city.

Being one of the largest rivers in America, and owing to its rail links and its wide-ranging tributaries, the Mississippi River was a natural avenue for transporting goods from the midwest of the United States to New Orleans and

General Grant at Cold Harbor, Virginia in June 1864.

other national and international markets. In the opening days of the Civil War few people considered that the war would be of extended duration, thus little Northern attention was focused on the importance of the Southern control of the Mississippi. However, as the war progressed the disruption of river traffic and the deviation from the river's traditional use bred discontent in the western states. Pressure increased in those states for the acceptance and recognition of the Confederacy, even to the idea of secession themselves, in order to resume free commerce on the great river.

In Washington, Lincoln recognized the growing discord and realized that the dissent would continue to grow unless the Mississippi was reopened. His strategy was simple, capture the river and open it for trade. The execution of this strategy was another matter entirely.

During the second half of 1862 several attempts were made to overcome Vicksburg as it was the primary fortification blocking the Mississippi. One venture involved the combined efforts of river fleets attacking from both north and south. Admiral David Glasgow Farragut was responsible for the capture of New Orleans during that action, and although some degree of success was initially achieved the problems of supply, cooperation between the services and the ample Confederate defenses along the river proved overpowering. It should be pointed out that although the action was not successfully completed, this was the first instance where a concerted effort was made to combine the army and the navy in one operation.

The many difficulties encountered through the use of flotilla tactics led to the use of basic assault tactics. Another

General William T Sherman, photographed by Matthew Brady.

Vicksburg before the siege.

attempt was made to capture Vicksburg through the use of overwhelming numbers of troops. This, however, proved equally ineffectual against the Confederate defenses. With the Confederate forces in possession of the high ground and the most strategic locations, the concept of landing an army and supporting it with fleet artillery simply did not function. Grant determined to devise a successful strategy.

His first plan was to bypass Vicksburg by cutting a canal across the narrow finger of land which formed the bend in the river on the western side, opposite Vicksburg. He received support for his plan from President Lincoln and Sherman's XV Corps was assigned the task of digging the canal. Once completed the canal would allow the free passage of ships outside the range of Vicksburg firepower. The canal would also allow for the future encirclement and isolation of Vicksburg in the Union scheme.

Several obvious flaws in the project became apparent as construction began. First and foremost was the fact that the Confederates could view the Union activity from their vantage point on the heights of Vicksburg. Their immediate retaliation to the impending canal was to reposition several batteries at Warrentown, bringing the southern mouth of the canal under range of their guns. The second major problem occurred in March 1863 when the river rose, breaking through the upper dam and flooding the canal and the surrounding lands. This natural disaster destroyed Union stores and equipment and completely disrupted Sherman's corps.

At General Grant's headquarters alternative plans were already being devised. In February 1863 a navy flotilla was sent down a tributary of the Yazoo River north of Vicksburg with the support of infantry columns. The troops were to capture Confederate dockyards at Yazoo City and secure all positions of high ground at Snyder's Bluff. This plan was thwarted by harassment from Confederate forces, who blocked the waterways and hindered the navy at every opportunity. The Confederates were assisted in their efforts by the natural silting of the narrow river passageways. The Union forces were forced to move at a snail's pace when speed and rapid deployment were vital.

By April the navy was forced to withdraw. Confederate troops had been successful enough in their delaying tactics to be able to reinforce their position, creating a formidable enough front to dissuade the Union forces from further attacks in that area. A second expedition set out in mid-March, with General Sherman taking part. This was equally unsuccessful. The fact that movement was slow, whether by water or land, meant that Confederate forces were always fully aware of Union intentions and able to act accordingly. The failure of these attempts to attack the city from the north caused Grant to again reassess his ideas and reevaluate his strategy.

However, despite the failure of those missions Grant learned a valuable lesson which would stand him in good

The Union forces tried to cut a canal across a loop of the Mississippi in order to approach Vicksburg. The canal was either flooded or silted and proved a wasted effort.

stead during the coming Vicksburg campaign. Forced to abandon their assault by the fact that Confederate forces had severed the Union lines of communication and supply, Grant discovered that his force could subsist quite well by living off the land during their retreat. He would implement this knowledge in the near future.

Grant developed a strategy which was not only daring but once set in motion was undoubtedly irrevocable. Two issues had troubled Grant throughout the campaign. First was the fact that despite all efforts his forces were forever in an adverse position when attempting to bring pressure against the Vicksburg fortifications. Second was the fact that the garrison was reinforced and resupplied with consistent ease. In his new strategy Grant decided to eliminate the support before concentrating on the garrison itself.

In mid-April Grant sent seven gunboats, a ram and several cargo steamers down the river past Vicksburg. This maneuver was accomplished under cover of darkness to minimize the effectiveness of the guns. From 20 April Grant began to move his army down the Louisiana bank of the river, constructing an effective roadway through the bogs and forests toward the river city of New Carthage. After great success in that region Grant's forces continued south along the river banks, yet by-passing Vicksburg, on a course for Bruinsburg. Simultaneously ships continued to run the gauntlet at Vicksburg, creating a sizable force south of the city. These vessels not only carried supplies for the army but would figure as major components in the next stage of Grant's strategy.

By the end of April Grant's forces had entered Bruinsburg and on 30 April he began to ferry his troops from the western to the eastern banks of the Mississippi. That maneuver took the Confederates completely by surprise. Thus far all Union attacks on Vicksburg had been from the north. Grant exploited the opportunity for surprise and now was threatening by land from the south, a contingency for which the Confederate command was not prepared.

The details of Grant's scheme were yet to be realized. As Confederate commanders considered the possibilities of Grant's next move against Vicksburg, Grant was concentrating on his prime objective – the isolating of Vicksburg. His first course of action would have to be a move inland to sever the Confederate lines of communication. This would mean that his own lines of supply would cease to exist. As the area south of Vicksburg had seen little land combat, Grant felt certain that he would be able to forage all necessary supplies.

On 1 May Grant sent part of Major General John A McClernand's XIII Corps to quell any Confederate resistance at Port Gibson. With Grand Gulf threatened on the landward side by the Union's XVII Corps, the Confederates decided it would be wise to evacuate those troops and join forces with troops sent from Vicksburg, holding a line along the Big Black River.

On 7 May Sherman's XV Corps took advantage of the Confederate evacuation, marching from Milliken's Bend and crossing the river at Grand Gulf. With that maneuver Grant shifted most of his army to the Vicksburg side of the river, and with Sherman moving rapidly to join him, Grant set about executing the next phase of his plan.

Rather than marching straight on Vicksburg from the

Above: The head of the canal opposite Vicksburg. This shows the swampy nature of the countryside.

Right: Skirmishing in the woods before Vicksburg.

south, Grant struck further inland, converging his forces on the Mississippi state capital, Jackson. General Joseph Eggleston Johnston, Confederate commander in the West, had at that time only two brigades at his disposal. Realizing that he would have to attempt to buy time, Johnston retreated northward to link up with reinforcements he expected from the East. Within a few days he hoped to be able to field an army of 30,000 men. Johnston also sent word to Lieutenant General John Clifford Pemberton, Commander of the Mississippi Military District, to take charge of combining the garrison forces of Port Hudson and Vicksburg. Johnston's field army and the combined force should have brought his command to more than 50,000.

Possessing what he thought to be double the number of men under Grant, Johnston felt certain that he could not only defeat Grant but maintain a strong Confederate dominance in the war in the West. However, Johnston was not aware that Pemberton had previous orders. Jefferson Davis had personally given the order that neither Port Hudson nor Vicksburg was to be left ungarrisoned. In following that order Pemberton left behind 10,000 of his troops to man the defenses at Vicksburg and, rather than move to the immediate support of Johnston's army, decided to take his smaller force and sever Grant's lines of communication and supply.

As Pemberton ignored Johnston's orders he came to realize that Grant had disregarded military convention and had no lines of communication or supply. Instead of disrupting Grant's rear area Pemberton followed the movement of Grant's troops toward Jackson, Mississippi. On 14 May Grant entered Jackson, destroying the Confederate stores and severing the Jackson–Vicksburg railroad. Grant was well aware that if he could defeat any of the Confederate armies in an open field battle Vicksburg would be temporarily isolated. On 16 May, after five hours of seesaw engagements Pemberton's forces were defeated at the Battle of Champion's Hill.

More significant than the defeat was the fact that Pemberton had made a grave tactical error. Instead of retreating toward Johnston to combine their strengths and attempt to pin Grant's forces between the field army and Vicksburg, Pemberton retreated to the mock safety of the Vicksburg defenses. In succumbing to the temptation of a safe haven Pemberton again divided his troops to cover his retreat. Over the next 24 hours that decision would cost him more than 1700 men and the loss of some 18 heavy guns as the Union troops swept away the rearguard at the Big Black River.

On 19 May, a little more than one month after Grant had set his new strategy in motion, his army was poised just outside Vicksburg preparing for the attack. Grant confidently believed that victory was at hand. He felt certain that his enemy was so demoralized by the past weeks' events and the recent defeat that panic would surely be racing through the ranks, and that an immediate assault on Vicksburg would probably overpower the defenses of the city.

In all the past month's displays of brilliant maneuvering and strategy this was Grant's first mistake. His error in judgment was based primarily on a lack of intelligence information concerning the garrison and an overconfidence attributable to easy victories. Although the defenders' morale had indeed been severely shaken, Grant failed to compensate for the determination that the Confederate forces gained in the realization that they must either make a stand for victory or surrender in defeat. They had no alternative with the Union forces encircling the city. This determination, coupled with the fact that 10,000 fresh troops had remained in the garrison, gave new heart to the Confederate troops who had already faced Grant's army. Thus the first Union assault was soundly repulsed and Union forces withdrew from the attack greatly bewildered by the staunch resistance which they had encountered.

On 22 May Grant ordered a second assault. He was concerned that Johnston's force was by then only some 50 miles east of the garrison. In spite of the fact that Johnston had a much smaller force Grant did not wish to allow him any time to put together an army which could arrive to relieve the city. At 1000 hours Grant ordered a heavy bombardment of the fortification along his army's entire front. He was confident that his second assault was better organized, with all three Corps concentrating their attacks simultaneously. Sherman's XV Corps attacked from the north, McPherson's XVII Corps from the east, and McClernand's XIII Corps from the southeast. Union forces pressed home a fierce attack against the defenders, but nowhere along the line was an actual breech in the defenses made. McClernand's XIII Corps did however manage to overrun several entrenchments, causing him to request reinforcements that he might carry his position. Grant, unable to have an overall view of the battle, had committed his reinforcements to renewed assaults by Sherman and McPherson. That commitment resulted only in increased casualties on the Union side without the gain of an extra foot of ground. Without reinforcements the XIII Corps could not hold their ground and foot by foot were driven back from the entrenchments.

The second assault had failed with three times the casualties suffered in the first assault. Grant hastily reviewed the situation. The first question he undoubtedly asked himself was whether or not the troops had lost heart. His answer, based on their performance was an emphatic 'no.' During the second assault each corps had managed to plant its flag on top on the entrenchments and had fought stubbornly to gain a victory. If the troops were not to blame it had to be the tactics. Two frontal assaults had gained nothing but casualties and meant that a third would also be unsuccessful. If assaults were unsuccessful then the only alternative left was siege.

Yet how successful could such a siege be? Grant had completely cut off the city of Vicksburg from any avenue of resupply or reinforcement. The surrounding land was in the complete control of Union forces and the Mississippi River had been blocked by Union war vessels. His campaign had until that point been successful, and he had managed to deliver the South a severe blow even if he had failed to take the fortifications at Vicksburg. But Vicksburg was the key and Grant would not be dissuaded.

In 20 days Grant had marched some 180 miles through enemy territory, had accumulated vast quantities of military supplies, captured a state capital and fought five major engagements, all on five days' rations. His forces had managed to capture more than 6000 enemy soldiers and 89 field pieces, all at the loss of less than 2000 killed and 7500 wounded of his 43,000-strong army. As Sherman is said to have pointed out, they had achieved a great victory even if Vicksburg held out. Not only had they encircled and isolated the fortification, but Grant was aware that Johnston's army was not in a position to offer any assistance to the defenders. The reserves that Johnston had counted on so desperately had been diverted to the East to support Lee in his Northern Campaign into Pennsylvania.

Grant was therefore faced with the problem of seizing Vicksburg as quickly as possible, denying the Confederate forces time to recover from his previous assaults. The mounting of a full siege was a prospect which Grant did not relish. He knew that siege warfare was a very specialized art and from his studies at West Point realized that whole armies could be wasted on a mismanaged siege. Grant had

On 22 May 1863 Grant ordered another attack which was preceded by heavy bombardment. After a day's heavy fighting the attack was seen to have failed.

no desire to end his campaign in that manner, yet to be so close to the prize and then to lose it would be more than he could bear.

As the troops began to dig themselves in Grant reviewed his command and found that he was very short of trained military engineers. He had a good number of men in his volunteer units who had built bridges, constructed roads and with Sherman's XV Corps had built a canal. However, very few of these men understood the business of con-

Following the failure of the 22 May attack Union forces built fortifications around the Confederate lines to prevent them from breaking out. The picture shows Sherman's Corps.

structing parallel trenches, mining and countermining, and lines of circumvallation and countervallation, all of which are an integral part of siege warfare. Grant was not to be found wanting. As a young cadet he had received training in the field of military engineering, as did all cadets no matter what branch of the armed service they would eventually enter. As he had no true Engineer Corps Grant decided to create one. He put a request to all units that all officers who were West Point graduates report to one of the four regular engineering officers to serve in the capacity of assistant engineers. With a man of ample capability to guide them, in the person of Captain F E Prime and his successor Captain Cyrus B Comstock, Grant felt certain that he could mold his officers and western volunteers into an engineering force which could rival any regular engineering unit.

Grant was also granted some breathing space in that while he assembled his engineering unit and his troops were digging themselves in for the siege, a truce had been called on two separate days so that the Union forces might recover and bury their dead. With Confederate troops assisting their Union counterparts in the recovery, Colonel H S Lockett, commander of the Confederate engineers, decided that he had a prime opportunity to examine the Union siege works. Lockett was quite sure that Grant was no fool. It would be in Grant's best interest to assign his engineering officers to command the recovery details, thus allowing them a close look at the Confederate entrenchments and fortifications. Lockett decided that he would perform the same role for the Confederates. Unfortunately, Lockett was consistantly hindered from seeing many aspects of the Union works by General Sherman, who kept Lockett engaged in courteous conversation throughout the day. This gave the Union engineers a certain advantage over the Confederate forces.

Grant's next most important problem lay in the fact that he had no true siege guns, except for his six 32-pounders. For the most part he would have to rely on his

Left: General John A Logan's
headquarters on 25 June 1863.
Logan was a Douglas Democrat
from Illinois and was a political
general.

Below: A view of Vicksburg during
the siege, seen from behind the
Union lines.

field guns to soften the fortifications. Admiral Porter did manage to transfer a battery of large caliber naval guns to the siege troops. Although greatly needed they were still far too few to make a great difference.

At that time Grant made a very wise decision. He turned the siege operation over to his engineers, maintaining control over the army as a whole yet allowing the engineers to formulate the detailed plans of attack on the various sections. In doing this Grant displayed two things. First and foremost he demonstrated that he was a capable and con-fident commander who was not afraid to allow subordinants to take charge and formulate the best avenues of attack according to their specialities. Secondly, it showed that Grant was well aware of the great magnitude of the task, realizing that it was too large and intricate an operation for one man and his staff to command efficiently. His best possible strategy was to apply a loose command over the army, giving it direction and purpose, while allowing the details of the plan to be handled at the lower levels of command.

Union forces (Grant)

Mid April 1863 Steamers sent to Hard Times

20 April Grant begins movement towards Bruinsburg

Mississippi R

Miliken's Bend

Sherman (XV Corps)

Arrived Dec 1862

29-30 April Demonstrations by Sherman

Yazoo R

Haynes Bluff

19 May, 1863 Siege of Vicksburg begins, 4 July Pemberton surrenders

Sherman

16 May Pemberton defeated

BRIDGEPORT

Champion's Hill

CLINTON

Johnston retreats north

Pearl River

Proposed canal

VICKSBURG

Confederate forces (Pemberton)

McPherson and McClernand

McClernand

RAYMOND

JACKSON

14 May Union forces enter Jackson

WARRENTON

Big Black River

McClernand and Sherman

Sherman and McPherson

NEW CARTHAGE

2 May Confederate units withdraw

AUBURN

McPherson

McClernand (XIII Corps)

ROCKY SPRINGS

McPherson (XVII Corps)

HARD TIMES 29 April

GRAND GULF

Mississippi R

7 May Sherman's XV Corps arrives

Grindstone Ferry

BRUINSBURG End April

PORT GIBSON 1 May

UNION FORCES

CONFEDERATE FORCES

EARLY APRIL,1863

MILES 0 — 10

KILOMETERS 0 — 20

The siege of Vicksburg

Sherman

Mississippi R

VICKSBURG

Pemberton

McPherson

Confederate defence line

McClernand (Ord later)

Grant

0 — MILE 1

© Richard Natkiel, 1981

Although the actual basic mechanisms of the siege did not necessarily reflect on Grant as an able military commander, the siege was highly important for several reasons. The concept of siege was not a new one, but the manner in which the siege at Vicksburg was executed gave a preview of the type of trench warfare which would become prevalent in World War I. The idea of two armies dug in, entrenched only yards from one another, with mining and countermining a daily routine, would be the blueprints of trench warfare in the future. The two initial assaults on Vicksburg serve to exemplify the devastating results of attacking troops in entrenched and prepared positions. The losses sustained by Grant's forces were only a preview to the number of soldiers who would be lost in 'no man's land' on the battlefields of France.

The whole concept of war was changing. Less and less frequently would armies meet in a short, decisive battle. More often battles would degenerate into a war of attrition. Had Vicksburg been in a position to resupply, and if the fortifications had been woven with more interlocking points on a grand scale of defense and support, it would have given a staunch resistance, more clearly displaying what was forthcoming in the art of warfare.

Another point concerning the siege merely confirmed that no matter how formidable or well conceived a fortification may be, once isolated and unable to be resupplied or relieved, that fortification is doomed. Grant's strategy of encircling his objective as well as removing any chance for support or relief was responsible for ending the siege of Vicksburg so quickly. His tactic of first removing hope

before setting about the basic details of the engagement would be used as the guidelines for many siege engagements of the future, most notably at Dien Bien Phu by General Giap.

Those strategies and tactics would echo in the future, as would the life led by Grant's soldiers fighting the siege. Life became a set routine of digging trenches at night, defending the newly built earthworks during the day, and trying to survive the snipers' bullets and the harassment of the enemy artillery. By 30 June they had produced miles of trenches encircling the fortification on all landward sides and had created positions for some 200 pieces of artillery. When it rained the trenches became muddy troughs, and in the heat of the southern summer sun became baked dust pits. The life of the Union soldier at Vicksburg was to sweat and dig all night and exchange a few shots during the day.

An unusual phenomena occurred to break the monotony for the Union troops in early July. Northerners, elated by the news of the successes at Vicksburg, flocked to the siege site. Friends, family, volunteers, politicians and others arrived to give aid and comfort or simply to view the proceedings. A carnival atmosphere prevailed before the troops returned to the inescapable task at hand.

It was the Confederate soldier who had to face the worst the siege could offer. The first problem confronting the defenders was lack of food. The fact that Vicksburg had a

The fight in the crater at Fort Hill after the explosion of the mine, 25 June 1863.

civilian population as well as a military one meant that rations dwindled rapidly. By mid-June the defenders' diets consisted mainly of mule stew, cane shoots and roast rat. Early in the siege yams and blackberry leaves were substituted for coffee which ran out quickly. Flour was eked out with cornmeal or ground peas, while they lasted. All food was strictly guarded but supplies were very limited.

The lack of food began to show its effects as Vicksburg defenders became so weak that their maximum efforts and abilities were consumed by the mere manning of their positions. There were stories that in the early days of the siege Union and Confederate soldiers, whose trenches were so close that they could throw hand grenades, managed to communicate long enough to toss hardtack in exchange for Confederate tobacco. As the siege dragged on such exchanges rapidly disappeared.

The Confederate's second problem dealt with another much needed commodity, ammunition. Most personal accounts written by Confederate soldiers at Vicksburg remark of the Union soldiers firing constantly at the Confederate lines with both artillery and muskets, while the Confederate soldiers had to horde their ammunition to be used at its most advantageous time.

Finally, and of grave importance to the morale of the Confederate troops, was the realization that relief was not forthcoming. Union forces were virtually in full control of the Mississippi River. Johnston's army, which was supposed to come to the aid of Vicksburg, could barely muster sufficient troops for an attack when it was most needed. As the defenders watched Grant's forces grow day by day, watched their rations dwindle, and watched for relief which they knew would not arrive, their spirit and will to fight slowly died.

On the night of 2 July General Pemberton called together his staff and most of his officers and informed them that the situation was desperate. He discussed whether or not they should surrender the garrison. Although several officers wanted to hold out as long as possible, in order to cause more casualties to the Union forces and to keep tied down the main Union army in the West, the majority of officers felt that it was only a matter of a few days before ammunition became so scarce that even this object could not be accomplished. Pemberton accepted the majority opinion and decided to surrender.

At about 1000 hours on the morning of 3 July flags of truce were flown over the garrison. Pemberton sent his aide-de-camp, Colonel Montgomery, and General Bowen, a divisional commander, with a message of armistice. Both sides took heart upon seeing the white flags. For the Confederates, even though it meant defeat, the bloodshed of a hopeless situation would soon end. Once surrender terms were properly ironed out medical aid and food for the beleaguered troops would be available within a matter of hours. For the Union soldiers it meant an end to a hard fought campaign and victory over what the Confederate president had termed an 'impregnable, unconquerable fortification.' Victory would indeed be sweet.

However, the terms indicated in Pemberton's letter were not in any way to Grant's liking. Pemberton offered a period of armistice and proposed that the two commanders set about laying the terms which would be required before

Fighting with hand grenades on the last day of the siege of Vicksburg before the terms of the surrender were agreed.

the Confederates would relinquish their position. Grant's reply was returned in no uncertain terms itself, and is recorded in the *Personal Memoirs of U S Grant*. He replied: 'Your note of this date is just received, proposing an armistice for several hours, for the purpose of arranging terms of capitulation through commissioners, to be appointed, etc. The useless effusion of blood you propose stopping by this course can be ended at any time you may choose, by the unconditional surrender of the city and garrison. Men who have shown so much endurance and courage as those now in Vicksburg, will always challenge the respect on an adversary, and I can assure you will be treated with all the respect due to prisoners of war. I do not favor the proposition of appointing commissioners to arrange the terms of capitulation, because I have no terms other than those indicated above.'

Unconditional surrender was the key to Grant's terms. At 1500 hours Grant and Pemberton met on a hillside a few hundred yards from the Confederate lines. The two generals, who had served together in the same division during the Mexican War, greeted one another as old acquaintances. Perhaps it was a result of past friendship, or out of respect for the valiant manner of the garrison troops, but more than that it was a reflection of Grant's military character which dictated the terms he was to see to his unconditional surrender.

Although the surrender was not finalized until 2000 hours on 3 July the ceasefire began immediately. Whereas Pemberton balked at the word 'unconditional' his troops seemed prepared to accept the fate which awaited them. Many soldiers from both camps had been recruited from

Missouri, and the Vicksburg campaign was one in which brother had literally fought brother. The troops took the opportunity to begin searching for friends and relatives in the opposing camp.

Finally, after 2000 hours Grant had sent his proposal for surrender to General Pemberton. The unconditional surrender stood but several modifications and provisions were introduced. First, the city of Vicksburg would surrender and the garrison would lay down its arms. The garrison force would be released on parole, with the stipulation that they would participate in no further action in the war unless properly exchanged for Union prisoners of war. Confederate officers would be allowed to retain their side arms and swords, along with their mounts. The army would be allowed to keep any personal effects such as food, rations or clothing, but nothing else. Civilian rights and disciplines were to be strictly maintained but all slaves would be forfeited and set free as called for in Mr Lincoln's Emancipation Proclamation.

It was obvious by General Pemberton's relief at the terms that he had underestimated his adversary. Grant was not one, once the battle had been won, to add humiliation or subjugation to the defeat of his foe. On the morning of 4 July Pemberton surrendered the city and garrison of Vicksburg and Grant's campaign was victorious.

The surrender meant that the Union forces acquired more than 170 pieces of artillery and some 60,000 small arms. The small arms quota especially pleased the Union command as many of the rifles were of more recent date than those supplied to the Union troops. Grant issued orders that the new Enfield Rifles be issued to his troops, replacing the antiquated US or Belgian rifles then in use.

Without a doubt, however, the main prize in the victory was the fall of Vicksburg as the main block on the Mississippi River. The fall of Port Hudson five days later opened the river completely and within one week Union shipping could leave the docks of St Louis and travel unimpeded to New Orleans.

The success of the plan which Grant formulated for the defeat of Vicksburg sets him in the ranks of the greatest generals in history. His policy could be said to have been somewhat ahead of his time. Like all generals, Grant suffered from outside interference. His superiors, politi-

A rare photograph of Vicksburg under Union fire during the early part of 1863.

cians and even the President hindered his success in the early days of his second campaign, and could be said to have cost him a victory in the first campaign almost a year earlier. There comes a point in the command of every great military leader when he must abandon what is considered acceptable and, as in Grant's Vicksburg campaign, take the 'bull by the horns' and set out to conquer rather than simply remove an obstacle.

Grant's early campaigns convinced him that any further attempts to take Vicksburg from the north or northeast would be a senseless waste of both time and lives. He set out to destroy the enemy's means and will to fight by staging a successful campaign against the surrounding key areas, such as the capital, Jackson. His daring and success set him apart as a master among the great minds of strategical and tactical brilliance. But the brilliance of one man's strategy is often overlooked when comparing his role to that of others of his era. Jackson's magnificent flanking maneuver at Chancellorsville and Meade's rapid rise to glory at Gettysburg are fine examples of well-executed, courageously fought engagements. Grant's campaign was a different type of warfare entirely.

Not only did Grant have to consider his objective, but each and every encounter which led up to that final engagement. In the space of time which was allotted to him he had to maintain the impetus of his army at its maximum, never losing the initiative, while keeping his enemy separated, isolated and off balance until his goals were accomplished. Gettysburg and Chancellorsville were crucial engagements, with ranging effects, yet the generals concerned were faced with dealing with a basic strategy, the execution of which would determine the success or failure of that one encounter. Grant's strategy was such that he had to execute each battle to facilitate the final execution of his plan at Vicksburg. There is often a great deal of chance and a certain degree of luck involved in any given battle, but in a campaign nothing can be left to chance. Planning, execution and sound strategy are the factors which dictate success or failure.

In an era of attack-counterattack, move-countermove,

General Grant meets the defeated General Pemberton at the State House in Vicksburg on the morning of 4 July. The loss of Vicksburg was a terrible blow to Southern morale.

Grant worked out a deliberate long-range plan for the defeat of Vicksburg, with the actual assault on the city as his final goal. He set about to accomplish three major goals before the assault on Vicksburg. First, to destroy Confederate supplies and ammunition stored in Jackson. Second, to cut the Confederate railroad lines of communication and movement. Third, to defeat any forces in the area which could reinforce or assist the garrison. The final act in Grant's strategy was the outright defeat of Vicksburg. With no food, no ammunition, and no hope for relief he expected the victory to be more easily obtained than it actually was. The first two direct assaults on the city were valiantly driven back. This however was more a result of the fact that 10,000 fresh troops were garrisoned there and the undeniable influence of the defense being a last-gasp effort. The point remained, despite the initial set backs in the assaults, that Vicksburg was virtually an island. Grant had removed all chance of outside support, save Johnston's distant force, and while he may have misjudged the Confederate defenders' initial state of morale, the outcome was obvious. Sooner or later Vicksburg would fall.

An interesting point in the campaign lay in the development of another as yet little explored military technique.

The Vicksburg campaigns, both unsuccessful and successful, employed the use and cooperation of the naval forces of the Mississippi in their strategies. While the slow moving ironclads were often made to appear foolish in their efforts to navigate Confederate patrolled tributaries, the armored vessels were often used to carry troops and supplies to key areas along the river banks. The guns on the decks of the river craft were well appreciated by land-based troops for the support they gave. Grant demonstrated considerable forethought in his application of the naval forces in the overall picture of his campaign, another preview of tactics of the future in the art of warfare.

Grant and his Vicksburg campaign are not merely examples of a great leader and a monumental battle, but are also examples of innovative strategy and tactics which can be considered ageless. Grant's concepts form the foundation for much modern strategy. Grant deserves to be remembered not only as a victor but as one of the founding fathers of modern warfare.

MEADE AT GETTYSBURG 1863

When considering crucial battles, famous generals and the success or failure of campaigns, seldom does one encounter a battle such as Gettysburg. In this campaign the victorious general is quite often referred to as little more than one of the many commanders in the fray. In most historical accounts, Major General George Gordon Meade has been a victim of severe criticism and injustice in a refusal to give credit to his leadership and judgment, as shown not only during the battle of Gettysburg but throughout his career as an officer in the Union Army. Too often reviews of the battle concentrate on the mystique of Lee and the invulnerability of the Army of Northern Virginia, overshadowing Meade's finest qualities. The fact remains that in a time span of less than one week General Meade did more to turn the tide in the Eastern Campaign than any other individual.

Although born at Cadiz in Spain in 1815, George Gordon Meade was brought up in Pennsylvania and eventually completed his education by attending the Military Academy at West Point. During his service in the Union Army Meade gained a reputation as 'the most professional looking soldier in the North.' Although this has often been misinterpreted as an insult to his abilities, Meade was indeed an extremely professional military man. A grave, stern man, often impatient with his subordinates, Meade was a dedicated commander who demanded perfection in himself and those who served with him. He was methodical in his approach to any course of action, and had the ability to quickly assess the essentials of a situation. Meade's self-discipline meant that he could be counted upon to keep a clear head in the most volatile of situations, particularly when he could operate from a defensive posture.

Critics often dwell on the fact that Meade's methodical approach made him unable to control a fast moving battlefield and therefore unsuitable to command the Army of the Potomac, particularly at that point in time. Meade himself realized his shortcomings, considering his own cautious nature and attention to detail fine attributes for an administrator, staff officer or corps commander, but not those required of an army field commander. However, knowing one's own shortcomings is often the greatest of attributes.

Primarily Meade must be accepted for exactly what he was – a simple soldier fighting for his country. This cannot be said of his predecessors, particularly Hooker, who appeared to visualize himself as the 'savior of the Republic.' Perhaps the greatest tribute paid to Meade came from the lips of General Robert E Lee. When news of Meade's appointment reached the Confederate headquarters, Lee is reported to have referred to Meade as 'a soldier who would not commit a blunder, but who would make haste to take advantage if I should commit one.' This comment demonstrated that the Confederate Staff realized that Lincoln had at last chosen a commander who knew his profession and whose abilities could not be taken as lightly as those before him.

The second of Meade's basic qualifications lay in the fact that he was not afraid to act. He was well aware that the task of his army was to check and ultimately defeat its adversary. As an administrator and staff officer Meade

General Ulysses S Grant was besieging Vicksburg at the time of the Battle of Gettysburg.

knew how to move an army; as an efficient general, he knew why. Taking command a mere three days before the Battle of Gettysburg, Meade marched his army from the border of Virginia, through Maryland, to the hills of southern Pennsylvania to meet his enemy. So positive an effort displays capabilities which were lacking in his predecessors.

The manner in which Meade assumed command of the Army of the Potomac is another reflection of the man. The Army of the Potomac, having taken the war into the South, failed to convert advantages into victory. In every major encounter Union forces bungled their opportunities and courted disaster. Morale was at an unprecedented low. In many units the confidence of the troops had deteriorated to the point where soldiers believed that the defeat of the Army of Northern Virginia was an impossible dream in the minds of those who sat in Washington.

Lee's invasion of Pennsylvania had brought the chaotic situation of command to its climax. In Washington Lincoln considered his options and personal preferences in appointing a commander who would set the Army of the Potomac back on its feet. The first possible choice as permanent commander of the Army was Major General Joseph Hooker, the acting commander. The second possibility was Major General John F Reynolds, considered a capable and aggressive leader. Finally, though perhaps not the strongest candidate, was Major General Meade.

In considering Hooker for the post Lincoln decided that the general's past record, particularly his indecisiveness, proved that he was not the man for the position. In fact, neither Lincoln nor his advisors had been proponents of the original decision to give him the command. The President, supported by General Halleck and backed by the Secretary of War, considered Reynolds the most appropriate man to assume command. However, Reynolds had stated that unless he was given full command and complete freedom of action he did not want the command. Lincoln's office declared him Commander in Chief of the Army, and he was not prepared to let the reins slip from his grasp. Unable to accept Reynolds' terms, Lincoln and his Secretary of War, Edwin Stanton, were left with the dilemma of continuing to tolerate Hooker's ineptitude or taking the risk of promoting Meade.

While these decisions were being made, Hooker, Reynolds and Meade were encamped, carrying out their separate duties during a lull in the fighting. Rumors had been circulating and most officers were aware that something of major importance was afoot. It was generally believed, indeed even Meade was convinced, that the foremost candidates for the permanent command position were Hooker and Reynolds. Meade so firmly believed that Reynolds could be the only choice that when one of his junior officers approached him with the suggestion that Meade was also being considered, Meade dismissed it as 'another ridiculous camp rumor.'

In the early morning hours of 28 June 1863, General James J Hardie, Chief of Staff to the Secretary of War,

entered Meade's camp dressed unobtrusively in civilian clothing. Finding Meade asleep in his tent, Hardie woke him and began to explain that as acting representative to the President, Hardie was commissioned to oversee Meade's immediate assumption of Command of the Army of the Potomac. Meade was unable to digest the information. Hardie slowly and with determined simplicity repeated his assignment to a stunned and speechless Meade. Upon regaining his composure, Meade is said to have become extremely agitated. He insisted that if anyone should succeed Hooker it should rightfully be Reynolds, and condemned the President's decision as an injustice to all parties concerned.

After several trying hours and many appeals that Hardie return and have the orders amended, Meade realized that as a soldier his first duty was to obey orders. He and Hardie then set out for Hooker's headquarters. Meade demanded that Hardie deliver the news to the general in private, believing that his presence would only cause Hooker more personal discomfort in an already delicate situation. Shortly thereafter Meade assumed command as quickly and unostentatiously as possible.

In a later interview Meade exposed himself by expressing his shock and lack of preparedness for the promotion. One of Meade's anxieties was removed when his long standing friend General Reynolds arrived to pay respects to his new commander. Meade and Reynolds discussed the twist in

Above: General Meade consults his generals at a Council of War on the night of 2 July in his farmhouse headquarters on Cemetery Ridge. Meade and his generals decided that in spite of the heavy casualties the Union forces should hold their ground.

© Richard Natkiel, 1981

events and Meade again expressed his wish that Reynolds had been given the command. Reynolds assured Meade that he was happy for his friend and would support 'with all earnest' his new Commanding Officer. The two generals then spent some time exchanging ideas concerning Lee's movements into Pennsylvania, parting only when other duties required their attention.

In the afternoon hours of 28 June Generals Meade and Hooker drew up the official change of command and General George G Meade embarked on his career as Commander of the Army of the Potomac.

Two important points reflecting Meade's character were apparent in his acceptance of the command. Firstly, Meade displayed an unselfish concern not only for the army but for the sensibilities of his fellow officers. Secondly, he showed a willingness, despite surprise and doubt, to accept the responsibility and attempt the seemingly impossible in true military fashion. Meade realized that he was no 'Prima Donna,' no 'savior of the Republic.' He was commander of an army with a responsibility which could not

be treated lightly nor with self-indulgence. The Army of the Potomac had at last acquired a leader who would serve it with pride and concern.

Meade's place in history was, of course, caused by his involvement in one of the most famous battles in modern history. On 28 June when Meade took command of the Army of the Potomac, the main force was located in and around Frederick, Maryland, and Lee had already moved the Army of Northern Virginia into Pennsylvania. Moreover, Lee's march north had been almost completely uneventful, with little or no resistance or pressure, except from local militia groups. Meade decided to begin his command with action. Unlike Hooker, who sent Union cavalry units to probe the direction and strength of the Confederate forces, Meade considered that the situation was too grave to allow the two armies to be separated by such a distance. On the day his command began Meade adopted the plan of moving directly north to stay in contact with and counter Lee's army, setting the Army of the Potomac on a definite and direct course of action against its opposition.

The effect of this decision on the Union troops cannot be overemphasized. He demonstrated to the troops that he was willing to take affirmative action. In keeping with the true soldier he was, Meade intended to turn his army into an efficient fighting force, not soldiers en masse fumbling desperately to block a Confederate assault on Washington. It is often asserted that the protection of Washington was Meade's only concern. In fact, his primary concern was the defeat of the enemy, rather than the protection of a city whose garrison and fortifications would have proved a powerful obstacle to the number of troops at Lee's disposal.

Another factor which gave a much needed boost to the morale of the Union troops was their return to an area which was sympathetic to them and their cause. Since the beginning of the war the Army of the Potomac had spent the majority of its time faced with hostile civilian populations, Lee's seemingly invincible army, declining morale due to failures in leadership and the attrition of war. Morale soared as the Union soldiers crossed the Mason-Dixon line to be greeted by cheering crowds and friendly faces. Food and drink were placed into the hands of the troops as they marched along the roads. Pennsylvania was proud of its native sons, whose numbers swelled the ranks of the army. Little did they realize that in a few short days a battle would be fought on the soil of their beloved Pennsylvania, led by a general who was himself an adopted Pennsylvanian. The new confidence within the army which resulted from the affirmative action and the move in a definite path toward the enemy would stand Meade in good stead in the days ahead.

By 30 June neither Meade nor Lee was aware of the exact location of their respective enemies, nor could they determine which army had the most advantageous position. The lack of tangible evidence with regard to the enemy's position caused Meade to worry over the possibility of Confederate raiders blocking the roads to Washington and Baltimore. However, his main concern lay in determining whether or not he could maneuver Lee into a confrontation on a battlefield which would be advantageous to the Union force. Lee on the other hand struggled with the problem of having to rely heavily on information gained through the questionable source of his spies and delayed intelligence gleaned from captured local newspapers. Stuart's cavalry, Lee's primary intelligence gathering source, had vanished into the Maryland and Pennsylvania wilderness. The majority of the remaining Confederate cavalry were occupied in guarding the passes of the Blue Ridge Mountains to keep the avenues of communication, supply and possible retreat open.

On the morning of 30 June Meade sent engineers to scout areas along the Big Pipe Creek, hoping to find a location which would prove suitable and advantageous to a defensively positioned Union force. He sent his III Corps to the town of Emmitsburg, just south of the Pennsylvania border. The I and II Corps were sent north to take position around the sleepy college town of Gettysburg. Meade and his headquarters staff were a day's ride behind the most forward troops near Taneytown. This gap was not a major concern as Meade believed it would be several days before

General James Longstreet was called 'Lee's old war horse' and was accused of procrastinating during the Battle of Gettysburg.

he or Lee would be prepared to commit themselves to the inevitable battle.

Lee's headquarters at that time was only some 10–15 miles northeast of Gettysburg. On that same morning he decided to detach a portion of his troops to Gettysburg in a bid to capture equipment and clothing said to be in storage there.

At approximately 0800 hours on 1 July Union cavalry under the command of Brigadier General John Buford, scouting along the road between Gettysburg and Cashtown where Meade believed Lee's forces were concentrated, encountered the Confederate troops which Lee had sent on a supply search. This chance encounter developed, through circumstance, from a mere clash between pickets into the battle itself.

Before conducting his reconnaissance mission along the Chambersburg Pike, Buford had received assurances from Reynolds that the I Corps would support Buford should contact with the enemy be made. The Confederate troops, under Major General Henry Heth, had been given the same verbal support by their III Corps commander, Lieutenant General Ambrose Powell Hill.

Upon encountering the enemy, Buford's cavalry dismounted. For more than two hours, with a single artillery battery for support, they held back the Confederate advance. By 0930 Reynolds' I Corps was fully aware of the confrontation and was on the march in Buford's support. What had begun as a minor skirmish was rapidly escalating into a major engagement. Neither Meade nor Lee made the decision to fight a major battle in the hills surrounding Gettysburg. It developed from the circumstances of combined support assurances and the aggressiveness with which Reynolds entered the fray.

Before 1100 hours the Union 1st Division of the I Corps was reinforcing Buford's cavalry, attacking Heth's column as it moved ever closer to Gettysburg. The strain on Buford's forces was becoming apparent. In spite of Reynolds' Divisional support, Buford's cavalry was forced to abandon its position on Seminary Ridge in the face of Heth's overwhelming superiority of numbers. Locked in the struggle, both factions were totally committed to battle.

As noon approached a Confederate sharpshooter, marking a Union general in his sights, shot and killed General John Reynolds as he rallied troops on the battlefield. By order of rank, command fell on the less able shoulders of Major General Abner Doubleday who, in direct contrast to Reynolds' forcefully aggressive nature, was a man of indecision. Groping to decide what his next move should be, Doubleday caused the Union forces to lose momentum along the entire front. In spite of the fact that Heth had slowed his attack in order to consolidate his forces and await further reinforcements, the Union impetus at Gettysburg was in danger of crumbling.

Major General Oliver Otis Howard, commander of the Union XI Corps, which had been advancing to join Reynolds' force, received word that Doubleday had assumed command of the I Corps. Unable to accept the thought of Doubleday in command, Howard immediately relinquished his own command to General Schurz and rode forward to relieve Doubleday of his burden.

At about the same time Meade received reports of the developing engagement. Although stunned by the news that his friend Reynolds was dead, Meade began to assert his role as commander of the army. He commenced with an action which caused much controversy yet gives an insight into his powers for the proper delegation of authority. Of the opinion that he had no one near the front whom he could entrust with the impending responsibilities, Meade sent Major General Winfield Scott Hancock to assume principal command of the three Corps which were engaged in combat. Hancock arrived at the front and informed General Howard of Meade's decision, whereby Howard challenged his right to assume command. It spoke well of Hancock's demeanor that he again quite simply informed Howard that he had his orders and would immediately undertake the command responsibility, at which point Howard withdrew as gracefully as possible.

General Winfield Scott Hancock was the commander of the II Corps and was sent by Meade to Gettysburg to take charge after Reynold's death.

As an officer of the Army of the Potomac, Hancock was a well-known figure, considered a courageous and sensible officer, though of less seniority than Major General Howard. Meade's decision to place Hancock in command was a bold act unprecedented in the rank-conscious Union Army. Meade had elected his course of action on the basic principle that Hancock was the most capable man for assessing the situation and keeping Meade well informed and abreast of the battle situation. Meade's conduct in this instance is one of several decisive moves which show him to have been a responsible commander. Hancock's arrival on the field of battle restored confidence, established order and held the Union troops in check. He was primarily responsible for converting the early, disastrous conflict into a well ordered defense around Cemetery Hill, causing Lee to postpone any thoughts of an assault at that time.

Meade's most important decision during that first day of fighting was his acceptance and continuance of the battle at Gettysburg despite the fact that his closest reinforcements were some distance from the battlefield. He had evidence that Lee's troop concentrations were much higher than had been expected. The decision to fight Lee's army with the Union I, XI and III Corps on the battlefield demonstrated that Meade was not afraid to challenge Lee's mystique. Chance had forced Meade's hand, but he would not tolerate the idea of retreat. In short, Meade was willing to take a calculated risk. Such is often the main ingredient needed to win great battles, and establish great generals. His conviction and aggressiveness in the initial stages of the battle established his control over the army and paved the way for the Union victory.

Meade finally arrived at the battle scene near midnight of 1 July, and personally assumed command. Surveying the situation and troop positions with his staff, Meade was again faced with a critical decision. He could continue with the engagement, in spite of the fact that he was aware that only three-quarters of his army could possibly reach the field by the morning of 2 July. Further time would be wasted in positioning the newly arrived troops, shuffling the units already in position, and reinforcing the weak sectors of the front. The time element was not particularly favorable. His alternative was a strategic withdrawal and regroupment in preparation for a battle more of his own choosing.

However, Meade considered that his army's position was tolerable. He was convinced that if his forces could defend their ground through 2 July, his reinforcements could strengthen him sufficiently to give him an advantage.

Predicting the enemy's movements is another quality inherent in a man of command capabilities. Meade rode over the battlefield at 0100, and after careful deliberation and a conference with Major General Howard, decided that the Confederates would be most likely to renew their attack with a major assault against Cemetery Hill. He concluded that their main objective would be an attempt at a sweeping maneuver to engulf the Union right flank.

The morning of 2 July saw the beginning of one of the greatest controversies of the battle of Gettysburg, and perhaps of Meade's entire command. Early on that morning Meade gave orders for Major General Daniel E Sickles to move his III Corps to a position of high ground on the army's left flank at a location known as the Little Round Top. Sickles was to hold that position and to place his artillery where it would have command over the entire battlefield in that sector. The controversy arose over Sickles' misinterpretation of his commander's orders. Whether deliberately or through simple misunderstanding, Sickles chose to elaborate on Meade's orders.

Comparing his position with an area of high ground approximately one mile beyond his position, Sickles decided to advance and occupy that alternate location. Unknown to Sickles as he began his relocation, Confederate forces commanded by Lieutenant General James Longstreet were advancing. Although the Confederates did not have complete superiority, they were maneuvering into a position which could spell disaster for Sickles' exposed Corps.

Officers watching the shift of Sickles' Corps from other sectors of the front were amazed to see the abandonment of the Little Round Top commence. Knowing of Sickles' ambitious nature and viewing the move as another of his personal ploys, General Hunt was goaded into openly referring to Sickles as 'a politician . . . a man after his own ends.'

General Meade was not a commander to sit in stunned surprise shaking a bewildered head at the scene unfolding along his left flank. Without delay or thought for his personal safety, Meade rushed to Sickles' position, his anger mounting as he sped to the exposed troops.

Above: Close fighting on the last day of Gettysburg, 3 July 1863.

Above and below: The fighting at
Gettysburg lasted three days and
was the decisive battle of the Civil
War. Both sides fought desperately
for every inch of territory.

General George Pickett.

Morale was perhaps the most major consideration as Meade weighed the possibilities open to him on that second day of battle. The location of the engagement was not of Meade's choosing, and with circumstances going awry so early in the day despite Meade's planning, he could have begun a withdrawal of his forces at the earliest opportunity. He could not forget however that the Army of the Potomac had become infamous in its apparent 'destiny with disaster.' Ill fate seemed ever present and ever ready to snatch victory from the Union army. A defeat of the III Corps would probably have resulted in a massive Union retreat. A defeat of the Army of the Potomac on northern soil would have compounded the legend of Lee's Army of Northern Virginia and meant a complete collapse in the morale of the Union troops.

Upon reaching Sickles, Meade lashed out a reprimand and demanded an explanation. Sickles defended himself by claiming that Meade had led him to believe that he was authorized to decide where best to station his Corps. Sickles felt that he was in complete command of his Corps and could best decide the most advantageous position. Meade stated quite firmly that when he positioned Sickles, Sickles *was* in command — in command to *maintain* that position. In the face of Meade's obvious wrath, Sickles agreed to return to the Little Round Top. Surveying the unmistakable approach of the Confederate forces, Meade replied, 'I wish to God you could, but the enemy won't let you!'

This early test of Meade's mettle as commander of the Army of the Potomac was an all-important factor in the outcome of the Battle of Gettysburg. The results of his success as a commanding general were bought and paid for in those moments of decision as he stood surveying Sickles' Corps stretched along the Emmitsburg Road. The most obvious problem was blatantly simple. Meade could not afford the losses which would surely result if Sickles attempted to reestablish his original position. Neither could he leave the corps unsupported in its position.

While the gravity of the possibilities weighed on him, Meade could not forget that on the battlefield one must take action with swift deliberateness as circumstances demanded, not when or where one might wish. Sickles' maneuver courted disaster for the army, but at all cost the Confederate move against his army's left flank had to be repelled. Meade sped away to find troops with which to reinforce the III Corps. He personally rode along the flank, positioning troops, giving encouragement and driving the reinforcements forward.

The manner in which General Meade handled the situation which Sickles had created was one of many actions which earned him the rightful title 'victor.' He was delivered what appeared to be a lost cause, acted promptly and with forethought, employed his reinforcements, and ensured that victory would not be lost due to Sickles' blunder.

Meade's obvious options were few. It required outstanding command abilities to assess the situation as rapidly as he did, personally relocate reinforcements and still maintain an understanding of the battle as a whole. His efforts converted disaster to his advantage, breaking the spell of the Army of the Potomac's destiny with disaster.

This is not to say that the Union forces went unscathed in their efforts to maintain a solid front. Losses to the left flank were a staggering 50 percent, which caused a considerable dilemma in the strength and morale of the entire army, as Meade had stripped troops from various sectors of the front. However, the determination with which they repulsed the Confederate assault helped to temper the Union forces and instilled a confidence in themselves and their new commander. Meade's decisions, actions, and

presence on the battlefield demonstrated courage and dedication which for once need not be in vain.

By the evening of 2 July Meade was again faced with a decision which could decide the fate of the army. The left flank had held, but casualties continued to remain enormous. The army's center and the right flank, which had seen the majority of the day's action, had repulsed the attacks but casualties in those areas had reached a point which prompted Meade's staff to suggest that the army disengage and seek a better position. This move would have given the army time to recover and reengage at a more favorable time and location. While the staff was

Pickett's charge at Gettysburg was the climax of the battle. Lee hoped that Pickett would break the Union center.

shrouded in gloom the spirit of the army itself was high. Corps commanders reported a strict confidence in the ability of their troops to fight and win the battle along the existing lines. Meade himself questioned the ability of his troops to withstand such heavy losses and retain the morale necessary for victory.

In the bleak hours of early morning on 2 July General Meade had directed staff officer General Butterfield to draw up plans for a withdrawal of the army. Later that night the corps and division commanders met collectively to express their conviction that victory would surely be theirs if they could but rob the Confederates of any substantial success along the front. After listening to and evaluating their opinions, Meade solemnly replied, 'Well Gentlemen, the question is settled. We will remain here. But I want to say that I consider this no fit place to fight a battle.'

Thus, Meade chose to act, despite reservations, on the faith he had in his frontline commanders, whom he considered to have the most direct perception of the army's ability to continue the battle. General Henry Slocum, commander of the XI Corps, is said to have been the man in whom Meade had the most faith and on whom he based the decision to remain. Slocum was later to write that though many criticized Meade's thought of retreat, it was not due to military incompetence nor 'a timidness for battle,' but as a result of the serious sense of responsibility Meade felt for the army and the lives of the men under his command.

It was also during that night's meeting that Meade and his staff decided that the Confederate army's main assault on the morrow would most probably be directed against the center of the Union line. Lee had tested the flanks and had been unable to breech them.

The first offensive on the morning of 3 July was Ewell's attack on the Union right on Culp's Hill. Devastated by Union crossfire, the Confederates were forced to withdraw after three hours. The expected attack on the Union center began after a two-hour artillery barrage, as 15,000 Confederate led by Major General George Pickett charged up Cemetery Ridge. Outnumbered and outgunned the attack collapsed with a loss of almost two-thirds of Pickett's force. With a number of his generals seriously wounded, Meade did not order a counterattack against the heavy mass of Confederate cannon.

The primary questions and criticisms which surface with regard to that final day of battle deal not so much with the actual actions fought as with Meade's conduct following the defeat of the Confederate Army. Meade has come under consistently severe criticism for his failure to follow-up the engagement with an offensive aimed at the destruction of the Confederate forces as they retreated south. There are those who voice the opinion that Meade helped to extend the war by at least one year. Armchair strategists who criticize Meade because he did not sweep down from his position to annihilate his enemy apparently fail to consider the true situation.

Both armies had fought one of the most costly battles which they had been or would be engaged in. Casualties and losses were staggering and great fatigue was felt by both sides. Accusations concerning Meade's lack of response were unfounded. Early on the morning of 4 July

he ordered Union forces under Commander French in Frederick, Maryland, to cut off the Confederate retreat to the best of their ability. Meade himself began to move his army against Lee, but he was thwarted on two accounts. First, the morning of 4 July brought a severe storm which turned the battlefield into a sea of mud. Second, and perhaps more responsible for the lack of eagerness with which the army viewed continued action, was the task of caring for the wounded and burying the dead. It may be claimed that such tasks are best left until the battle is truly won, but these concerns seemed to have more priority in the minds of the men of the Army of the Potomac than engaging an enemy which was already defeated. Knowing

General Hancock (on horse, left center) directed the defense of the Union center. Moments later he was badly wounded.

Meade for the 'fine old soldier' that he was, Lee was certain that he would not allow the wounded Confederate troops left behind to go unattended. Although Meade sent patrols to reconnoitre the enemy position, the tending of wounded and prisoners seemed more appropriate that day than a vainglorious counterattack. By 5–6 July the Army of the Potomac was once again on the move, but the chances of contacting the retreating Confederates were nil.

Those who have experienced war, particularly actions of long duration or suffering heavy losses, realize that comforting thoughts stem not from who has ultimately won or lost but the relief that the battle is over. It takes time to mentally and emotionally prepare for final victory or defeat, and as the Battle of Gettysburg was not the last battle to be faced, time was needed to prepare for what lay ahead. Meade did what lay in his power to conduct himself and the army in the most competent military manner. The Battle of Gettysburg had been too costly and too wearisome to execute the counterattack which Meade's critics think he should have attempted.

Meade's place as a great commanding general, with Gettysburg the pinnacle of his career, has long been over-shadowed by Lee and the mystique which surrounds the

The fighting was so intense and
the bombardment of lines so
massive that visibility was poor.
The flower of Lee's army, some
15,000 men, was lost at Gettysburg.

Army of Northern Virginia. However, without a doubt Meade conducted himself and his army with great distinction and honor in what can be considered one of the great battles of American history. The conditions and accomplishments of Meade's command have been exceptionally well documented by Francis A Walker, Brevet Brigadier General of the US Volunteers. It is difficult to elaborate on his description of Meade's handling of the situation at Gettysburg, as he follows precisely the main points of Meade's success.

First and foremost, Meade was in command of the entire Army of the Potomac for only three days before the Battle of Gettysburg began. The command he assumed was not one over an army of efficient, aggressive troops. Thrust upon him was the task of bringing cohesion to an army which had long suffered from a lack of competent leadership and deteriorating morale.

Meade was in fact nowhere near the battlefield when the battle began and was actually considering the possibility of giving battle in another location entirely. It was Reynolds who forced his hand and committed Meade to battle at Gettysburg. In effect, Meade inherited a battle, as he inherited the army, rather than executing an engagement according to his own strategy. Fortunately he had the necessary level-headed adaptability to circumstances which the commanders before him, particularly Hooker, had lacked.

Meade's immediate decision upon assuming command was to move the army northward in pursuit. This was

perhaps the most influential factor in the success he would achieve. After many years the Army of the Potomac was again fighting on and for northern soil. A large number of the men, including Meade, Reynolds and other officers, were Pennsylvanians that were not merely headed toward another battle, but a battle for home and state, a battle of Pennsylvanians for Pennsylvania.

Meade had an ability to understand not only the situation but also his commanders in the field. His ability to select the right man for the job was emphasized with his dispatching of Hancock to the front to take full command and do what was necessary to save the day. Meade chose Hancock not only for his abilities but as a man who would report to and carry out the express wishes of his supreme commander. Also, the fact that Hancock was not the senior-ranking officer demonstrated that Meade was concerned with effectiveness and capability, not with tradition and rank distinction. Meade continued to display a keen evaluation of, and regard for, his field commanders in his decision to remain at Gettysburg on the strength of their convictions. Too often a disregard for the opinions of such officers leads to a slanted perspective on the part of the commanding general, as amply seen during Hooker's reign over the army at Chancellorsville.

Meade's determination to maintain a defensive strategy also contributed to his eventual success. A defensive posture was more appropriate considering the terrain on which the Union forces took position and the lack of positive knowledge of the deployment of enemy troops.

Above: After the battle: a Confederate soldier lies in a crude breastwork in one of the niches in Devil's Den.

Above left: Cameras could not take action shots but after the battle the dead were commemorated in a series of historic photographs.

Meade's personality and his military concepts also had much to do with the decision to remain defensive. He believed that when truly in doubt, if the opportunity favorably presented itself, defend. Meade did not lose the initiative to Lee, he forced it upon him, causing Lee to gamble all in assaults against the Union lines. With only three corps in position by the end of the first day, Meade took the best possible option. Defense was not the more glorious option, but Meade was concerned with results, not glory.

By 2 July, in spite of Sickles, Meade had positioned the Union Army in a solid convex line facing Lee's forces. This caused the battle to separate into multiple fronts and engagements and made it easier to shift troops from one area to another. He could reinforce endangered areas and combat the Confederates in piecemeal fashion rather than face one massive line assault.

Many high ranking Union officers were killed or wounded during the days at Gettysburg, including Reynolds. The heroism and accomplishments of those who lost their lives have been stressed in many accounts. However, as with Sickles' blunder at the Little Round Top, it was Meade who entered into direct contact with the troops to rally and deploy them. The heavy loss of troops and officers is often overstated while Meade's involvement is understated.

The two principal criticisms levelled at Meade as Commander of the Army of the Potomac during the summer of 1863 are he mismanaged the episode with Sickles and charges that he allowed the Army of Northern Virginia to escape destruction. Meade's reaction to criticism was indicated by the manner in which he pursued his command in the best interest of the men and army as a whole. He believed that individual actions and results were rudimentary in the winning of battles and ultimately the war. Perhaps he lacked the flamboyance of other officers of the day, but Meade was no glory seeker. He refused to be manipulated by critics and detractors, content to apply his skills to the best of his ability for the good of his troops, his army and his country.

General George Gordon Meade was, in the classic sense, a great general and a worthy victor. One word is the key in the evaluation of Meade's character. That word is 'soldier,' as defined in the *Random House Dictionary*, 'a man of military skill or experience.' In the true context of the term soldier, Meade applied his skills to the best of his ability in the brief period before and during the Battle of Gettysburg. He was bound by his sense of honor, duty and service to the position he held.

Meade will never compete with other flamboyant figures of his era, yet he was without a doubt every inch the soldier, the general, necessary to accomplish the feats required during that decisive time. He was truly one of the great, though little appreciated, generals of Civil War.

VON MOLTKE AT SEDAN 1870

t is strange to realize that a man whose name, perhaps more than any other, is associated with Prussian militarism was himself not even a German but a Dane. Helmuth Carl Bernhard, Baron von Moltke, born at Parchim in Northern Denmark, was the son of a Danish general and began his own military career in his own country's forces.

It was at the age of 22 that he transferred to the army he was to serve with such distinction. The joint reformer of the Prussian army with von Roon, he later became the strategic architect of victories over his own native country in 1864 and over Austria two years later. Yet it was his victories during the late summer and early autumn of 1870, when he was himself as old as the century, which were the most resonant. France, long regarded as the greatest among the military powers, found herself deposed by the nation which was regarded at that time as being among the least.

Moltke's contemporaries and colleagues included not only von Roon, the Prussian War Minister, but also Otto Eduard Leopold von Bismarck, who if not the sole creator of German unity was certainly the man who contributed most to its realization. Following the defeat of Austria, hitherto unquestioned leader of the German-speaking peoples, 20 states north of the River Main joined Bismarck's North German Confederation with his own Prussia as its head. He realized, however, that only some external intervention would persuade the states of the Catholic South to overcome their religious aversion to uniting with the Protestant North.

One such intervention could be a war between Prussia and France. If this occurred the French armies would be compelled to strike through South Germany. In coming to

Napoleon III, Emperor of France.

Count Otto von Bismarck.

its aid, Prussia would also assert her own physical presence there and in fact Bismarck had gone so far in persuading the Southern States of the menace they faced from France that they had united with Prussia in a series of mutual defense treaties.

At the same time, he had looked to the condition of the Prussian army which he had himself helped to reform in 1862, while Moltke was to draw up the plans for encompassing France's defeat. What he finally proposed involved crossing the Rhine with the large forces available to him through the Confederation, driving a wedge between the principal forward bases of Metz and Strasbourg and thus dividing the enemy's forces.

Although quite prepared to incite the French to action, Bismarck had reason to hope they might themselves oblige by providing an excuse for war. The French had been growing increasingly ambitious. The spirit behind this new mood was Charles Louis Napoleon, nephew of the great Napoleon, who. elected President of the Republic in 1848, had proclaimed himself emperor under the title of Napoleon III, four years later.

His desire to add further luster to the family name had already led him to rebuild a sizeable chunk of Paris and, with the assistance of his elegant, Spanish-born consort, Eugénie, to make it the center of fashion and style it has been ever since. It had also led him into a number of activities less innocuous such as his futile attempt to install the Hapsburg princeling, Ferdinand-Maximilian, as client-emperor of Mexico.

So long as the German Confederation was restricted to the Northern States, Napoleon was prepared to cast a benevolent eye upon it. Matters would be different, however, as Bismarck realized, once a strong and united Germany pressed on France's borders.

William I of Prussia acceded to the Prussian throne in 1861 and became the first German emperor.

A potential challenge occurred in 1870 when Napoleon's ally, Queen Isabella of Spain, was deposed. In the July, Bismarck, knowing they would acquiesce, suggested to the Spanish Parliament, that they give the vacant throne to a member of the Sigmaringen-Hohenzollern family. A cadet branch of Prussia's own Hohenzollern dynasty and having some claim to the Spanish crown, Bismarck rightly judged that the French would not tolerate a potentially hostile power across the Pyrenées.

He was right. Angry speeches in the Chamber of Deputies were matched by angrier leaders in the Paris press. The capital had only just stopped laughing at Offenbach's *The Grand Duchess* in which figures recognizable as Bismarck and the Prussian General Staff were parodied. In such a mood, prudence flew out of the window. Instead of discreetly indicating to Spain that she was running the risk of incurring its displeasure, the French government at once revealed the Prussian machinations and was thereby brought into direct confrontation.

Nonetheless, French persuasions at first achieved their objective when the Prussian monarchs, Wilhelm I and Augusta, who disliked Bismarck, prevailed on the Hohenzollern candidate to withdraw. There the matter could and should have rested. The French press and the more right-wing politicians, however, were still baying and would only be satisfied by an abject confession of Prussian guilt. The French ambassador, Benedetti, was therefore instructed to obtain the King's public acknowledgment that there would be no repetition of the Spanish claim; this was tantamount to an admission of Prussian involvement. The furthest Wilhelm would go was a statement that the renunciation had had his approval. The king was both old and unwell. The discussions with Benedetti took place while he was undergoing a cure at Ems. Pressed by the importunate ambassador, he told him with exasperation that he should not be troubled with matters which were his ministers' responsibility. That evening he telegraphed Bismarck a summarized version of the interview, no doubt to prepare him for a possible encounter.

When his message arrived Bismarck was entertaining Moltke and von Roon to dinner. He saw it as just what he needed. Without making any textual changes, but by skillful editing he managed to convey the impression that the King had virtually broken off diplomatic relations. 'It will be like a red rag to the Gallic bull,' he predicted, before releasing it for publication. If in nothing else, Bismarck showed a matador's finesse in judging the reactions of his Gallic bull. Amid the angry bellows of the French Assembly war credits were voted eagerly.

He could now have his war under ideal conditions. The world at large which thought – and continued to think – that France was being paranoically touchy in detecting Bismarck's hand in every turn of events, saw it as the frivolous villain, especially after Bismarck revealed an earlier French plan to divide Belgium between them.

The French expected a brief and glorious war with a rapid advance across the Rhine to neutralize the South German States. Even Britain though openly favoring Prussia, took a similar view. The French army was admittedly smaller than the Prussian numbering about 300,000 men. Moltke expected to field 330,000 men if the Southern States remained neutral, 360,000 if they did not – as proved the case.

France's advantage lay with its vaunted 'professionalism.' It was an imperial power and required a standing army ready to be dispatched to any outpost of empire at short notice. To achieve this with a conscript army meant a long period of service and if this was not to drain the nation of its manhood, it had to be selective. Only 100,000 men, chosen by lottery, were conscripted every year, but until 1868 they had to serve seven years with special bonuses for reenlistment.

As a consequence the French regarded the Prussian army where every single able-bodied man was called up and served a mere three years, as little more than a *levée en masse*. This, of course, ignored the essential differences. For Prussia was a nation state, albeit a recently founded one, and required an army which could be mobilized quickly to guard the integrity of its own frontiers; one with a large pool of reserves, in other words. These the French army lacked, as men who had served with the colors for seven years and often much more, were unwilling to face recall.

There were other, deeper deficiencies. Splendid as they were on the parade ground, the French troops were drawn from the lowest and poorest elements of the peasantry, those unable to buy their way out of the call-up. The officers, men of the bourgeoisie, no less brave than their troops, lacked initiative, while the General Staff was frankly incompetent and openly relied on '*le Système D*,' D standing for '*débrouillage*' or 'muddling through.'

It could scarcely compete with Moltke's almost inhumanly efficient Prussian General Staff and this began to affect French conduct from the moment the war began. The nation's greatest advantage lay in the fact that with its standing army it should have been able to field the greater force initially. It was widely assumed, at home and abroad, that the declaration of war would be followed by an immediate invasion of Germany. This was prevented by '*le Système D.*' From the start there were commissariat failures which left units without cooking equipment and sometimes without food. Men were pushed hither and thither all over France and sometimes shipped off to Algiers and brought back.

Meanwhile Moltke could hardly believe his luck as he made his final preparations, unhindered by enemy action. In fact, the French had no real plans for an invasion of South Germany, indeed no plans of any kind save for those drawn up virtually in his spare time by General Frossard, the Emperor's military tutor. In character these were purely defensive. An Army of the Rhine would stand guard over Strasbourg and an Army of the Moselle over Metz. They would therefore be exactly where Moltke wanted them. There were, however, to be two reserve forces, an Army of Châlons and an Army of Paris. The backbone of the latter would be the *Garde Mobile*, proposals for which had been formulated in 1868 as part of General Niel's army reforms. It was to be an elite corps of the National Guard, ready to be sent anywhere, and lists of eligible men had been drawn up. The men involved had been rounded up when mobilization began. Though untrained civilians, they were at once dispatched to various units. Sullen at finding themselves snatched from civil life and left with no means of filling their time, they quickly became a drunken rabble, burdening every commander they were sent to and endangering general discipline.

Then, at the very last moment, what plans the French did have were scrapped. The Rhine, Moselle and Reserve Armies were merged into one cumbrous body assigned to hold some 200 miles of frontier. At the same time, Napoleon appointed himself Commander in Chief with Leboeuf, the Minister of War as his Chief of Staff. To watch over affairs of state in his absence, he appointed the Empress as Regent.

Napoleon's love of the army, certainly as great as his august uncle's, was not equalled by his talent, let alone experience. Charles Louis had never held command, could only read a map with difficulty and, now at 62, suffered from a chronic bladder weakness which required the constant presence of a surgeon to relieve it.

On 2 August, a French force under Frossard defiantly crossed the border and occupied Saarbrücken. This gave Moltke a nasty moment until it was clear it had been done solely to give the army employment and did not presage a concerted attack. On 4 August, Moltke himself moved. The Prussian Third Army, under the Crown Prince Frederick-Wilhelm, took the minor fortress town of Wissembourg, the French commander dying in the action. To meet this threat, the armies had to regroup and Saarbrücken was promptly abandoned, Frossard omitting, as he did so, to burn the town's bridges. It was now obvious to Napoleon that while his armies would not be in any position to invade for months, the unthinkable was happening and the Prussians were marching into his own country. With this realization he seems to have lost all interest in the campaign.

Further blows fell before there was any chance of a French regroupment. On 6 August Frossard was forced to withdraw from a line he had taken up from Spicheren to Forbach. The loss of the latter was particularly serious as it was the main supply depot for the French offensive. At almost the same time, the Prussian Third Army, followed up the capture of Wissembourg by that of Froeschwiller ridge. The enemy was visibly interposing himself between Metz and Strasbourg.

Military logic dictated only one course: a rapid retreat to positions which would allow for reconcentration and the formation of a continuous line. Logic was not paramount. The regime of Napoleon III had from the outset faced opposition from republican and liberal opinion, while his main support had come from the bourgeoisie and the conservative peasantry. This support had been steadily eroded largely as a result of the ill-advised adventures which were regarded as breaking his promise to restore peace to the country. To make matters worse, the Paris press had hailed the occupation of Saarbrücken as a major victory. When this was followed not merely by retirement but by three defeats for French arms, it looked as though fury would be boundless. To forestall this, on 12 August, the emperor gave up command of the armies to Marshal Bazaine.

Bazaine's prescription was indeed withdrawal and he successfully eluded Moltke's pursuit. Then, for reasons of political expediency, he was instructed to stand and fight. He took up a position at Borny where the astonished Prussians, believing their enemy in retreat, blundered into them. The daylong battle ended with the elated French holding their positions, but the truth was they still had to retreat and had lost time by taking a stand. Furthermore, the French troops had so spent themselves that when, the following day, they began to stream into the fortress of Metz they could not be dislodged from its refuge. On 16 August the Prussians reached them. From behind their fortifications the French rained down slaughter, but Bazaine was

Marshal Bazaine was the Commander of the III Corps at the start of the Franco-Prussian War. Napoleon gave him command of the Army of the Rhine.

Left: Strasbourg under fire. After the disastrous battles of 6 August the French armies retreated leaving Alsace and Lorraine.

Right: Marshal MacMahon was the Commander of the French I Corps. He had gained his military experience fighting in Algeria and was in command of Algerian troops.

Below right: At the Battle of Beaumont Failly's V Corps was taken by surprise and suffered 7000 casualties. He was replaced by Wimpffen after the engagement.

Below: A Cavalry action at Buzancy on 27 August 1870.

concerned that he might be besieged and tried to extend his line leftward toward the rest of the army. The result was a defeat which had just the effect he had tried to prevent.

The situation was not irretrievable as there was still the Army of Châlons. If this could be drawn back to form a protective cordon in front of Paris, survival was still possible. Even the *Gardes Mobiles* might be persuaded to fight since they were largely drawn from the capital. Militating against this course was not only the political situation, but also the ambitions of the Empress-Regent. Her husband had slipped out of Metz and was now at Châlons, a forlorn wreck, frequently in pain and hardly the sort of leader to inspire confidence in the ragbag of soldiery the Army of Châlons had become as stragglers from the previous debacles were absorbed into it. Nonetheless, both the Empress and the War Minister, Palikao, urged Napoleon to participate in a great relief expedition on Metz. It was this or the final collapse of the regime, they insisted.

The commander of the Châlons Army was Marshal MacMahon, a soldier experienced enough to realize that he was being asked to consign to hopeless battle an army which should have been kept intact at all costs. However, he could hesitate no longer when news came that Bazaine was attempting a breakout. Decency required that the Army of Châlons advance and stretch forth a helping hand. In fact, there is no evidence Bazaine had any intention of breaking out.

MacMahon suffered a further reverse. The pro-government press in Paris, to answer accusations of inertia against government, dynasty and army, saluted the departure of the relief force with a fanfare of headlines which had the unhelpful effect of telling Moltke, previously mystified, what his enemy was up to. Twist, turn, double-back on themselves as the French might, they never lost their pursuers who were often at their destination before them. At Beaumont,

the V Corps, under Failly, was surprised, showed little
stomach for the fight and retired. This was the last blow to
MacMahon's tortured and weakening nerves. He pulled
back to the little town of Sedan, up the Meuse and behind
the shelter of the Belgian border. There, too, Moltke had
not only divined his intentions, but was preparing to
thwart them.

Sedan lies in the valley of the Meuse. On its south side is
a marshy plain, criss-crossed by streams, while wooded
slopes surround its other sides. A main road passes through
the town, roughly following the meandering line of the
river. Somewhat less than a mile from it, however, at the
hamlet of Floing, is a crossroads with a second road going
eastward and away from the river to a junction at Olly
Farm. Here the road sweeps back southwest to meet the
Sedan road once more at Bazeilles. In other words, it forms
a kind of large triangle with Bazeilles, Floing and Olly Farm
as its three extremities and Sedan midway along its base
line.

It was within the limits of this triangle that MacMahon
disposed his forces. The VII Corps, under Douay, took up
a position along the ridge from Floing to the Calvaire d'Illy
which lay just below the point of the triangle at Olly Farm.
Then the I Corps, under Ducrot, occupied a line running
from Olly Farm halfway toward Bazeilles. Lebrun's XII
Corps continued the line down to and including Bazeilles.
The V Corps, battered at Beaumont, was kept as a reserve
in the center.

This last unit was under the command of Failly who,
because of his dismal performance at that battle, was about
to be replaced. His successor was to be Wimpffen, formerly
a colonial governor in Algeria, who had returned hotfoot
on the declaration of war in search of glory in the field.
Besides succeeding Failly, however, he was also instructed
by Paris to take over as Commander in Chief should the
misfortunes of war overtake MacMahon.

How MacMahon intended to fight the battle has never
been entirely clear. He was adamant, in his briefing of the
corps' commanders, that he had no intention of being
bottled up in Sedan as Bazaine had been at Metz. In any
event, supplies and ammunition at Metz were plainly in-
adequate for a prolonged struggle. Rather he seems to have
envisaged a kind of rearguard action, pulling back along
the banks of the Meuse toward Mézières, a move taking him
away from Metz, the fortress, which as the Empress was
quick to point out, he was supposed to be relieving.

If there was on the French side that uncertainty which
had marked their conduct of the entire war, there was none
on Moltke's. His plans for what he appreciated was the last
and, thanks to the ill-judged retirement on Sedan, decisive
phase of the war were complete before MacMahon began
making his dispositions. The total area available to the
French forces was a narrow wedge of land. On one side
was the River Meuse and on the other the Belgian frontier.
Bismarck had already dispatched a warning to the Belgian
government to see that no French unit was allowed to

Right above and below: The I Bavarian Corps in action at Bazeilles on the
morning of 1 September. Led by von der Tann the German unit attacked
prematurely at 0400 hours following up some heavy bombardment of
the town. After fierce fighting there was a stalemate.

escape by that route and to make assurance doubly sure the Third Army was ordered to pursue into Belgium if necessary. This unit was also allotted the task of holding the strip of land between frontier and river. On 19 August, the commander of the Second Army, Prince Frederick-Charles, had complained that his force, consisting of six corps and two independent cavalry divisions was grossly unwieldy. Three of its corps and the cavalry divisions had accordingly been taken from it to make another army, the Army of the Meuse, under the command of the resourceful Crown Prince of Saxony. This was to advance along the river's bank, cutting off escape across it.

On the night of 31 August, Moltke ordered Blumenthal, commanding the XI Corps, to cross the Meuse and close the remaining opening, that to the west. 'Now we have them in a mousetrap,' he told the king. The selfsame belief was expressed by Ducrot, commanding the French I Corps, in somewhat earthier language: 'Nous sommes dans un pot de chambre et nous y serons emmerdés.' As night fell, one after another of the Prussian watchfires punctuated the darkness, staking out the limits of the French perimeter.

MacMahon talked airily of maneuvering under the nose of the enemy as he prepared for the withdrawal of the morrow. 'Tomorrow,' Douay, commander of the VII Corps told him, 'the enemy will not give you time' – a statement which coming events would soon confirm.

Throughout the campaign, the *mitrailleuse*, a multi-barrelled, quick-firing forerunner of the machine gun, dubbed by one Prussian commander 'that damned coffee-mill' had taken severe toil, while the French *chassepot* rifle had proved superior to the Prussian needle-firing gun. Unfortunately from the French point of view, both required that the enemy come within range. This he was often able to avoid doing as the Krupps' steel, breech-loading guns of the Prussian artillery far outranged the French bronze, muzzle-loading weapons. Firing salvo after salvo from positions well out of reach the former could tear gaping holes in trench and earthwork, frequently reducing the defenders to cowering impotence. On the night of 31 August, the Bavarian I Corps, under von der Tann, began just such a bombardment on the French position at Bazeilles as the preliminary to attack.

All the same, there is reason to believe Moltke was in no hurry. He wanted his trap right in front of the mouse hole by moving his two wings round the enemy before he did. What frustrated him was the overeagerness of von der Tann to attack.

That the Prussian Army had become a sharper and more accurate weapon with each engagement was largely due to deep differences of philosophy between French and Prussian General Staffs. Ever since the days of the first Napoleon, the one had been designed to be the responsive instrument of a single, brilliant, dominant will. Field commanders were assigned their positions, took them up and defended them, if necessary, to the death. No one ever moved to the assistance of a comrade, however hard-pressed, unless ordered to do so and such were the jealousies the system engendered that it was not uncommon for one commander to watch, gloating, as his brother-in-arms suffered disaster. Under Moltke's tutelage, he and his headquarters were merely a nerve center. The system of staff training he had inaugurated was based on two precepts, the first being that field commanders should develop an almost telepathic sensitivity to the needs of the campaign or battle as a whole, referring to higher authority as little as possible.

Obviously this had its defects and could result in individual officers taking too much upon themselves. One repeated offender was the commander of the First Army, Steinmetz, who in the early stages of the Battle of Spicheren, for instance, defied orders by pursuing an enemy he believed in full retreat (which he was not), thus risking a separation between himself and Second Army next to him.

Such manifestations were, of course, to be expected in as new an army as that of the North German Confederation where many of those now subservient to Moltke had formerly held command in state armies and were, besides, often members of its landed gentry, more accustomed to rule than to obey. Nor was it easy for him to dismiss them, since doing so might offend local susceptibilities. The problem was usually avoided because experience showed that close collusion and the adherence to strategic intentions produced the best results. This was not always the case.

At 0400 hours, through a cold and misty darkness, the V and XI Corps, forming Moltke's wings, began their crossing of the Meuse at Donchéry, the junction of all rail lines and roads running westward. There was no resistance and by 0730 hours they were astride the Sedan-Mézières road. Believing themselves the first unit to take the field they were surprised to hear firing from an easterly direction.

It came from von der Tann's Bavarians who had attacked prematurely, while the western exits were still open, and were now locked in a ferocious struggle with French Marines, among the finest troops in the erstwhile Army of Châlons. In a very short time Bazeilles, or such parts of it as were left unburning from the artillery bombardment, was ablaze from end to end. As daylight came the positions were virtually deadlocked. Later, von der Tann was to

Right: The capture of three *mitrailleuses* by the Saxon Infantry Regiment August-Frederick. The *mitrailleuse* was Napoleon's secret weapon but unfortunately few French poilus knew how to operate it.

Below: On 1 September at 0600 MacMahon was injured in the leg by a shell splinter as he rode to Bazeilles. He was evacuated and he chose Ducrot to replace him.

justify his action on the grounds that he was afraid the French were slipping away in the darkness.

However, as Lebrun, the XII Corps commander, could see for himself, there was no escape: the Prussians were covering his whole front. The next village to Bazeilles in the northeasterly direction was La Moncelle and beyond this Daigny, both along the road to Olly Farm, the apex of the defensive triangle. Soon enemy artillery was occupying the slopes of the hills on the far side of the Givonne valley. A column of Saxon troops took Moncelle, joined up with von der Tann's Bavarians on their left, and another column to the right was threatening Daigny. The defense here, by Zouaves, a French colonial unit, was so tenacious it took four hours to capture the village.

Already, the French had suffered another mishap which because of the confused state of staff organization had more far-reaching effects than was necessary. MacMahon riding out toward Bazeilles just after the Bavarian attack began, was struck by a shell splinter and had to be carried back to Sedan. This, of course, was the situation in which Wimpffen was to take over. He had not yet arrived, nor was there any warning of his coming or of the orders from Paris he bore.

In these circumstances, MacMahon's chosen successor, Ducrot naturally took over.

Appreciating just what was happening, at 0800 hours he gave orders for a withdrawl by the V and XII Corps as the prelude to a general disengagement and withdrawal westward. He had not yet learned that the Germans were occupying Donchéry, blocking the western exit.

The plan was never tested, for no sooner had orders gone out than Wimpffen arrived on the scene and, full of vigor and determination which made him an incongruous figure in the present company, declared himself to be Commander

SITUATION AT DAWN, 1 SEPTEMBER, 1870

FRENCH — GERMAN

POSITION OF GERMAN UNITS SHORTLY BEFORE END OF BATTLE

① ATTEMPT OF FRENCH CAVALRY TO BREAK OUT EARLY AFTERNOON

② LAST ATTEMPT OF FRENCH TO BREAK OUT ('BATTLE OF THE LAST CARTRIDGES')

ROADS — WOODED AREAS — RAILWAY

MILES — KILOMETERS

© Richard Natkiel, 1981

Right: French troops scramble across marshy ground.

Far right above: The 105th Infantry Regiment at Daigny, near Sedan.

in Chief. The Empress and the Paris politicians had impressed on him the need for victory and, accordingly, he announced there would be no withdrawal. Those units under extreme pressure would be reinforced and in due course they would turn to the offensive.

If Ducrot's answer typified the mood of the defenders, it also had the merit of realism. He told Wimpffen, 'You will be lucky, *mon général*, if by this evening you even have a retreat.' As commentators like Michael Howard have pointed out Wimpffen was actually ensuring the total destruction of the French army.

As it happened, the Prussian V and XI Corps, now advancing beyond Donchéry were experiencing some difficulty, the product of von der Tann's overeagerness. The second of Moltke's basic precepts was that of marching to the guns, which, in contrast to the French habit of waiting for orders, produced a build up of strength wherever a struggle was raging. Its defect was that it could also produce severe traffic jams. When the V and XI Corps heard the firing from the east, every available unit began marching toward it with the consequence that infantry, cavalry, waggons and guns converged on the roads and required an hour to disentangle themselves. Nonetheless, by 0900 hours, while the XI Corps was advancing on Floing, the V Corps were crossing open country in the direction of Fleigneux. The delay, however, had had the effect of leaving a gap and realizing this the French cavalry had been sent out to keep it open by checking the Prussian advance.

One of the lessons of the present war had been to demonstrate the futility of cavalry charges against infantry armed with the rapid-firing, longer range modern rifles. Men and horses were cut down long before their foe was within saber range, while at the same time the artillery was firing into them. A few managed to escape via Fleigneux and the Ardennes Forest, but, soon after, this gap too was closed when the Prussian Guard Corps marched up to take position facing the apex of the defensive triangle.

Moltke need have done no more than wait for a result, using probing attacks to find weak points in the enemy perimeter and exploiting them in his own time. The sun had come up on a glorious day and perhaps it was this, combined with the panoramic view of the battlefield which the German position afforded that led him to succumb to the temptation to turn this, the world's first truly modern battle, into an exhibition of his own virtuosity. As the morning air grew warmer a procession of notabilities began mounting the hills near Frenois. Among them were not only the Kings of Prussia, but also Bismarck himself with Moltke and von Roon and their staffs, various Foreign Office officials, the military attachés of Britain, Russia, the United States and a gaggle of German princes whose titles recalled those states which by the end of the day would have taken such an irrevocable step toward dissolution into the larger entity of Germany – Leopold of Bavaria, William of Württemburg, Frederick of Schleswig-Holstein, the Duke of Saxe-Coburg, the Grand Dukes of Weimar and Mecklenburg-Strelitz. Bringing up the rear were the newspaper correspondents, whom Moltke was delighted to have as witnesses and heralds to his triumph.

Lingering mist still hid the more distant parts of the

Left: The destruction of the French cavalry at the Battle of Sedan.

Right: Prussian infantry overrun French *mitrailleuse* positions at the height of the battle.

Below: The Prussian Guard artillery, under Prince Kraft zu Hohenlohe-Ingelfingen, deploying above the Fond de Givonne where it faced the French I Corps.

landscape. As it rose, the spectators saw that what lay below them far outshone their own splendor: a panoply of war such as was never again to be arrayed, men in their thousands, marching, wheeling, advancing cautiously but boldly over open country. Everywhere there was a brilliance of color. The Zouaves, in tasselled caps and embroidered jackets, the glinting helmets and breastplates of the *cuirassiers*, even the humble French infantry in dark blue *képi* and tunic to set off their bright red *pantalons*; the German regiments in Prussian blue with glinting *pickelhaube*. Behind them were horse-drawn ambulances, supply waggons and gun teams, dragging weapons and limbers into positions. Guns seemed to be aimed at every point of the defensive concentration, while a line of them ran almost the entire length of the south bank of the Meuse below the spectators' line of vision.

The contrast in mood on the two sides was stark. Napoleon was in agony from his bladder and without hope of relief since duty demanded he should be seen by his troops. To this end, his face rouged to cover the pallor of sickness, he mounted his horse and spent the morning riding from one unit to another. Though he constantly came into the view and range of the enemy, hoping for the bullet which might end pains as much moral as physical, by lunchtime when he returned to his quarters this anodyne had eluded him.

There was one small hope. Wimpffen realizing that, whatever else, he was not short of men, had decided he would break out, but eastward toward Douzy and Carignan rather than west and toward Mézières. His first inclination was to make the attempt right away, then he decided to wait until darkness. With his plans thus crystallized, he rode over to see how the men who would have to hold his exit door at Bazeilles, were faring. Their commander was not unhopeful: he would hold as long the corps to his right did so and Wimpffen promised to reinforce this with men from the I Corps. By the time his rounds were finished, even the Commander in Chief understood the truth of his position. If he was to break out, he must do it at once, and at 1300 hours he sent out messengers to begin mustering the troops. At the same time, Napoleon was invited to take his place at their head. Long convinced the war and so this particular battle was lost, he declined the honor.

Nor was there much sign of men or officers, though at Balan, between Sedan and Bazeilles, Wimpffen assembled enough to mount an attack which compelled the II Bavarian Corps to ask for reinforcement.

He had not yet abandoned the thought of the breakthrough when the line of the VI Corps broke and he found himself engulfed in a tide of disorderly withdrawal which was more like a rout and belied its commander's promise to hold. Douay blamed the reverse on the failure of his right, but the truth was that Wimpffen's reinforcements, if they had ever arrived, had not been able to take up their positions before they were swept up by a German infantry advance. Ducrot, who rode up to see for himself what was happening, came upon hosts of stragglers in the Bois de la Garenne which lay behind the position. An attempt was made to rally them and a line of sorts actually formed from a hotchpotch of regiments. It held for two hours, then at 1500 hours began to break up as men sought the shelter of the woods, still under fire from some 90 Prussian guns.

Another crisis developed behind Floing, where the
defenders had staved off every attack from the village for
six hours. It was almost exactly as Wimpffen was giving
his orders for the breakout that their guns were silenced by
the superior German ones, however, and soon after, the
Prussians began reaching round the defenders' flank.

There were many acts of sacrificial, if vain, gallantry
that day, but none was more conspicuous than that of the
French Lancers. The Germans were now beginning to
appear on the plateau above Floing and had to be repulsed
at all costs. Not only this, but the French commanders
were returning to the idea of a breakout westward once
more. The cavalry would, therefore, act as the broom to
sweep the way.

General Margueritte, their commander, left immediately
to reconnoiter, while his squadrons formed up under shell-
fire. As his horse picked its way down the slopes toward
Floing Margueritte was hit by a bullet which smashed his
jaw and ripped his tongue. With the lower part of his face
a mass of blood, he rode up the hill, pointed with one arm
toward the enemy, then collapsed.

A cry of 'Avenge' went up from his men and they spurred
to rush the slopes, bursting in upon the German skirmishers
who broke up before them. That was their sole achievement.
The infantry stood their ground inflicting such slaughter
with their rifle fire that the cavalry was forced to split up
and go round it instead of overpowering it. They became
more and more separated from each other as they tried to
find their way through the enemy lines and back to their
own lines while all the time the killing went on, so that for
weeks after the battle the carcasses were found, often miles
from the battlefield.

Some came back over the hill's crest, nevertheless, and
Ducrot could only ask General de Gallifet, who was now
commanding them, if they would try again. 'So long as
there's one of us left,' the cavalry general told him. Twice
more they were unleashed down the hill.

Watching from his imperial grandstand, Wilhelm was
compelled to exclaim in admiration, '*Ah, les braves gens,*' a
phrase recorded in the memorial to them which stands on
the site. Their last attempt came at 1500 hours. As they
went, Ducrot and his staff rode among the infantry urging
them to follow, to seize such initiative as the Lancers'
bravery had given, perhaps to break through. But it was in
vain. They did not lack the courage; they were exhausted
and utterly disspirited. As Gallifet and his last brave few
reached the valley, the enemy ceased fire; officers raised
their swords in salute and the *braves gens* rode away.

Perhaps it could be said that the Germans felt able to
afford such gestures. All along the French lines were signs
of disintegration. As it became increasingly obvious that
the Germans were not to be stopped, men abandoned their
positions. The charge of the Lancers was almost the last
throw of the battle. However, Wimpffen, taking Lebrun with
him, returned to Sedan and somehow scraped together a
force some 1000 strong with a few guns, and advanced
toward Balan. On the way they collected a few more un-
vanquished spirits and attacked the village with such
ferocity that the II Bavarian Corps was driven from it and
men and guns had to be rushed up to prevent exploitation
of the attack. There was none since no one would follow
Wimpffen and Lebrun beyond the village.

This – the Battle of the Last Cartridges – was truly the
end. All round the fields silence fell in the brilliant coppery
evening light. Men of the French II Corps who had taken
shelter among the trees of the Bois de la Garenne, there to be
ruthlessly shelled, came out, half-dazed bands of stragglers,
to give themselves up.

Ever since the Emperor knew the day was lost, his one
concern had been to end the carnage, and even before
Wimpffen and Lebrun's shortlived rally, he had ordered
that a white flag should be hoisted over Sedan. It was only
at this point that Moltke spotted it and sent one of his
officers, Bronsart von Schellendorf, to ascertain its mean-
ing. He was taken to Napoleon who sent him back with a
member of his own suite, bearing a letter to the Prussian

Above: The surrender ceremony after Sedan. From left to right: General Faure, Count Nostitz, General Wimpffen, von Clair, Polbielski, von Moltke, Oberst Verdy, Count von Bismarck, General Castelnau and Oberstleutnant Bronsart.

Above far right: A cartoon of the end at Sedan showing General Ducrot waving a white flag.

king. The two armies had just fought what was the first engagement in a new, yet more dreadful epoch of warfare, yet the air of a great royal tournament imparted to the occasion by the hilltop spectators was maintained in that missive. 'My Brother,' it ran, 'not having been granted death in the middle of my troops, it only remains for me to place my sword in Your Majesty's hands. I am Your Majesty's true brother, Napoleon.'

Wilhelm's answer, dictated by Bismarck, continued the strain: 'My Brother, in regretting the circumstances in which we meet, I accept Your Majesty's sword.' There followed a reminder that what had been at stake had been more than a piece of gingerbread encrusted with a gilded fleur-de-lis, the traditional reward of a knightly tourney. Napoleon was asked to send plenipoteniaries to negotiate

the capitulation of his army. On his side, Wilhelm designated Moltke.

It was an inevitable final humiliation for Wimpffen that he should have been sent by Napoleon. He tried to evade it, but got short shrift from his brothers-in-arms who reminded him that he had been happy enough to command an army he thought might bring him glory.

The following day, 3 September, the two sides met at a chateau on the Meuse. There was little to be negotiated. Wimpffen was simply passing his forces, such as had survived, into captivity. Including those taken during the battle they amounted to 105,000 men, to this could be added 1000 waggons, 6000 horses and 419 guns. Prussian losses amounted to 9000 officers and men.

Among those taken into custody that day was a young officer, Joseph-Simon Gallieni, who was to profit by and later to put to successful use what he learned of German military organization. Another, and perhaps the least reluctant to leave France, was Napoleon himself with all his entourage.

The fruits of Moltke's victory are well known. The fall of the empire; its replacement by the republic; the formation of the national army to try to prolong the struggle; the Siege of Paris; the Commune and the brutal massacre with which it was repressed.

Following the victory of Sedan, the Prussian army became the world's model and the shouts of the Feldwebel echoed across the parade grounds of Japan, Turkey, Russia and Latin America, leaving as their permanent legacy the goosestep. Despite his Danish origins, Moltke was, like Clausewitz, a peculiarly German phenomenon, for it is a national characteristic to believe that everything – musical composition, human history, the universe, the fluidities of the battlefield – can be reduced to a single, all-embracing theory. This led Moltke to blunders in predicting enemy reactions. Believing they would comport themselves according to the exigencies of military logic, he overlooked the other, more human factors.

He was a gifted man rather than a military genius and his gifts were of two kinds. First, he recognized (as the French General Staff failed to) that the nature of war had changed. The battlefield was no longer to be ruled by the will of a single commander who, like Raglan at Balaclava, overlooked the entire action from his vantage point as if it were taking place on chessboard, sending out his aides with orders to this or that commander. The lengthening range of weapons increased the distance between the contenders.

If the Commander in Chief was to impose his will, he must do it before battle was joined. It had to be imprinted on the minds of subordinates.

His other gift was for sheer organization, for painstakingly meticulous preparation. The victory of Sedan was no strategic tour de force; there are those who claim the result could not have been otherwise. History shows they are wrong. One has only to think of the overweening confidence of the French chivalry before Agincourt or of the Russian before the Russo-Japanese War. Moltke did not throw away his advantages as they did. He did all that was required, making full use of his numerical superiority and the longer reach of his guns.

It might be added that he was the mind behind the entire campaign whose objective was to harry the enemy, driving him to inevitable, irreparable error. This the French made when they decided to make a stand with their whole army at a place where they could easily be surrounded. The French situation – an unpopular regime, embarked on an ill-considered and unpopular war and desperate for victory, and, when that eluded them, desperate to mask the magnitude of the catastrophe – made its great contribution to Moltke's victory.

HINDENBURG
AT TANNENBERG 1914

The reputation of Field Marshal Paul von Beneckendorff und von Hindenburg, which was to carry him to be Commander in Chief of the German Armies in the last two years of the First World War, was made by a single victory. When he died in 1934, by that time president of his country and having seen Hitler come to power, a grandiose mausoleum was erected on the battle's alleged site as a resting place for his remains.

Tannenberg was a significant victory, a blow to the enemy gut from which he was never to recover. The question is how much was all this due to Hindenburg?

In August 1914, Germany faced two enemies. To the west there was France. To the east there was Russia. The two were bound together by the 1892 treaty. The forces the latter could deploy were enormous: 6,800,000 men, divided into 114 infantry and 36 cavalry divisions. In comparison Germany's 87 infantry divisions, to cover both fronts, seemed paltry.

The answer to the predicament of a two-front war had been provided by General Count Alfried von Schlieffen, the German strategical genius and the Army Chief of Staff from 1891–1905. The Russian Army would take months to mobilize its forces because of its great size. Germany's plan must, therefore, be first to defeat the more readily mobilized western armies – and he provided the blueprint for doing just this – and then to turn in full strength on the eastern one.

If the Russians were able to mobilize quickly enough, there was only one place where they could mount an attack. This was East Prussia, which stuck out into Russian Poland. There was only one way they could attack it; by advancing one army in a westerly direction from Lithuania and a second in a northerly direction from Poland. For most of their approach march these two armies would be separated from one another by the Masurian Lakes in the southeast corner of East Prussia. The German defenders would simply strike with all available strength at the first Russian army that came within reach, incapacitate it, and having the advantage of superior internal communications, switch their forces to turn on the second.

When war came, the Germans felt they had greater reason for confidence than they had had in 1905 when von Schlieffen's plan was adopted. Now the southern part of the Russian front was guarded by their Austrian ally with its 49 infantry divisions. Their commander, Conrad von Hötzendorf had great offensive plans of his own, which should have kept the Russians busy.

This being so the High Command felt few qualms about entrusting the defense of the region to a single army, the Eighth. Numbering some 200,000 men, it consisted of three corps of regulars and one of militia or *Landswehr* drawn, in accordance with German practice, from men of the locality so that they had a vested interested in its defense.

However, there was one factor the Germans failed to take account of simply because they knew nothing about it. Under a secret protocol added to the original Franco-Russian Treaty of 1892 was a Russian undertaking that if war broke out they would field an army of 800,000 men by the fifteenth day of mobilization, while the French would respond in the west with a force of 1,300,000.

The Russians can only have made this commitment tongue in cheek. The size of the army was a reflection of the size of the country, across whose length and breadth its reserves were scattered and it was notoriously ill-served by railroads and roads, while the system of mobilization was of Byzantine complexity.

It was events in the west which compelled the Russians to keep their word. In Belgium and France, things had gone desperately awry. An attempted offensive toward Germany by the French armies of the right had failed, while the German forces threatening their left were nearly twice as great as their peacetime intelligence estimates had made them.

Through its ambassador in St Petersburg and its military mission at Russian headquarters in Baranovichi, the French demanded that the Russians fulfill their treaty obligations. On 6 August the Russian Commander in Chief, the Grand Duke Nicholas Nicholaievich, the Czar's uncle, ordered the armies of his Northwestern Front, facing East Prussia, to launch an attack to relieve their ally, though 'only when sufficient strength was available.' By 14 August, under pressure from increasingly plaintive French appeals, this caution was omitted and immediate moves were ordered.

The Northwest Front commander, General Yakov Grigorievich Zhilinski, had by chance been the man who had signed the secret protocol. Now it was to be his misfortune to have to fulfill its stipulations.

The Russian armies took their names from the towns in which they concentrated and Northwest Front had two at its disposal. The 'Vilna' or First Army, under Pavel K

Czar Nicholas II of Russia.

Rennenkampf and the 'Warsaw' or Second Army, under Alexander Samsonov. Rennenkampf was a dashing cavalryman with a roving eye, who had earned an international reputation in command of a force during the Chinese Boxer Rising. Samsonov was a solid, good-natured, competent, but unimaginative officer. The two loathed one another — to such an extent that during the Russo-Japanese War of 1904 they had come to blows in front of the assembled military observers of the neutral nations at Mukden railroad station, hardly a promising basis on which to embark on a battle which would require the closest possible cooperation.

The Russian plan was the same as the one von Schlieffen had foreseen. Rennenkampf's Vilna Army would advance in a westerly direction to engage the enemy frontally; Samsonov would advance on a northern axis to cut off its retreat behind the Vistula, and with luck envelop it. The only way to circumvent the Germans' execution of Schlieffen's response was by exact timing. The Second Army must arrive on the battlefield as the defenders were reeling back from the blow delivered by the First.

That this was unlikely to be achieved in practice was amply demonstrated in trial runs. Samsonov had the greater distance to traverse and this through terrain which, with its forests, marshes and lakes, lent itself to defense, while the Germans had improved on nature by building railroads and paved roads for the quick movement of troops.

The Russians were proceeding with such haste that some of their corps were not up to strength, while there was a shortage of ammunition for the big guns, themselves in short supply, and of such other necessities of modern war such as telegraph-wire for signalling. Not even the field-bakeries and kitchens on which they prided themselves were available in sufficient numbers to feed the forces they had to support.

Nonetheless, with the French growing daily more restive, Rennenkampf began crossing the East Prussian border on 17 August — within three days of the Grand Duke's order. This was not, in fact, his first incursion. Jealous to retain his reputation for dash he had sent Cossack raiding parties into the area in the first week of the war.

The results had been two-fold. The German High Command might be prepared to view with equanimity the sacrifice of a border village or two, perhaps even of a small town, in pursuance of its greater strategic objectives. However, this took no account of the feelings of the sacrificial victims. The Germans, and particularly those living near Russia, had a mortal terror of the 'Mongol hordes,' as if they still lived in the time of Genghis Khan. At the first sight of Rennenkampf's wild horsemen many of them fled. East Prussia was the Junker heartland. The first Hohenzollern, the dynasty currently ruling the country, had been crowned at Königsberg (now Kaliningrad) and East Prussia contained the hunting forests in which the Kaiser annually enjoyed himself, so that he was familiar with many of the leading local families. Some of them had reached Berlin and were begging for prompt and effective succor. Helmuth von Moltke, the German Commander in Chief, found himself besieged with demands that he move troops from the Western to the Eastern Theater at the very time when events in France were taking a turn for the worse.

The other result was one which worked to the detriment of the Russians. In the process of decamping, the population near the frontier took with them anything movable, including telegraph poles and railroad rolling stock which the invaders desperately needed. Rennenkampf found himself moving into a region totally deserted and offering little on which his troops could subsist. He advanced, regardless. His was thus the 'first Russian army to come within reach' according to Schlieffen's prescription.

Command of the German Eighth Army was exercised by General Max von Prittwitz und Gaffron, known for his corpulence. He owed his position less to proven military skill than to the stock of scurrilous stories about his brother-officers with which he kept the Kaiser entertained. However, he had on his staff the leading German expert on Russian affairs, Colonel (later General) Max Hoffmann. Scarcely less corpulent than his commander, he was also ambitious, intelligent and possessed of a penetrating wit which often made him enemies.

Prittwitz's response was to follow Schlieffen's textbook. He dispatched the greater part of his strength far forward to make a stand before the town of Gumbinnen (now Gusiev). There the XVII Corps, under August von Mackensen, would attack the enemy center, while the I Corps under Hermann von François, would reach round his flank. A single corps, the XX, under Scholtz, was sent south to hold or delay any enemy forces which advanced from Poland.

Both François and the troops he commanded were East Prussian. Inflamed by patriotic feeling, he decided of his own accord to push still further forward, to Stallupönen, only five miles from the Russian border. There he engaged the First Army and, by the end of the day, sent it back across the frontier. Although his disobedience had had the result he intended, it had also upset Prittwitz's intention of a defense before Gumbinnen and could have led to the other units being dragged forward, too. He therefore ordered

François back and, by pure chance, as they had made no attempt at reconnaissance, the Russians struck on the next day.

The I Corps' flank attack was such a success that Rennenkampf contemplated going back over the border once more. He was saved by the failure of Mackensen's attack on his center. The troops of XVII Corps actually collided with the Russian artillery which fired salvo after salvo into them. The more determined units were torn to shreds; the less determined broke in panic and fled. The attack had to be called off, the Germans retired and the town of Gumbinnen fell.

Rennenkampf, though he did not appear to have realized it, had won a strategic victory. There was, however, much

Top: Hermann von François was a brilliant commander but was not very good at following orders.

Top far left: General Pavel Rennenkampf.

Far left: General Alexander Samsonov. Samsonov and Rennenkampf were supposed to act together at Tannenberg but their mutual antagonism totally jeopardized the Russian position.

Left: The mobilization of Russian troops at the outbreak of World War I.

Left: The Czar addressing his troops in 1914.

Right: Major General Erich Ludendorff, the strong man behind Hindenburg.

Below right: Russian dragoons cross Tilsit on their way through East Prussia.

Below: Supplies for troops in the Front at Warsaw Station.

crowing in St Petersburg and a parade of captured guns. Having court connexions he was anxious to maintain, he even sent a German machine gun to the Czar, who put it on display.

After this blow, Prittwitz received a second: another Russian force was advancing from the south. This, of course, was Samsonov's Warsaw Army. The summer of 1914 had been exceptionally dry and the terrain through which he was moving, which in winter could be a quagmire, was now dry, ashy sand into which the men's boots sank, while the guns and their limbers were continually bogged down. There was a shortage of food and forage because, as had happened on Rennenkampf's front, the first approach of the enemy had led to a mass exodus of local population, taking everything they could with them. All the same Samsonov was keeping to schedule, though at punishing cost to his troops, and Scholtz's XX Corps was being pushed steadily back, leaving the deserted little country towns to the Russians.

Prittwitz was faced by the fact that while his action at Gumbinnen had failed, Samsonov's army was likely to fall on his flank at any moment. Before taking up his appointment, Moltke had told him that he must at all costs avoid being locked up in the fortress of Königsberg, but that he might in extremity fall back behind the Vistula. In the deepest depression, therefore, he telephoned High Command at Koblenz and told them that this was what he now proposed to do. However, he doubted his ability to hold the river line as the summer's drought had reduced its waters to a mere trickle.

Moltke, already under pressure to reinforce in the east at the expense of the west, came off the telephone no less depressed. He had been opposed to Prittwitz's appointment in the first place and saw his misgivings justified. He first ordered one of his own aides to call the various Eighth Army corps' commanders and find out whether they shared Prittwitz's pessimism and then himself gave thought to the matter of a replacement, a man to save a critical situation.

His mind turned at once to a Major General Erich Ludendorff, commanding a brigade in Belgium, who when the advance was delayed by the resistance of the fortress of Liège, had captured it by the simple expedient of knocking on the front door and demanding its surrender. The problem was that Ludendorff had no title and this might make for difficulties in his dealings with fellow officers and subordinates who had.

Then his mind turned to Hindenburg, on the retired list but still only 67. He was admittedly neither a particularly distinguished nor a particularly intelligent soldier, but if made nominal commander he could, at least, supply the 'von' while Ludendorff supplied the brain. He forthwith set about reaching Belgium.

In the meantime, a deep discussion had been going on at Eighth Army headquarters. While Prittwitz was on the telephone, Hoffmann suggested a solution to their current problem. After the losses at Stallupönen and Gumbinnen, Rennenkampf would be in no position to pursue in strength, he believed. This being so, the defenders' response should be to leave only screening forces in front of Rennenkampf and, making use of their excellent communications, swing the weight of their force over to Samsonov's front, defeating him before he was past the barrier of the Masurian Lakes and could form a continuous line with the First Army.

An attack on Samsonov, however, might cause Rennenkampf to react at whatever cost to himself in order to save his brother-in-arms. But Hoffmann had been a witness of the famous fisticuffs on Mukden station and knew this would not happen.

The proposal was put to Prittwitz when he came back into the room. At first dubious, he was gradually won over to it, and orders amending those sent out earlier were dispatched. Unfortunately, no one thought of telling Koblenz of the changed arrangements. There, the telephone calls to Prittwitz's corps' commanders had been completed and the consensus view was that although serious, the situation was not yet desperate.

Ludendorff, meanwhile, had been contacted and was on his way to headquarters in a fast car. Hindenburg had also been reached, but it was symptomatic of Moltke's attitude that he had not bothered to bring him to Koblenz for briefing.

After his interview with Moltke and another with his Supreme War Lord, Kaiser Wilhelm II, Ludendorff entrained for the journey east. At Hanover, he was joined by Hindenburg, the first ever meeting between the two men who were later to be so closely associated that they were to speak of their relationship as 'a happy marriage.'

Solely to undermine Prittwitz, Ludendorff's only action had been to telephone the Eighth Army commanders from Koblenz and tell them to act independently until his arrival at headquarters.

There Prittwitz was in a positively cheerful mood. With no sign of movement on Rennenkampf's part, the transfer southward to forestall and defeat Samsonov had begun. In fact, Hoffmann's analysis had been perfectly correct. Not only had the First Army suffered 20 percent casualties, but what was worse in view of its shortages, it had fired off the allocation of artillery shell for the entire campaign in the Gumbinnen battle. Unable to pursue, Rennenkampf, for reasons of his own, had omitted even to send out scouts and so had no idea where the enemy was making for.

In the early afternoon, Ludendorff and Hindenburg arrived at Marienburg where the Eighth Army headquarters had been set up. Prittwitz, who had no knowledge of his own replacement until that moment, shook hands with his fellow officers and gave up his command to the newcomers, in Hoffmann's words 'without any complaint at his treatment.'

Told of the new orders, Ludendorff simply confirmed them, though, according to the evidence not without a great deal of persuasion. By the following day, the 24th, he seems to have conquered his apprehensions. For one thing, he now had an insight into Russian intentions. Short of telegraph wire, Rennenkampf was forced to use radio to promulgate his orders and, though sent in code, these were of such a puerile nature, that the Eighth Army cryptographers had no difficulty in deciphering them. These confirmed that he was not going to move.

Instead of striking at only one of Samsonov's flanks and preventing the junction with Rennenkampf, as had been proposed earlier, Ludendorff decided to strike at both and the pace of the transfer from the First to the Second Army front was increased accordingly and the attack's scope widened.

Samsonov was now encountering increased opposition and duly reported this to Northwestern Front command. There Zhilinski, convinced that the greater German forces were retreating before the First Army, accused Samsonov of cowardice and urged him to hurry as his slowness was endangering Rennenkampf – a suggestion which contained, of course, not an iota of truth. Zhilinski continued in his mistaken belief about relative German strength on the two fronts even after a Russian flyer had reported a massive movement toward the south in which every conceivable form of transport, including taxicabs, was being used.

On the night of 24th the Germans had a momentary shock when Rennenkampf again began moving. However, from the decoded radio messages it soon became clear that instead of advancing westward, he was veering north and toward Königsberg where he believed the enemy to have gone. This was taking him away from Samsonov and, by widening the gap, making the possibility of a link up more difficult.

Samsonov was facing a dilemma of his own. As the forces in front of him increased, the need to find Rennenkampf's left flank, which he believed would be stretching out to him to form a single line, became ever more urgent. At the same time, he was being impelled forward under Zhilinski's orders.

As his right was groping in the dark for Rennenkampf,

Left: Russian heavy artillery unit in 1914.

Below: German troops advancing through East Prussia to the Russian border to protect their homeland.

Above center: A German defensive
position on the shores of a
Masurian Lake.

Right: German infantry in a
defensive position during the
Battle of Tannenberg. They have
built trenches in a farmhouse.

Far right: Russian troops pressing
home an attack.

FRONT LINE, EVENING 25 AUG 1914
"   "   "   "   29 AUG   "
RUSSIAN ATTACKS
GERMAN COUNTERATTACKS
RUSSIAN RETREAT
GERMAN FORTIFIED POSITIONS
HELD DURING RUSSIAN ADVANCE

0   MILES   30
0   KILOMETERS   50

IV Corps
NORDENBURG
Alle
First Army
(Rennenkampf)
Angerapp
ANGERBURG
BARTENSTEIN
II Corps
RASTENBURG
1 Cav Div
BISCHOFSTEIN
LÖTZEN
Masurian Lakes
XVII Corps

G   E   R   M   A   N   Y
BISCHOFBURG
SENSBURG
Eighth Army
(Hindenburg)
I Res Corps
ALLENSTEIN
BARTELSDORF
NIKOLAIKEN
VI Corps
E   A   S   T
OSTERODE
P   R   U   S   S   I   A
4 Cav Div
JOHANNISBURG
III Res Corps
PASSENHEIM
HOHENSTEIN
ORTELSBURG
FRÖGENAU **XX Corps**
KURKEN
JEDWABNO
TANNENBERG
XIII Corps
XV Corps
XXIII Corps
ORLAU
WILLENBERG
USDAU
NIEDENBURG
I Corps
LAUTENBERG
I Corps
SOLDAU
Second Army
(Samsonov)
R   U   S   S   I   A
MLAWA
P   O   L   A   N   D

Left: Russian casualties after Tannenberg.

Right: Russian troops surrender. Some 92,000 prisoners were taken by the Germans.

Below left: Hugo Vögel's painting of the German commanders at Tannenberg. General Hoffman is looking through a rangefinder and to the right stand Hindenburg and Ludendorff.

it was becoming further and further separated from the rest of the army. Concerned about the thinning in his line this was leading to, he therefore ordered the VII Corps, on his extreme right to close up. He then realized, after the order had gone out, that this would leave his right flank open, and he was forced to countermand so as to make it a flank guard.

His communications were in an even more parlous state than Rennenkampf's. Not only was he lacking in telegraphs, but each of his corps was using a different code and the First Army headquarters did not have all the requisite keys. He was compelled to send out his orders by radio and *en clair*. They were monitored without trouble by the enemy.

Soon after his VII Corps had begun retracing its steps, it ran into a German force. The only explanation of its presence the Russians could think of was that it must be a scattered unit in retreat from Rennenkampf. This could only mean the two Russian armies were about to meet.

It was nothing of the kind. It was part of Mackensen's XVII Corps which was beginning to reach Samsonov's front. As the battle flared up along the VII Corps' line, the corps to its left was embroiled. At the same time, Scholtz's XX Corps, which had turned from retreat to attack, was holding Samsonov's center, making it impossible for it to give assistance to the struggling units to its right. By nightfall, a breach six miles wide gaped between Second Army's center and the Masurian Lakes, and Mackensen's men were beginning to sidle round it to reach the Russian flank.

The Russian I Corps, under Artamanov, was sent to fill the gap but arrived too late and fell back across the frontier under withering German artillery fire. A third German corps was now reaching the south. This was François's I, which had the greatest distance to travel. Insubordination among German commanders was a malaise which had afflicted the army from the time it was formed under the united flag of the North German Confederation in the time of the first Moltke. François had already given a demonstration of it at Stallüpönen. Now, under orders to attack the Russian left wing at Usdau, he made a token gesture in that direction before wheeling to strike at their flank at Soldau, his excuse being that his artillery had not arrived and this made a frontal attack too hazardous and costly. His action was later to be justified since it was actually to seal the fate of the Second Army and of its commander.

The struggle had now been raging for two days. On the 27th, it reached its climax. The artillery of the I Corps arrived and François began an all-out assault at Usdau. The Russian troops, tired from their long, arduous marches and hungry from lack of supplies, fell back. A pursuit was ordered as far as Neidenburg, this placing the I Corps in the Russian rear, a move checked, though only temporarily, by a counterattack.

The brutal truth was that more than a counterattack was needed. The only way in which the Russians could extricate themselves was by a hasty withdrawal of their forces back to the border.

Samsonov did the opposite, either because he was still smarting from accusations that his own tardiness was endangering Rennenkampf or because while the First Army was advancing, as he still believed it to be, he did not want to be the one to instigate retreat. With his left folded back on itself and his right under threat he continued to push his center forward. It soon came into contact with Scholtz's XX Corps once more. It succeeded in pushing it back, but with severe loss and at the cost of further fatigue to the men.

Nonetheless, news of this repulse to the XX Corps so unnerved Ludendorff and Hindenburg that they considered abandonment of the entire plan and even sent François instructions to withdraw back to support Scholtz.

In fact their advance had led the Russians deeper into the trap, as the I Corps' commander was quick to point out.

It is true that at this stage Samsonov seemed to have realized that there was no alternative to retreat. His troops, however, were already taking the law into their own hands and first in small bands, then in ever growing numbers, were finding their way back across the frontier.

Their escape route was not open to them for long. Having reached Neidenburg, François' troops pushed further east to Willenburg, setting up a line of outposts across the Russian rear. The area was largely one of forests, totally unfamiliar to the invaders who, lost and confused among the trees, found themselves under machine-gun fire from the I Corps' picket line whenever they emerged from cover.

They had stood as much as was humanly possible and, on the whole, had fought with exemplary if futile courage.

Now, they began giving themselves up in their thousands.

Riding out to discover for himself the exact situation, Samsonov got caught up in the tide of retreat. Then, with his immediate staff, he got lost in the forest himself. In the confusion, he was able to slip away, unmissed, until a single shot was heard. His companions found their Commander in Chief had shot himself.

Yet even at that stage the Russians' position was not totally lost. Artamanov's I Corps which had retreated over the frontier, was now on its way back, reinforced. In any case, Mackensen's XVII Corps had not yet joined with François in the Russian rear, leaving an escape route still open, had the Russians been able to fight their way out. There was still Rennenkampf who, had he attacked vigor-

ously, would have found the way to the heart of East Prussia open to him.

None of these things happened. In consequence, Samsonov's army suffered an enormous defeat, one of the worst in military history. Of its five corps, two and a half were annihilated. Ninety thousand of its men were taken prisoner. Total Russian casualties in the first East Prussian campaign were 310,000 men and 650 guns, the equivalent of seven and a half corps.

At the height of the battle, the Eighth Army Staff had set

A Russian field battery after the battle. The three corps which were encircled during the battle included Martos' XV Corps and Kliouviev's XII Corps which were considered among the best in action.

up temporary headquarters in a farmhouse at Frogenau, a few miles from where the battle was being fought. Someone pointed out that not far away was the village of Tannenberg. Here in 1410, the Teutonic knights had suffered a great reverse. This, surely, was the revenge. Accordingly, the great defeat of Samsonov's army was called the Battle of Tannenberg.

By his inactivity while his old enemy was writhing, Rennenkampf had merely ensured his own ultimate defeat. For, with the threat of the Second Army removed, the Germans could, à la Schlieffen, turn on him in full strength. This they shortly did, pushing him back across the frontier from where his Cossack bands once more began their forays, though there was little enough for them to find.

Even before this, recriminations against the First Army Commander had begun. In a play on his German name, he was rechristened 'Rennohne-Kampf,' ran-without-fighting. There was even a suggestion of treason, which, of course, was totally without foundation. All the same, in contrast with the speed with which Prittwitz had been replaced, it was not until the early November that the Czar confirmed his dismissal as commander.

Yet, taking the war overall, the defeat of Tannenberg was not without effect. Two days after his appointment of Hindenburg and Ludendorff as saviors of East Prussia, Moltke was still wondering if he had done enough. Two corps on his Western Front – the XI and Guard Reserve – seemed underemployed, since both the French and British forces in front of them were in full retreat. He sent them east.

On 6 September the Franco-British forces, taking advantage of the German offer of their flank along the Marne, swung from the defensive to the offensive. The British Expeditionary Force found itself advancing into a 30-mile gap. It had been left by the removal of the troops sent to Ludendorff. It was German apprehensions about this gap which in the end persuaded them to disengage and retreat behind the Aisne, removing the threat to Paris.

Just after Tannenberg the French liaison officer at Russian headquarters, who had done so much to spur them to adventure, commiserated with the Grand Duke who, with breathtaking chivalry, told him, 'We are happy to make such sacrifices for our allies.'

What of Hindenburg's part in the battle which is regarded by the German people as his special victory. All the moves toward it had, as we have seen, been taken before he even entered the scene and had been confirmed by Prittwitz. Both Hindenburg's account and that of Ludendorff make it very clear that they had considerable trepidation about the battle. Certainly, the latter was prepared to abandon the whole enterprise when a Russian threat appeared.

The Eighth Army staff were, naturally, perfectly well aware of the truth. Hoffmann best sums up their feelings. After the war, it would sometimes fall to his lot to show awed visitors over the house at Frogenau which had served as headquarters. Taking them into one room he would tell them, 'This is the room in which General Hindenburg slept before the Battle of Tannenberg.' And into another, he would say, 'And this is the room in which General Hindenburg slept after the Battle of Tannenberg.' And into a third, 'And this is the room in which General Hindenburg slept during the Battle of Tannenberg.'

Rarely can a general have slept so greatly to his country's and his own benefit.

JOFFRE
AT THE MARNE 1914

To the modern mind, accustomed to protracted wars ending only when one side has been bankrupted and physically devastated, the idea that a struggle between two great nations could be decided in a mere month or two seems hardly credible. Yet before 1914, the long war was thought to belong to a past growing ever more remote. Countries had their standing armies, usually backed by a large pool of reserves; their General Staffs drew up plans of campaign, periodically revised, which envisaged two or three battles culminating in a final and decisive one. In theory, that was to be that. In practice, what is more, it sometimes was.

The idea that the army and its first-line reserves might serve only to give time for the economy to be geared to war and for enormous armies, drawing on a nation's entire manhood, to be mustered had occurred to none. There was nothing outrageous, therefore, in the German plan to defeat France in the six weeks between 1 August and 15 September 1914. Indeed, they would be improving only slightly on their 1870 performance. A quick, decisive end was also a necessity, for they would be facing not one but two enemies. To their east was Russia, bound to France by the Treaty of 1892. The western foe had to be neutralized in the period of grace granted while the unwieldy Russian war machine creaked into action.

The plans for achieving this had been drawn up by General Count Alfried von Schlieffen, Chief of the German General Staff from 1891 to 1905. What he proposed had the merit of originality. Instead of the obvious route of an advance across the Rhine, as in Moltke's plans of 1870, he advocated the longer one through Luxembourg and Belgium. The armies would march almost to the coast before wheeling west to advance into France with the extreme right, as Schlieffen put it, 'brushing the Channel with their sleeves.' In this way, like the trunk of an enormous elephant, the German phalanxes would reach round the waist of the French defense, pick it up and, presumably, deposit it lock, stock and barrel in the German prison cages.

The French were, as a matter of fact, aware that the Germans might have some such intention, but, though they had hardly distinguished themselves in recent wars, felt they could face the next with confidence. For one thing, they had as allies not only massive Russia, but also Britain which besides its command of the seas, had an indubitably successful, if comparatively small army.

For another, the French had not merely a counterplan, but an entirely new military philosophy. The plan was the acme of simplicity: their army was simply going to march into Germany by the shortest route, advancing across the old battlegrounds of 1870, liberating the lost provinces of Alsace and Lorraine, and crossing the Rhine. In sum, while the Germans advanced their left, the French would hurl themselves on their right. The more they strengthened the one, the more they would weaken the other – *et voilà*, the road to Berlin would lie open.

What transformed this mere intention into something different was their new found philosophy. This, with equal simplicity, stated that the absolute key to military success was *l'attaque*. The next war would be won by *l'offensive à l'outrance*, offensive to the uttermost. The French army, resplendent in blue tunic and red trousers, inspired by their

General Joseph Galliéni, Military Governor of Paris.

sword-brandishing officers, would advance without consideration of losses, and would overcome by sheer élan.

As the French response to the Schlieffen Plan, it was given the sternly businesslike title of Plan 17 and in July 1911 its execution, should necessity arise, was entrusted to General Joseph Jacques Césaire Joffre, then 59. This paunchy figure with a thick white moustache, who looked like a healthy Norman peasant dressed in a general's uniform, had not been the first choice for the post. The man the government originally wanted was a very different man, Joseph Simon Galliéni, who had refused it on the grounds that as a colonial soldier his appointment might be resented by the Metropolitan army.

However, when necessity did arise, the French intentions suffered two terrifying reverses. First, all the enormous French courage of their *offensive à l'outrance* was sacrificed in a useless carnage which should have convinced all observers that in this new war the weapons of defense – machine gun and barbed wire, to say nothing of fire power – were more potent than the most indomitable will in *l'attaque*. Within a short time, the struggle resolved itself into one of attrition of a kind to become familiar along the whole front. Its effect on German intentions was virtually nil. By the end of the month, the French First and Second Armies, their flower destroyed, were holding a line north of the Moselle in what was rapidly becoming a secondary theater. Worse still, the advance of the German right which was to have been little more than a march into French custody took on an entirely different character. For one thing the invaders were nearly twice as numerous as French intelligence estimates had made them.

In a desperate effort both to succor their Belgian ally and to halt the rolling German masses, Joffre ordered the Fifth Army under Lanrezac to strike at the enemy flank as it moved toward the French frontiers. On 22 August Lanrezac was caught at Charleroi, defeated and thrown back. To maintain continuity of line, the two French armies next to him, the Fourth and Third also had to retreat. On 24 August a million German troops began crossing the borders, a line of reapers 75 miles in width consisting of four armies. In the way of their advance, like a clump of poppies in a harvest field, was the French capital, Paris.

Later to be credited with a policy of 'masterly inactivity,' on this occasion Joffre reacted with laudable promptness. On 25 August the armies facing the German advance were to undertake a slow retirement, seeking as they did so to harass the enemy and delay his advance. At the same time a Sixth Army would be formed from troops railed from Lorraine to take their place on the left, along the Somme, a position which should pose them on the flanks of the invaders. It was planned to achieve this on 2 September – Sedan Day – which would mark the start of a general offensive.

There was a snag. To the left of Lanrezac's Fifth Army were the four (later five) divisions of the British Expeditionary Force with only a thin screen of French cavalry and territorials between them and the English Channel. Liaison between the British and French armies was almost

General Alexander von Kluck, Commander of the First Army.

non-existent. The Commander of the BEF, Sir John French, deeply suspicious of his ally, unable to pronounce their place names, let alone speak their language, still had ringing in his ears the instructions given to him when he left Britain: he must not allow his army to be sacrificed.

When, on 23 August, the day after it had taken its place in the line, the BEF was surprised on the march by the Germans miles forward of where they were thought to be, the British held their own at the Battle of Mons but, totally outnumbered, were forced to retire. Even more alarming, Sir John discovered that instead of forming part of a solid line with the French Fifth, he was actually on his own and Lanrezac was in full retreat after Charleroi. If, as he suspected and perhaps half-hoped, 1914 was to be a repetition of 1870, it was now his overriding duty to save his forces. While it is untrue, as the French alleged and continued to allege, that he began forthwith to make for the Channel ports, he certainly decided to set as great a distance as possible between himself and the advancing foe.

He had, of course, totally misread the situation. What was now happening was the reverse of 1870. Then total defeat had largely been due to the fact that for political reasons the French armies had failed to retreat and maintain a line when military necessity dictated that they should have done so.

On the German side, General Alexander von Kluck, commanding their First Army on the far right, had come to a similar conclusion to Sir John, but in his estimation, not only the French, but also the British were worsted, and in this belief he pushed his men relentlessly forward.

They pursued with such speed that on 26 August they caught up with the BEF's II Corps, under Smith-Dorrien, at Le Cateau. Compelled to give battle, the corps mauled their tormentors, but only at the cost of 20 percent casualties and further retreat.

Since Kluck was able to continue his advance, the flow

Sir John French, Commander in Chief of the British Expeditionary Force.

of euphoric communiqués from his headquarters went on uninterrupted. These, however, were being received with increasing skepticism by the German Commander in Chief, Helmuth von Moltke, nephew of the hero of Sedan. As great a pessimist as Kluck was an optimist, Moltke was asking himself why it was, since the Franco-British forces were supposed to be retreating in disorder, there were so few prisoners and so little booty. He had an uneasy suspicion they might actually be escaping his trap and luring him into one of their own.

It must be remembered he had other causes for anxiety. There had already been delays and modifications to the original plans. First, the line of fortresses on the Belgian frontier had proved more intractable than had been supposed. Then, the Belgians themselves had failed to collapse before the Germans' might and there were rumors they were being reinforced by the British. Though grossly exaggerated, these caused Moltke to detach some of his forces to stand guard over Antwerp. This reduced the breadth of the intended swing on the English Channel, which now had to be carried out further inland than Schlieffen had stipulated. On top of all this, came stories of Russian troops reaching France in numbers which increased with each retelling. Pure legend as they were, until denied, they were enough to unsettle still further Moltke's never very strong nerves.

And there was worse. The armies of the Czar which, it had been confidently estimated, would require three months to mobilize, actually began invading East Prussia on 17 August. Schlieffen had not ignored this eventuality and had catered for it. What he had not catered for was the panic into which the arrival of the Cossacks in German territory threw the local population, leading to a demand for massive reinforcement of the forces there.

These doubts at enemy headquarters would, naturally enough, have been balm to the souls of the harassed British and French commanders, had they known of them. As it was their horizons were dominated by what they saw before them – a remorseless advance toward the capital.

The question of the moment, therefore, was Paris and how it should be treated. We know that militarily Joffre viewed Paris as just another city 'comme les autres,' that he did not believe its loss betokened the end of the struggle. We also know, of course, that he was preparing the way for his own riposte to the German invasion and one in which Paris played no part. However, the sacrifice of the city was hardly likely to appeal either to France's popula-

The German armies swept through Belgium according to the plan laid down by Schlieffen. On 23 August 1914 they reached Mons and the British cavalry had to retreat.

tion or its leaders. Their misgivings were not merely emotional. The strategist might see Paris as 'comme les autres,' but from the point of view of morale it was, after all, the capital. The effect of its loss would be devastating. There was one man who realized this.

When Joffre had been appointed Commander in Chief, his predecessor, Michel, had been offered as a sop the military governorship of Paris. The War Ministry had as little faith in him in his new post as in his previous one and on 24 August replaced him with Galliéni, Joffre's former rival to the post of generalissimo. Tall, austere, bespectacled Galliéni looked like an eccentric university professor among the French generals and because of his strangely variegated

uniform was regarded by the British as little more than 'a clown' — a judgment they, like others, were soon to revise. Now 65, recently bereaved of his wife, he was already suffering from the cancer which was to kill him within two years.

Though he believed that Paris could and should be defended, his acceptance of the post of governor had been conditional. To man the 100-mile perimeter round the city would require an army of three active corps, far more than its garrison could muster and this, in any case, was being milked by Joffre for his coming attack on the German flank. There followed a protracted struggle to persuade Joffre to part with some of the men he was husbanding for this, but the government had little recourse since it had voluntarily

Top: Prince Rupprecht of Bavaria was in command of the Sixth Army.

Top left: General Joseph Maunoury was put in command of the newly formed Sixth Army which was to protect Paris.

Left: German transports taking bridging equipment during the march to the Marne.

foregone much of its own power in military matters.

Among the lessons which the French believed they had learned from 1870 was that strategy and politics made poor bedfellows. Then, the armies had embarked on hopeless adventures simply because the politicians had overruled the commanders. To avoid a repetition of this, at the beginning of the present war France had been split in two. The Zone of the Interior was the province of the politicians; the Zone of the Armies was ruled by Joffre as by a dictator. The trouble was the latter was fluid. As the armies moved back so did their zone. By 28 August it encompassed Paris and within it the control of government and municipality had ceased. Thus Joffre refused Galliéni's requests on the grounds that a fight for the capital was no part of his plans.

The resolution of the dispute was due to the enemy. Kluck's army had been on the verge of victory over Smith-Dorrien's British II Corps when night fell. Under its cover, the British decamped with such efficiency the Germans were totally nonplussed. Aggrieved, as though he had been unfairly tricked, Kluck set off in pursuit. But where had they gone? Toward the Channel Ports, no doubt. It was, therefore, in this direction that he ordered his army to march. The British were not making for the ports at all; they were pulling back toward Paris. Far from finding his

enemy, Kluck was moving away from them.

On the other hand, his route was taking him toward the French, for it was in this area that Joffre's Sixth Army, newly arrived from the northeast, was beginning its concentration. To avoid a head on collision, it too had to be moved toward Paris and so became the force Galliéni had been demanding.

Kluck's chase after British shadows was having another effect: it was widening the gap between himself and the army to his left, Bülow's Second. The Second Army had already run into trouble from Lanrezac's Fifth Army which had been ordered to turn and fight to reduce the pressure on the British. When Bülow's position became critical, Kluck wheeled to come to his aid. The move was made with the blessing of Moltke, who was worried about the fanning out of his forces as they had advanced deeper into France, and the thinning of the lines it had brought about. At the same time, he had himself contributed to this weakening as, in response to cries of help from East Prussia, he had sent two of the corps from his right to the east, although the attempted Russian 'march on Berlin,' never more than a hasty improvisation to aid France, had been stopped and one of their armies destroyed.

What he now realized was that these miscellaneous

Left: Taxis and cars were requisitioned in Paris to take troops to the Marne Front.

Right: French prisoners take a rest as they are marched from the front, 26 August 1914.

Below: Belgian cavalry and infantry evacuate Antwerp and fall back to join the BEF in early September 1914.

moves in the west added up to the entire abandonment of Schlieffen's grandiose plan. Instead of the broad sweep of the armies far to the north of Paris and its formidable defenses he was now forced to a compromise with something infinitely more modest. His Fourth, Fifth, Sixth and Seventh Armies would concentrate on that part of the French Army on the far side of Paris. The capital's garrison was to be held in check meanwhile by stationing Kluck's First and Bülow's Second Armies in line facing west.

The outstanding flaw in these arrangements was that Kluck was ahead of Bülow and advancing southward and so upon Paris. Considerable shuffling of enormous bodies of men would be necessary to comply with Moltke's orders and Kluck saw them as denying him the chance of decisive victory. There was, in any case, little time to make such complex redeployments.

In the meantime, Galliéni was preparing for what everyone in Paris and outside it expected: a second siege. In the days following his appointment he worked tirelessly to

prepare, knowing he was short of men and that the capital's defenses were unready. Charges were laid on bridges, even those scheduled as works of art; every conceivable means of infiltrating the city was barricaded, including sewers and drains; ammunition was stockpiled as it came from the factories; cattle and sheep were brought in to graze in the Bois de Boulogne and in such other open spaces as the city offered.

Through this Joffre was single-mindedly refusing to allow himself to be diverted from his own plans by the city's needs. What he now wanted was to create a stable line and this, of necessity, required that the British cease their retreat. To persuade them to do so he paid a personal visit to Sir John French at the new headquarters he had established at Compiègne. His efforts were entirely wasted. The British Commander in Chief intended to retire to St Nazaire in the west for reinforcement and reequipping over the winter. While he did not make Joffre privy to these plans, he argued that his army was exhausted and reduced by its losses and so would be unable to take its place in the line for some ten days. The losses, though small by later standards, were, it was true, considerable, but as to exhaustion, the British troops had had far more opportunity for rest than their French brothers-in-arms or, come to that, the Germans. During the time that Lanrezac's men had been struggling to relieve the pressure on their ally, the British Army had quite simply slept.

Nor did French's estimate of his condition tally with that of his field officers or the men themselves. Both believed they were at least a match for the Germans and were longing to show their mettle. If the consideration of any of these points caused Sir John any hesitation, he certainly did not allow them to weaken his resolve.

All the time the crisis was developing by the day. On 30 August Paris experienced the first of the daily air raids to which it was to become accustomed when a handful of bombs were dropped from the cockpit of a single-seater *Taube*, causing some casualties mainly round the Gare de l'Est area. Besides its more lethal spawn, it also deposited leaflets warning the Parisians that they were now besieged 'as in 1870' and had no alternative to surrender.

The message of the leaflets had very little effect, but it brought home – in view of the short range of the aircraft of those days – how near the enemy was. In fact, Kluck's advance guards were only some 20 miles from the city gates and this being so Galliéni warned the government it might be necessary for it to leave, though it was a further three days before the move was actually made.

Expectation of the coming battle for the city grew by the day and a kind of nervous tension, half-excited, half-apprehensive grasped its citizens or such as had not left. All realized it would affect fundamentally the course of the war, a view those who remembered events before and after the Siege of Paris could only confirm.

It was at precisely this moment, when France needed to draw together all her strength that relations with the BEF reached a crisis. In a dispatch to Lord Kitchener, the British War Minister, French was proposing nothing less than the abandonment of the struggle and a return home with his armies now some 150,000 strong. Horrified by the military and political consequences even the suggestion of such a move could have, Kitchener donned his field marshal's uniform and hastened through the night of 31 August–1 September toward Paris. The result of his meeting with Sir John French was to secure his undertaking to 'conform with the movement of the French Army' – and no more. In his interpretation, Sir John was given the widest latitude. ·

Infuriated by Kitchener's 'political' intervention, he actually interpreted it by continuing his retreat, though managing in doing so to keep some kind of tenuous contact with his French neighbors, at least initially.

So much for Joffre's efforts to secure a continuous and stabilized line as a springboard for his own offensive. In justification, it has to be said that French was convinced Paris would fall; that France would be defeated. Thereafter an angry – and victorious – Kaiser might well decide to turn on Britain. Then it would have reason to be grateful to him for saving the army.

The conviction that Paris was soon to fall was one shared not only by many of French's fellow-Britons, but also people in France. In a matter of 24 hours, Kluck's armies had halved the distance separating them from the city.

Then came a succession of indicators, at first hardly credited, which betokened a dramatic and unhoped for shift in German intentions. Between the day of Kitchener's visit and 3 September, it became increasingly plain that Kluck was, after all, going to bypass Paris. Instead of advancing in a southwesterly direction and so toward the city, he was veering southeastward. He was, of course, marching to take up his assigned position in Moltke's new plan.

On 3 September Maunoury, commander of the Sixth Army now part of the Paris garrison, reported that there were no Germans west of Paris along a line reaching out as far as Senlis. This was confirmed by British air reconnaissance.

That Kluck believed he could make such a turn under the noses of the enemy could only be accounted for by his conviction that they were incapable any longer of responding to the challenge his exposed flank offered them.

Galliéni, however, was not the man to miss such an opportunity and at once saw that, instead of merely defending the city, the men under his command were going to be in a position to strike a decisive blow. On 3 September he told Maunoury to begin cavalry and air reconnaissance and at 0900 hours on the 4th, ordered him to prepare for a move against the German flank. If this was to be more than a parry it required greater strength than he disposed,

Left: German officers take a break from the advance during September 1914.

Far left: BEF gunners attack.

Far left below: Shrapnel hits the 1st Middlesex First-Line Transport at Signy on 8 September 1914. Nine horses were killed and the man with hands raised was badly wounded in the incident.

Below: German Jäger troops use a mobile phone. World War I saw a revolution in military communications.

while, in any case, the large-scale offensive for which he thought the opportunity was presenting itself, would need the sanction of Joffre to whom he was subordinated.

He hurried to General Headquarters only to find the Commander in Chief in an intractable mood. Joffre was still considering his own plans for the blow to take place well to the northwest of Paris and the farthest he would go was to promise to think over Galliéni's proposals. Leaving his chief to this meditation, Galliéni next made for Compiègne and the British Headquarters where Sir John French was absent and he saw the even more cautious Chief of Staff, Murray. It was absolutely plain that nothing would shift the British from their planned withdrawal and they even went so far as to say that had they known of the condition of the French Army they would never have entered the conflict.

For Galliéni it had been a thoroughly depressing and largely wasted day. Or so it must have seemed.

Nonetheless, despite outward appearances, Joffre had not been entirely unmoved by the arguments presented to him. He went so far as to address a letter to Franchet d'Esperey, who had succeeded Lanrezac as commander of the Fifth Army, asking him, though without implying a sense of urgency, whether he thought his forces could join in a general attack with any hope of success. Franchet's answer was that they would be in no position to do so in less than 48 hours. In the meantime, they, like the British, were continuing a retreat which would take them even further from Paris.

Even though Joffre was coming round to Galliéni's view, there was a danger, increased with every passing hour, that he would be too late since the Sixth Army was advancing alone against a much stronger enemy. What was more, the armies on its flanks were actually marching away, leaving an ominous gap. The situation clearly gave the advantage to Kluck.

At this late stage Joffre began to move, as did, even if reluctantly, the British Commander in Chief. Galliéni arrived back at his own headquarters in Paris after his discouraging interviews with Joffre and Murray late on the 5th. He found a message from the former awaiting him. Permission for the counteroffensive was granted, but it was suggested that it should be south, not north, of the Marne as Galliéni wanted. He rang Joffre and by sheer vehemence won him over. That night orders were issued for a general offensive to begin on the 6th. Joffre promised to obtain British co-operation in the attack.

The battle order on the eve of the Marne Battle ran, left to right: the French Sixth Army, whose sector began roughly on a line with Paris and extended southwest of the Ourcq to Lagny, then the BEF from Lagny along the River Grand Morin, then the French Fifth Army, north of the Seine and to the marshes of St Gond. The Fourth Army had originally stood next in line, but its tenacious defense of a sector south of the Ornain had caused it to draw upon its own left along the Marne to reinforce. To fill the gap thus created, Joffre had inserted a so-called Detachment Foch, named after its commander, General Ferdinand Foch, and this had become the Ninth Army, still commanded by Foch, whose sector ran for much of its distance southwest of the St Gond marshes.

Beyond the Fourth Army's sector, from the confluence of the Marne and Ornain rivers, that of the Third Army ran up to Verdun and then followed the French fortress line to Nancy.

With one notable absentee, all these armies from the Ourcq to the Meuse were to turn about and go over to the offensive next day. Along this extensive line, the crucial area was that on the French left up to the St Gond marshes where Kluck was exposing his flank. It was here that there was one army which apparently had no intention of participating in the attack. The BEF's front, though small, chanced to stride the point of junction between the German First and Second Armies. It had been from here, just because there was no sign of enemy activity, that Moltke had taken the two corps he had sent east a day or two earlier.

Aside from the opportunities which existed for them because of this, the possibility that the British would absent themselves was a dreadful one for Joffre to contemplate. Not only did it virtually divide the attack in half — with a hole in the middle — but it also allowed an opportunity for the enemy to outflank his attackers and convert the offensive into the most appalling of catastrophes. Yet for most of the 5th, his efforts to make the BEF commander

Left: General Pau was the Commander of the Army of Alsace during the Battle of the Frontiers.

Center left: General Franchet d'Esperey was given command of the Fifth Army at the height of the battle.

Far left: General de Castelnau was in command of the Second Army in 1914.

Right: 'The Last Gunner' at Mons commemorates the bravery of a soldier who held off the advancing Germans despite the fact that the other members of his crew had been killed.

Below right: General Joseph Galliéni, who must take the credit for saving Paris.

change his mind proved unavailing. Not even when he asked the French government, now evacuated to Bordeaux, to appeal directly to Britain's was he any more successful.

When Joffre's order to his own forces to begin the offensive was promulgated, a copy of it was delivered to Compiègne, in accordance with established practice. Its bearer reported back that the British seemed lukewarm to the whole enterprise. To depress French spirits still further news came that day that Sir John French was proposing to move his own headquarters further back, to Fontainebleau. In fact, at those headquarters one British officer, General Sir Henry Wilson, a loyal and unswerving friend to France, was just beginning to persuade his commander.

At 0930 hours Joffre could stand the suspense no longer. He had appointed as his personal chauffeur a French racing driver. With him at the wheel, he set out on the 150-mile journey to see Sir John. He arrived at 1400 hours and presented himself before his ally's Commander in Chief. Normally a laconic man, what now poured from Joffre's lips was a passionate and eloquent appeal. It ended with the words, 'Monsieur le Marechal, the honor of England is at stake.' At these words French is said to have blushed, struggled to say something in Joffre's own tongue as a tear welled up and coursed down his cheek. Despairing of his French, he burst out, 'Dammit, tell him we will do all we can.'

If the British were no longer to be absent from the battle, they still had to retrace their steps. So, to some extent, did Franchet d'Espérey's Fifth Army. Yet strangely, as Basil Liddell Hart has pointed out, the British absence at the beginning actually helped rather than hindered the successful outcome as it further convinced Kluck he was dealing with a beaten foe and so could afford risks he would not otherwise have taken.

Two armies were, however, in position on the 6th. These were Maunoury's Sixth and Foch's Ninth. The latter's performance is instructive since he was to end the war as Commander in Chief of the combined Anglo-French forces. Under orders to hold the southern outlets of the St Gond

marshes as the Fifth Army put pressure on Kluck's right, what he actually did was to mount a private offensive of his own. This very nearly ran into trouble from a determined German counterattack which was only held by a combination of devastating French artillery fire and reinforcement provided by Joffre and Franchet d'Espérey himself. All the same, it continued to pose a threat to the French offensive right up to the end of the battle.

For Kluck, it was Maunoury's attacks on his right which were the major cause of anxiety. To meet them, he moved his II and IV Corps from behind the Grand Morin to his right, leaving only a thin screen to hold the gap up to Bülow's front.

There was a lingering morning mist over the battlefield in that area between the French Fifth and Sixth Armies where the British were to attack and it was through this they began their advance. The effect can only have been eery. On either side of them battles were raging, but here there was silence and desertion. The chilling, uneasy suspicion of commanders is perfectly understandable, but it was without foundation. They had simply struck in an area which the enemy had denuded to try to meet the threats elsewhere. The British were being offered the chance of slicing through the thin links attaching the First to the Second Army and so bringing total disaster to the invaders. All that was needed was for them to speed up their advance. They did the reverse. Convinced they must be walking into a trap, they slowed down, painfully reconnoitering every mile of the way.

While the British were hesitating, Kluck's II and IV Corps were now making their presence felt. By the 7th, Maunoury's advance seemed to have been held and Galliéni turned to every available means to find reserves to send in.

On the 8th, a fresh division reached Paris, a total of some 6,000 men. They were 40 miles from the front and the railroads choked. It was then that there occurred the most famous legend of this legend-encrusted battle – that of the taxis to the Marne.

The idea was not entirely original. The Germans had already used taxicabs as a means of transporting troops when they made their famous switch from left to right in

Left: German soldiers during the exhausting action which brought the German armies so close to Paris.

Right: Generals Joffre and Foch at the end of 1914.

Below: French troops in a forward trench during the Battle of the Marne.

East Prussia. In any case, Galliéni's headquarters had earlier commandeered 100 taxis for its own use, so it was no sudden brainwave. To this 100 a further 500 were added and, each with five men aboard, they raced, swerved and honked their way to the front, making the journey twice. The romantic view of war, survives on the idea that the tide of battle can be turned by the single, timely and dramatic gesture. Reality is rarely so obliging and the taxis of the Marne are no exception. Though there was no lack of success, courage or élan on the part of either of the attacking armies, what brought the final change of fortune was an act of the German High Command.

With confused reports reaching him, the already unnerved Moltke decided to send a personal representative to take stock. The chosen man was Lieutenant Colonel Hentsch, who when he departed on the 8th had already been given full power to coordinate a retreat if necessary.

Hentsch went first to the Fifth, Fourth and Third Armies, all of whom were holding their own, if without confidence about the final outcome. When he arrived at Bülow's headquarters he found only a deadening gloom. That day the Second Army commander had received reports from air-reconnaissance of columns, that both the British and the French were marching in his direction. What it meant was that the gap between his own and Kluck's forces had at last been discovered and was being penetrated in such strength as threatened to cut them off from one another. In response to this he had ordered retreat.

At the First Army headquarters, Hentsch found similar depression. Its commanders wanted to break off the battle and orders for a retreat had gone out. These, Moltke's representative confirmed, but adding that the direction taken should be northeastward so as to bring the First and Second Armies together. By the 11th, the order to retire had been extended along the entire German line. By the 12th, the Battle of the Marne was over. The German armies were behind the Aisne.

If the British and French could look on themselves as victors, they were only partially so – a fact to be agonizingly reaffirmed by the events of the next four years. The Marne was a victory of lost opportunities such as even the vicissitudes of warfare can rarely exhibit. Some of these have already been discussed, but there was a still more important one. The French line formed roughly the three sides of a box enclosing the Germans. Had sufficient strength been applied at the top edges of the two open sides, at Senlis on the left and Verdun on the right, the Germans could well have faced the direst disaster. Pressure came only from one side and Sarrail, commanding the Third Army, on the right, asked in vain for reinforcement.

He was certainly entitled to it. By his stubborn defense of Verdun, which he had been expected to give up, he had helped to frustrate Moltke's revised battle plan, as well as preventing the movement of forces westward and against Maunoury.

Almost without exception every crucial battle has generated its long and often acrimonious debate. On the one side the defeated commanders declare that had their advice been heeded at this or that point the result would have been different. On the other, those of the victors, each vying to prove himself the instigator of the successful train

of events. It would be amazing if the Marne, whose results were so far-reaching, should have been an exception. Indeed, the battle remains something of an enigma because the arguments of the claimants are so difficult to substantiate or refute and they themselves so numerous.

They include Foch, whose true role we have seen, but the principal of them must, of course, be Joffre and Galliéni, both of whom have their jealous partisans, as if one or other was totally and alone responsible for the victory from inception to enemy retreat. In fact Joffre, in view of his later profession of prescience, showed a surprising reluctance to make the first moves. Certainly he intended to go over to the offensive and was laying plans and making preparations to that end. However he had in mind both a different place and a different time. If, in the realization of his intentions, the French capital should, by chance, fall he was prepared to accept this with equanimity.

It was Galliéni who first saw the necessity of holding the capital and it was his *coup d'oeil* which took in the opportunity Kluck was so imprudent as to offer when he turned his flank and tried to slip past the defenders. Joffre was slower to react, but he had, it should be remembered, been through great disasters and knew a further one could spell the destruction of his country. To his credit it must be recorded that once convinced, he wholeheartedly supported Galliéni and gave the orders for a general offensive. It is possible that had Galliéni been Commander in Chief, as he might so easily have been, the result of the battle would have been more decisive. When the laurels for the Marne victory are handed out, there should, therefore, be not one, but two wreaths.

PETAIN
AT VERDUN 1916

At Christmas 1915, the German Commander in Chief, Erich von Falkenhayn, wrote his customary annual report to his Supreme War Lord, Kaiser Wilhelm II. The year had not been without achievement. In the west, every attack by the Anglo-French coalition had been held; in the east, there had been the stunning, apparently unending chain of victories which culminated in defeats for the Czar's army along their entire line and would shortly bring the country to the peace table. For the foreseeable future, it could be said that the Russian threat to the German homeland had been removed. If a similar result could be obtained in the west, the war would be finished with Germany the victor. The trouble was that this desirable state of affairs had eluded German arms as consistently as it had those of her enemies. The problem was simple: the amalgam of trenchline, barbed wire and well-placed machine gunners so greatly favored defense as to nullify every assault. Even the old maxim that victory went to the biggest battalions applied no longer. The greater the numbers of the attackers, the greater their slaughter.

What was the answer? Various ideas had been devised by both sides, including the ill-fated Anglo-French Gallipoli attacks intended to outflank the enemy far to his right. Falkenhayn in his report to his Kaiser offered yet another and in its originality it deserves to be seen as one of the most brilliant plans of the entire war. So far, all endeavors had been directed toward the seizure of militarily important objectives. Not only had these been strongly defended, but given the nature of trench warfare even if a withdrawal were forced, it had always proved possible to dig more trenches further back and all that could be gained before the impetus of the attack was lost would be a narrow band of territory.

Falkenhayn proposed that, instead of going for the comparatively flexible trenchline, they go for a fixed objective whose loss the enemy dare not contemplate. In other words, it would not necessarily be a truly strategic objective at all, rather one whose capture would be politically disastrous. What especially distinguishes this notion was Falkenhayn's apparent understanding, an understanding unique among generals of both sides, of the totally changed nature of modern war. The morale of the army was also the morale of the people, and the politicians, as the people's representatives, were vital. If their confidence was shaken, this might spread to the whole of the fighting forces.

However, this quality of originality is one which has largely been attributed to Falkenhayn by the hindsight of later writers, and the real enigma is whether he had really thought this far ahead or whether he simply wanted to obliterate what was in fact a menacing salient. If, in so doing, this also produced depression and perhaps a collapse of morale that would be a bonus, but not one Falkenhayn was so sanguine as to expect.

The salient in question, at Verdun, bulged out between Avocourt in the north and St Mihiel in the south with the town itself at its very heart, a fortress city blocking the Valley of the Meuse, whose origins went back to Gaulish times. However, since 1870, it had become the center of a double ring of some 21 forts which had been dug out of the chalk and reinforced with concrete. Of these, 10 stood

A German 21cm Mörser ready to shell French fortifications at Verdun.

on the west bank of the river and the rest on the east. The latter included those which the world was to know so well: Fort Douaumont, Fort Vaux, Fort Souville, Fort Tavannes. This ring of defenses stood on the north side of the salient while most of its south side was made up by the Plain of Woevre, itself backed by the Meuse Heights.

The reason why this salient poking into the enemy belly had survived was precisely because of the fortresses. Yet the French General Staff had so far failed to appreciate this that they had actually drained them of much of their garrisons and were in the process of taking away their guns as late as January 1916.

The policy rested on the thesis that fortresses, however strong by earlier standards, could not withstand modern artillery. The proof was said to be the experiences of Belgium in August 1914 and of Russia in the spring of 1915. This overlooked the fact that the Belgian forts had actually provided a very important first line of defense seriously dislocating the German timetable and thus facilitating defensive deployment. The Russian forts, on the other hand, were out of date and derelict from lack of funds devoted to their maintenance. The coming battle was to show that the Verdun forts were the most impressive.

Unfortunately for the military-intellectuals, the French people and politicians had not caught up with the latest vagaries of their thought. To them, therefore, the fortresses of Verdun remained as the epitome of their nation's will to resist. Joffre, having not deigned to explain what he was doing and why, found as soon as danger loomed he had to reverse his policy or risk censure and possible dismissal. In the process, countless young men died in 'the Hell of Verdun.'

Whether or not Falkenhayn's plans had the radical intention later attributed to them, they were accepted by his Supreme War Lord with as much enthusiasm as he propounded them. The assault would be entrusted to the Fifth

Left: A German 38-cm gun in April 1916. Heavy artillery was used either in long bombardments to prepare terrain for the infantry or at the last moment to break gaps in the wire.

Right: The effects of the long bombardment scarred the landscape around Verdun.

Below: German troops rush through a gap in the wire.

Army under the German Crown Prince, Wilhelm, known derisively to the British public as 'Little Willy.' Its aim would be to force the French into a bloody defense of the fortresses by attacking along the northern side of the salient.

There was early disagreement between the Commander in Chief and his immediate executive commander, the Crown Prince, who wanted a wide-fronted assault on both sides of Meuse where Falkenhayn himself wanted the initial assault to be limited to the east back only and got his way.

Successful as the attack in Russia in the previous spring had been, it was felt that a number of lessons had been learned from it. In that battle secrecy and, therefore, surprise, had been subordinated to the requirement of overwhelming force. One of the ways in which German intentions had been revealed had been by the digging of advanced trenches opposite the positions to be attacked as the means of reducing the distance which would have to be crossed. In the event, such was the effect of the enormous bombardment, the Russians were in no state to man their trench defenses anyway.

In France, Falkenhayn wanted, if possible, to retain the element of surprise and, with the Russian experience in his mind, decreed that no advance trenches should be dug. The shock troops would rely on the artillery barrage alone to give them cover as they raced across no man's land, in some places as much as half a mile wide.

Falkenhayn also set great store by attacking at the earliest possible moment. The closer to spring and the campaigning season they came, the better they could expect the French to be prepared. Indeed, they might preempt with an attack of their own. The date was set for 13 February, the attackers hoping for the best as far as weather was concerned.

The Germans' desire for total surprise was not realized. French intelligence got wind of the planned attack in late January and passed their information on to GQG (*Grand Quartier Général* or General Headquarters) where it was ignored. Joffre had decided that the next enemy offensive was going to be in Champagne and no intelligence would change his mind.

Thus, the French defensive system at Verdun comprised a group of forts bereft of guns and troops and a single trenchline, backed up by a subsidiary trench which was only partly usable. There was a considerable shortage of men and materiel; wire was incomplete in many places; and very little shell-proof cover had been prepared. As the signs of enemy activity grew more obvious, while still insisting it was part of a bluff, Joffre sent some reinforcements in the form of two *Territorial* (reserve) divisions. Mercifully, the Germans did not get the weather they had hoped for and were forced to postpone until 21 February.

Nonetheless, even with this respite and the addition of two corps, sent at the last moment, there were only three divisions on the right or east bank of the Meuse, with two on the left and a further three to the south of the fortress-area facing east. There were no reserves at hand.

On the 21st, the attack came, heralded by the explosion of a 14-inch shell on the Archbishop's Palace. The barrage, along a 15-mile front lasted the entire day reaching its height at 1600 hours. Three-quarters of an hour later, on a 'dry, cold day,' the shock-troop squads of bombing parties made their dash across no man's land, probing for the weakest points in the enemy defenses. They struck along a four-and-a-half mile front between Bois de Haumont and Herbefois on the east bank of the Meuse.

In fact, as Basil Liddell Hart says, this narrow frontage favored the defenders who, unlike the Czar's peasant soldiers of 1915, did not wilt and turn tail under the bombardment. The initial assault was actually something of a disappointment with two of the attacking divisions back at their start line by nightfall. However, a footing was gained in most French trenches and one regiment of 2000 men suffered losses of no fewer than 1800.

That sector of the line of which Verdun formed part came for administrative purpose under Groupe d'Armées du Centre or Central Army Group (GAC for short), under the command of Langle de Cary. On the night of 21st he was an extremely anxious man. If the German succeeded in breaking through here, in the very center of the French line and successfully turned a flank a great disaster threatened. They did not, of course, appreciate at this point that

Falkenhayn's real intention was to compel them to fight for the forts, rather than to force a breakthrough.

Joffre, at Army headquarters, however, seemed unperturbed. The attack at Verdun was a feint. The real attack was coming in Champagne. In 1914 with German phalanxes apparently invincible in their march on Paris, he horrified the politicians by his declaration that to him, as a strategist, 'Paris was a town like any other.' He did not propose to hazard his forces in its defense. He had similar thoughts about Verdun which was only a minor provincial town and not the national capital. As in 1914, he was once more to find himself outmaneuvered by the politicians whom he loathed and against whose power he had done his best to insure himself. The fall of the Verdun fortresses would inflict an intolerable blow on French morale. Unwillingly, he was forced to recognize that he must fight for the area he had himself done so much to demilitarize or else there would be no war left to fight. This volte face was only to come about after further disasters.

On the 22nd, the Germans widened the front of their attack. Although the dual pressures of artillery and continual infantry assault produced an advance of only about three and half miles, the French trenchlines were crumbling away and many of their second positions falling. Even more worrying, a battalion of North African Tirailleurs holding a crucial sector of the line broke and fled, leaving a gap filled only with difficulty. Langle de Cary then decided much to Joffre's annoyance to evacuate the Plain of Woevre on the south side of the salient though it had not yet been attacked. They now had their back against the Meuse Heights, but Langle de Cary was so pessimistic he doubted whether the east bank of the river could be held at all. While this was happening, the Grand Quartier continued in its conviction that the attacks were a diversion and insisted on holding back the greater part of their reserves. GAC was assisted only in the most niggardly way.

In December 1915 Joffre had been given as Chief of Staff, General de Castelnau, who by chance was a former commander of GAC. He had watched events with singular disquiet throughout, but never more so than on the night of 24 February as the evidence of Langle de Cary's depressed state of mind began to emerge. He took the unprecedented step of actually awakening the Commander in Chief from his slumbers to suggest a visit from the Grand Quartier must be made at once. Having got permission, Castelnau drove through the night to see the GAC commander, arriving to find he had been preceded by a telegram from Joffre ordering that the front north of Verdun be held at all costs. Any order to retreat would result in a court martial for the officer responsible.

Fresh catastrophes were on their way at the very moment that Castelnau was at the front. For it was on that day that Fort Douaumont fell and that by a humiliating incident. The drawbridge had been left down and a patrolling German unit simply walked in. Its garrison, consisting of 23 gunners who manned its single usable turret were taken prisoner as they slept, having let it be said, collapsed from exhaustion. This was the kind of event whose effect on public morale the government most feared.

What emerged from Castelnau's visit was the certainty that Verdun could only be saved if GAC's forces were augmented by reinforcements capable of holding the entire left bank against German attacks. If Falkenhayn's intention was indeed that of bleeding the French, they were now playing into his hands. GQG decided the scale of reinforcement called for nothing less than an army and decided on the Second under the command of Henri-Philippe Pétain, then 60 and a general. He had begun the war as a colonel and even this promotion had come late. Born at Cauchy-la-Tour in the Pas de Calais, he had been successively a lieutenant in the *Chasseurs Alpins* and a captain attached to the general staff of the XVI Corps at Marseilles. In 1902 he served as an instructor at the École Normale du Tir, at Chalons and by 1906 was an assistant instructor at the War School. In 1912 he got his colonelcy and shortly after the beginning of the war was given the temporary rank of brigadier general. He had fought in Belgium and on the Marne.

During his army career he had shown certain gifts, though none outstanding. Indeed he was hardly the sort of officer likely to rise to prominence had it not been for the exigencies of war. By nature he was cautious and dour, characteristics which reflected themselves in a tendency to rely on strategic withdrawal rather than offensive action in the face of a superior enemy.

Why then was he chosen for a task which seemed to call for precisely opposite qualities? The explanations are innumerable, but one is forced to agree with Richard Griffiths that it was probably simply because his Second Army had been taken into the army reserve. Whatever the reason, he was chosen and was summoned from the bed of a Paris brothel to receive his new orders.

After a meeting with Joffre, he drove to the little French town of Souilly which he made his headquarters. At midnight he was in full command. Not long afterward he found himself back in bed, not this time with a mistress, but with double pneumonia. This did not stop him from setting to work with a vigor which would have been astonishing in a healthy 40-year-old. Although an attempt to retake Douaumont, ordered by Castelnau failed, he began establishing that form of defense he has often been credited with inventing: 'the elastic defense.' (In fact, it was the Germans who first used it in September 1915). In essence it consisted in a three-layer line. An 'Advanced Zone' was intended to cushion the first shock. Behind this was a 'Battle Zone' in which the real struggle took place, and behind that a

Above: Officers enjoy themselves at the Cafe de la Paix in 1916. There was some bad feeling that the people back home were enjoying themselves while the soldiers were dying.

'Reserve Zone' into which the defenders could withdraw if necessary. As the advancing Germans began to encounter this system the going became harder and harder. By 28 February their attacks had been halted and, according to their own sources, a deep depression was setting in.

What was more French reinforcement was beginning to arrive. This, however, posed its own problems. All but a single light railroad being in German hands, there remained only the narrow Bar-le-Duc to Verdun road. A brilliant and determined engineer, Major Richard, was given the task of making this single artery sufficient for all needs. He divided the road into six sections each with its own improvised workshop for the repair of vehicles. So that there was no obstacle to movement, any vehicles that broke down were simply manhandled off the road. The stream was unending: one driver in the early days sat at his wheel for 50 hours at a stretch. The statistics of the achievement are incredible. Every day 1700 trucks travelled down the road in each direction, an average of one every 25 seconds. Between 27 February and 6 March, 190,000 men, 23,000 tons of munitions and 2500 tons of military materiel were brought up. Even when a sudden thaw on 28 February caused the trucks to sink to their axle-trees in mud, it was somehow kept open, Richard drafting in men to throw gravel under their wheels. It was little wonder that the 40-mile stretch became known as

La Voie Sacrée, the Sacred Way.

With the road working efficiently, it proved possible to rearm the forts, while artillery, directed by Pétain personally, mounted 'offensives' meant to compensate for deficiencies in infantry. Pétain also saw that, despite difficulties of transportation, the only way men could tolerate the strain of the battle was by speedy replacement. This meant that the Second Army would have to go beyond its own resources of men and therefore brought him into collision with Joffre who could see his entire forces going through the Verdun 'mincer.' All the same, Pétain got his way and in this, many observers, believe lies the ultimate success of the French. The Germans entrusted the entire battle to the Crown Prince's army, replacing casualties as they occurred. It was their morale which dropped first. If the troops were quickly relieved, commanders got more cavalier treatment. At the first signs that the strain was telling they were summarily dismissed.

Pétain's gifts for the defensive were being exercised to the full and, strange as it may seem in the light of the accepted image of Verdun, he was actually extremely sparing of human life. Unfortunately, this was negated by the demands from above for offensive action, such as the attempt to retake Douaumont, which brought heavy French losses, usually without result.

While the French were doing exactly what Falkenhayn was supposed to want them to do, that is pouring men on to the battlefield and throwing away lives in futile attempts to recapture objectives of purely prestige value, the German Commander in Chief found his own ideas so revolutionary that he could not cope with the implications and he began to think in terms of territorial gains. On 4 March the Crown Prince called on his army to try to reach Verdun 'the heart of France.' This time the assault was to be made on both

Below: François Flameng's view of Les Eparges and Woevre, east of Verdun, drawn before 1916. During the fighting at Verdun the German line ran between those points.

Left: The destruction at Fort Souville following intensive shelling, 26 July 1916.

Right: The damage inside Fort Douaumont.

Below: The battlefield outside Fort Douaumont. The fort fell to the Germans on 25 February but it was recaptured by the French on 24 September 1916.

sides of the river.

The reason for this was that Pétain's artillery 'offensives' had proved so destructive that the Germans realized they could not advance on the east bank as long as they were threatened by the guns of the west, in particular those of Côte de Poivre and the Mort-Homme ridge.

The bombardment began that very day and continued for two more. On the 6th the infantry began scaling the hillsides. They came up against stubborn resistance from the French employing their 'elastic defense' system. Furthermore, the defending artillery used with matchless skill, succeeded in destroying all the German 17-inch howitzers and blew up an entire gunpark with 450,000 rounds of heavy shell, an achievement which affected the attackers for the whole of the rest of the battle.

By the 8th the two hills were still in French hands. By the 9th the Germans had so far admitted failure as to convert the struggle into one of attrition. This second date has frequently been regarded as that which marked the end of the Germans' hopes, though fighting was to continue until the end of the year.

By the end of March Falkenhayn was plainly losing faith in the result himself and looking for another place to attack. On the other hand the Crown Prince still believed in ultimate victory and continued the effusion of his men's blood.

As the physical battle was turning against the attackers, so was another. No less than their barbarities of 1914, the Battle of Verdun and the dogged French resistance swung world public opinion against the Germans. The French did their utmost to exploit this. Army cameramen braved the thick of the fight to secure dramatic newsreel shots which were shown all over the world. The Russian Czar, who was given a Royal Command Performance, was so moved that he ordered his spent and ill-equipped forces to mount a vast

offensive round the area of Lake Narocz in Lithuania. The result was a complete bloody disaster, the Russians losing between 110,000 and 120,000 men. It probably made a greater contribution to the army's disillusionment and so to the revolution than any other single one of the Russian's ill-managed offensives.

There was one other unlooked-for result. This was in the German High Command itself and its origins were also on the Eastern Front. The joint commanders there, Hindenburg and Ludendorff, noting the failure to gain a decision at Verdun, were soon whispering in the ear of their Supreme War Lord whenever he chanced to visit their headquarters. Time, surely for a change at the top and who better to succeed as Commander in Chief than the two men whose every effort had been crowned with triumph, as witnessed by the latest Russian disaster round Lake Narocz.

Early April found the Germans once more on the attack. The chosen sector this time was south of Douaumont in the Bois de la Caillette. For two days, 10–11 April, the shock waves kept coming at the defenders. They produced little in the way of results and the losses were horrific. On the second day a counterattack was ordered, though there were a mere 100 men available for it. The small company retook all that had been gained so painfully. The German commander was relieved, but this could do nothing to cure the underlying malaise: it was not any longer the French who were displaying the symptoms of demoralization.

At the end of April, Pétain's area of command was extended as he took over the leadership of GAC with one of his most aggressive lieutenants, General Robert Nivelle, taking command of the Second Army. The change only reflected the growing renown of Pétain and the feelings of confidence he had inspired in all circles, not least those of government. This was scarcely to the taste of Joffre and

GQG. Not only was Pétain outshining them, he also made no secret of his distrust and dissatisfaction with their conduct of the struggle as a whole and was now in a position to find influential listeners for his complaints.

In these circumstances Joffre's order that Douaumont be retaken seems very like an attempt to regain the limelight. Pétain was strongly opposed, but Nivelle and his own subordinate commander, Charles Mangin, were enthusiastically in favour and the assault was launched on 22 May. It was a failure for which, despite his opposition, Pétain took full responsibility. The effects of this ill-timed offensive actually went further than the immediate disaster. Within days the Germans were themselves attacking once more and succeeded in capturing the objective which had previously eluded them: the Mort-Homme ridge.

Above: the mud and chaos around Fort Douaumont.

Top left: An aerial view of Fort Douaumont before it was pounded to rubble by German shelling.

Top right: General Nivelle was Pétain's subordinate and after Pétain's promotion to command the Group of Armies of the Center, was in command at Verdun.

Left: Inside Fort Douaumont following its capture.

Right: French poilus struggle across the battered landscape which has become featureless from the intensive bombardments.

In the first week of June, the Germans were pressing southeast of Douaumont toward Fort Vaux. A garbled telephone message (the German military telephone system was notorious) had led to a report appearing in the German press that the fort had fallen no less than three months' earlier and, indeed, two of the officers who were supposed to have taken it had actually been awarded the *Pour le Mérite*, the highest military decoration, for their feat. Now it was really in the front line and the struggle which centered upon it was to take its place in French military annals beside the Foreign Legion defensive battle at Camerone in Mexico.

Permanent garrisons had been installed in all the forts and Vaux was held by 300 men under Commandant Raynal. Resistance continued after the Germans had succeeded in surrounding it and even after an attempt at its relief by Nivelle had failed. Adding to the trials of the defenders was the fact that they could not reach the latrines. The attackers declared that they were as much repelled by the stench emanating from the fort as by the hail of fire which greeted them. In the end surrender was forced by the exhaustion of water supplies. On 7 June a small handful of men, unshaven, filthy and ragged emerged from their stinking holes to be greeted by Germans with arms at the present. Raynal himself was received and congratulated by the Crown Prince.

This was a low ebb in French fortunes comparable only with the early days of the offensive and there is no doubt

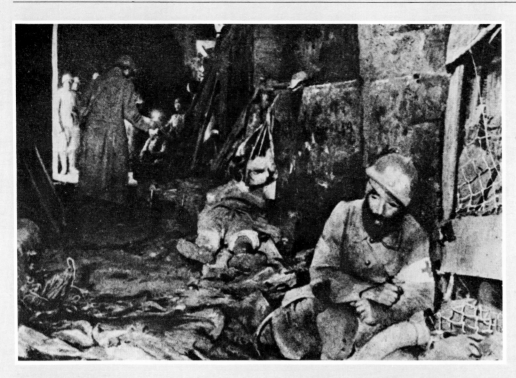

Left: The central corridor at Fort Vaux, which fell to the Germans on 7 June.

Right: French prisoners are questioned after being taken at Verdun.

Below: German troops inch their way forward.

that at this time Pétain was sinking into gloom and was ready to criticize GQG for lack of support. Actually his strictures were without foundation. In January a meeting of the Chief of Staff of all the Allies, including Russia, had taken place at Chantilly, and plans were laid for coordinated offensives on both Eastern and Western Fronts.

The western effort was to be a combined Anglo-French one on either side of the Somme and originally the French were to have had the greater share in it, their 40 divisions, to the British 25 striking along a front of 25 miles. Such was the drain on the army created by Verdun that Joffre

was forced to serve notice that only 16 of his divisions would be fit to participate and that their frontage must be reduced to eight miles. Thus, it could not be said he was failing to respond to Pétain's appeal for reinforcements.

However, in June came fresh German blows with Forts Souville and Tavannes which formed part of the inner ring of defenses, as objective. During the preparatory bombardment a new form of shell, filled with phosgene gas, was used. It paralyzed the French artillery and in the subsequent assault Belleville Height and the village of Fleury were both taken while the advance was approaching the two forts.

Pétain was forced to beg Joffre to speed up the Somme offensive. The decision no longer rested with the French Commander in Chief, however, since the British were now playing the predominant role. There had already been repeated calls for relief action and Haig had to some extent responded by taking over a greater length of line to allow more troops to be sent to Verdun. On the other hand, he was understandably reluctant to fritter away the forces he was amassing for major action in minor, improvised attacks of doubtful value.

As the fall of Souville and Tavannes would threaten the

entire defensive structure it was necessary to contemplate a large-scale withdrawal including the sacrifice of the town of Verdun itself. Plans were drawn up in the deepest secrecy and even when Joffre somehow found four more divisions to send to the front it seemed unlikely that this would change the course of events.

However, on 26 June, Pétain received a piece of news which welcome as it would have been only a short time before, at this moment presented him with new difficulties. The preparatory artillery bombardment for the Somme offensive had begun Joffre told him, but as a result it was imperative that the east bank of the Meuse was held at all costs. He undertook to take full responsibility himself for what might follow in pursuing this course.

He was not asked to bear it. On the 24th, Falkenhayn's nerves finally gave out and he stopped the flow of ammunition to the Verdun front. On 1 July, the Somme offensive opened and if this disappointed in its result at least it had the effect of giving the men of the French Second Army much needed relief.

There was one final, desperate assault on Souville in early July, but at GAC Pétain had sensed that the crisis was over. The problem he now faced was that of keeping his aggressive-minded lieutenants in check and as early as 11 July, they had launched an attack which produced no tangible results despite considerable losses. No more offensives were to be attempted until adequate strength had been recruited, though planning to this end was begun. Preparations were meticulous. Pétain put himself in charge of overall planning, with Nivelle in charge of detail. To reduce casualties as far as possible, artillery was to be extensively employed and Mangin, an artilleryman in origin, was made responsible for arrangements.

It was late September before the Commander in Chief of the GAC decided that the time to strike was arriving. It was late October before it came. On the 24th, a bombardment of withering ferocity fell upon the German trenches and it culminated in the use of the new 'creeping barrage' by which the guns registered so that their shells exploded just

ahead of the advancing infantry forcing the defenders to stay in their dugouts.

The whole operation was handled with the greatest efficiency and though only three and a half divisions were used in the attack, their success was brilliant. Within a short time the forts of Douaumont and Vaux were back in French hands. Mangin's troops who conducted the attack took 6700 prisoners and German losses in killed and wounded were proportionately high.

On 15 December there was yet another French thrust, which, like the last was limited in its objectives. Of the five German divisions in line, four were from the Somme front, and it is indicative of their shortage of reserves that it was necessary to 'rest' troops by sending them to a sector hardly less active than the one they had left. The results were even more spectacular than those of October. Over 11,000 prisoners and 115 guns fell into French hands and one of the features of this phase of the struggle was the success of the air force. French flyers had been playing an increasingly significant part and now had total air supremacy.

It could be said that this was the end of the battle. The cost to both sides had certainly been enormous. The entire strength of the Second Army was 24 divisions, yet no fewer than 65 divisions of the French Army had travelled the Voie Sacrée between March and June. This large number was, of course, a result of Pétain's policy of speedy rotation and in fact the Germans had used only 47 divisions up to August, so their troops spent more time at the front.

French losses amounted to 315,000; German to 281,000. It is instructive that whereas, in the early part of the battle the ratio of French to German casualties was of the order of 8:7, in the final offensives of October and December, it had completely reversed itself to 7:8.

Before one considers the victor of Verdun one must first ask oneself whether it was a victory. This has always been a controversial question, even in France where there is the most enormous, justifiable pride in Verdun. It is a little difficult to understand why. If an attacking force achieves its objectives, that, certainly, is victory. If a defending force

Left: French prisoners from Verdun.

Right: A dead soldier. By May the number of French casualties had risen to 185,000. The final cost of holding Verdun for the French was 275,000 men.

frustrates them and finally compels them to abandon their endeavors, that is one of another kind – a defensive one. When, in addition, the defenders, taking the offensive themselves, recapture all that has been snatched from them who can deny that they have shown their supremacy? Although the words of King Pyrrhus may apply, 'One more such victory and we are undone,' the Germans having failed in their aims, the Second Army achieved a victory.

It was also a victory of another kind. It galvanized the French spirit. Far from being broken by the disasters of the weeks of late February and early March, they were if anything exulted by them. They did not end the conflict with a sense of imminent defeat, but of ultimate decisive triumph. It was the German spirit which began to flag, both here and at the Somme.

If this counts as victory then its laurels certainly belong to Henri Philippe Pétain, a man who perhaps more than any other First World War general, understood the importance of morale. In the last stage of the First World War Pétain began writing his own account of Verdun. In it he describes how he used to watch the young French soldiers marching to the battlefield, confidence displayed in their very tread. Then he describes their condition when they returned, often only in a matter of days: 'Their gazes, impenetrable, seemed fixed on a vision of terror; their walk and their attitudes betrayed the most complete exhaustion; they were weighed down with terrifying memories; they scarcely replied when I cross-examined them, and in their troubled minds the joking voices of old soldiers awoke no echoes.'

Of course in the Battle of Verdun as in every other battle there was, on the victor's side, an element of luck without which the decision would have gone the other way. At least twice, fate smiled on the defenders. The first time was when the Germans were compelled to delay the start of their offensive because of bad weather. The eight-day reprieve enabled the French to reinforce in some degree. The second was when Falkenhayn chose to attack on the east bank only, allowing the guns of the west bank to interdict the assault.

This does not diminish Pétain's achievement. Given command of this crucial, embattled front when everything seemed about to be lost he did all that could possibly have been asked of him. Nor did he complain at the hopelessness of the task as others had done and were to do later. He went to the front, established his command post at the Mairie of Souilly and coolly and methodically set in being his 'elastic defense' against which the enemy threw himself in vain. He instituted his artillery offensives. He improved communications. He introduced the rotation of troops. He rearmed the forts. Most of all he obeyed to the letter Joffre's injunction that there was to be no retreat.

Throughout the struggle, the French, supposedly at their poorest in defense, held back attacks from vastly superior forces. This alone was a fantastic achievement and a tribute to Pétain's ability to inspire confidence in his troops. As a consequence, two weeks after the first assaults had been launched, he was already causing the enemy deep heart-searching and making him recast his aims.

Finally when the moment was right, he swung from defensive to offensive. Even then he curbed his impetuous and overambitious subordinates, Nivelle and Mangin, who wished to make every engagement into a march to Berlin, and persuaded them to limit themselves to lesser, more attainable objectives, a form of tactics which was to be generally adopted by everyone, including the British once it had sunk in that the Somme and Passchendaele were catastrophes.

The scale was, of course, infinitely smaller, but one is to some extent reminded of Wellington and the Peninsular War. Where Pétain differs from Wellington, however, is that the success of Verdun did not prove to be repeatable in bigger terms. When he became Commander in Chief of the French armies in succession to Joffre, then Nivelle – and perhaps this was another result of Verdun – his natural caution and defensiveness took over and not until bestirred by Foch as Allied Generalissimo in 1918, did he bring himself to think offensively.

HAIG AND THE BLACK DAY 1918

Writing his memoirs during the autumn and winter of 1918–19, Erich Ludendorff, a man not given to linguistic flights, coined a phrase. '8 August (1918) was,' he wrote, 'the black day of the German Army in the history of the war.' It is a phrase which historians have employed to exhaustion ever since.

Just exactly what he meant by it is made clear in the chapter which he began with those words. It was the day when the British, Australian, Canadian, American and French forces were released in a massive offensive between Moreuil and Albert, the latter perhaps the most battle-scarred and fought-over town on the entire Western Front. The defenders behaved in ways which, the author describes, he would 'not have thought possible in the German Army.' That is to say, they behaved as troops everywhere behave when they know they are totally, irrevocably overpowered.

In fact, their behavior was astonishingly restrained compared with what had happened in other armies on similar occasions. If their collapse was less complete than might have been expected, it was enough finally to snap their commanders' nerves. Only six days later, on 14 August, the German emperor, Wilhelm II, ordered that peace feelers should be extended. Some 12 weeks after that he was a crownless exile, cooling his heels at a Dutch frontier post, begging his neighbor monarch to grant him sanctuary.

Yet through almost the whole of that year the stars of both the German army and of its commander had seemed to be in the ascendant. Ludendorff was 53 and effectively master not only of the military machine, but also of the government.

Everywhere, except in the West, German arms had been crowned with triumph. Rumania, which had imprudently joined the war on the side of the anti-German coalition, the Entente, the previous year, had been forced to make peace. Negotiations to the same end were currently going on with Russia's post-revolutionary Bolshevik government. The campaign of unrestricted submarine warfare was producing such drastic losses to her shipping that it seemed as if Britain would soon be subjected to a blockade as harsh as that Germany had experienced through the whole war, though it was true one of its results had been to bring America into the war.

The victories in the east, besides giving Germany access to the grain wealth of the Ukraine, also freed the forces engaged there and the not inconsiderable numbers in prisoner-of-war camps, a total, all in all, of perhaps a million men.

By contrast, the position of the Entente had never looked poorer. Besides the Russian defection, there had been mutinies in the previous spring which had infected half the French Army. These had been quelled but its reliability in an emergency was uncertain.

In Britain the carnage of Third Ypres had led to such doubts about the generals' ability to conduct the war that the politicians had intervened. David Lloyd George, the Prime Minister, had insisted that reserves must remain in Britain so that the Commander in Chief was not tempted to throw men into yet another 'Big Push' without prior consultation. This, added to enormous casualties, meant the British Expeditionary Force was so short of men that

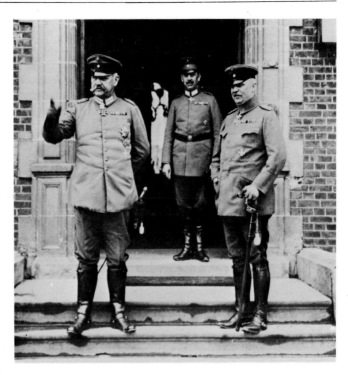

Field Marshal von Hindenburg and General Ludendorff in May 1918.

divisions had been reduced from 12 to nine battalions. There were only 26 of these reduced divisions holding a line roughly from Ypres to Soissons. Furthermore, their defensive deployment was in the process of being changed. They were now to be organized 'in depth' on the German pattern, with an advanced line to break the impetus of an attack. There would be a 'Battle Zone' in which the main struggle would take place and a fall-back or 'Reserve Zone.' Unfortunately, these changes were far from complete and in many places the Reserve Zones existed only on maps or as turfs removed from the ground to show where they were to be.

The sole light amid the gloom was America's involvement, but the British and French were making exactly the same complaint the French made about the British in 1914 and 1915, they were being desperately tardy about arriving. Thus, Ludendorff could report to his emperor with some confidence on 13 February 1918, 'the Army in the West is waiting for the opportunity to act.'

Germany needed to act quickly. The trickle of American troops would, if later rather than sooner, become a flood. The augmentation of the Royal Navy by that of the United States was likely to reduce, or even nullify, the effect of the U-Boats. France, notwithstanding her losses at Verdun in 1916, was recovering and making heavy drafts upon her colonial empire. Britain seemed to possess a bottomless pit of reserves from her dominions.

Germany, on the other hand, was fast reaching the end of her manpower resources. If she did not use her temporary advantage to inflict a decisive reverse, she must sue for peace. At best, she could only hope for an indefinite prolongation of the war of attrition, a possibility the German people, including the armed forces, seemed unwilling to resign themselves to.

Ludendorff had divined, rightly, that at present the British were the major adversary. Once their forces had been crippled, France would be a smaller challenge and might well be inclined to make an end. Deep in the British rear lay the three main Channel ports, Dunkirk, Calais and Boulogne, with the shortest sea routes from Britain. Not only were they vital to the movement of men and supplies, their loss would also mean that the BEF would be in the trap most dreaded by British military planners. At the same time, the Americans would only be able to reach France by the much

longer routes further down the channel. Ludendorff had deluded himself that the Americans were unwilling allies (though this was far from true, once committed they were determined to see the war out) and that faced by such difficulties they might decide the fight was not worth the candle.

He knew that what he had in mind was incredibly ambitious, requiring the kind of continuous advance against the

Left: Field Marshal Sir Douglas Haig with General Rawlinson, General Byng, General Lawrence and General Birwood at Cambrai on 31 October 1918.

Below: German artillery moves forward during the Battle of Kemmel in April 1918. The final German offensive was launched on 21 March 1918 and was supposed to win the war before American troops arrived on the front in force.

enemy no offensive on either side through the whole course of the war had so far been able to produce. He did not underestimate this in his report to the emperor. 'It will be an immense struggle,' he admitted, 'which will begin at one point, continue at another and take a long time.' On the other hand, though 'it was going to be difficult,' he promised that it would be victorious.

His British opposite number, Field Marshal Sir Douglas Haig, was four years his senior. A Scot, related to the famous whiskey firm of Haig, he was educated at a British public school and then at Brasenose College, Oxford. He was a cavalryman and had seen service in the Sudan, South Africa and India. In August 1914 he had been in command of the I Army Corps which fought at Mons, on the Meuse and at Ypres. By 1918 he had been Commander in Chief of the British forces on the Western Front for nearly three years, having succeeded Sir John French.

He has sometimes been described as an unimaginative soldier, this epithet being applied to him because of his inability to find an answer to the problem of assaulting an enemy whose forces lay behind broad belts of barbed wire which they could protect with machine guns. Since, however, no commander in any of the belligerent armies found a total answer to this problem it is perhaps a little less than fair. His greatest weakness, apart from vanity – a fault of which few commanders are free – was in a certain hidebound orthodoxy. Believing that, whatever temporary aberrations might appear, the cavalry would always come back to their own once the infantry had broken through, he was suspicious of innovation. Nonetheless once he had

been won over he was very willing, perhaps overwilling, to use any new weapons which were thrust in his hand. The early weeks of 1918 saw him waiting with his now attenuated forces for the enemy attack he knew must come and about which, despite German attempts at secrecy, increasing information was arriving at his headquarters.

By the third week of March Ludendorff's preparations were complete. Something like 750,000 men opposed a British force about 300,000 strong. In the early hours of the morning of 21 March 2500 guns opened up along a 44-mile front from Croisilles to La Fère using not only high explosive, but also gas shell.

Churchill, who chanced to be present, has described the tumult in his usual graphic prose, 'The enormous explosions of the shells upon our trenches seemed almost to touch each other, with hardly an interval in space or time. Among the bursting shells there rose at intervals, but almost continually, the much larger flames of exploding magazines. The weight and intensity of the bombardment surpassed anything which anyone had ever known. . . . Daylight supervened on the pandemonium and the flame picture pulsated with a pall of smoke from which great fountains of the exploding "dumps" rose mushroom-headed.'

Over that spring and summer such bombardments were to become almost commonplace. Indeed, they were surpassed. On 25 April the bombardment was so concentrated that, though it lasted only two and a half hours, the men were reduced to gibbering imbeciles. The artillery bombardment was, of course, only the precursor. It was followed by the attacking waves of infantry. The Germans had assembled their large forces into two army groups. That of the Crown Prince Rupprecht of Bavaria comprised the Fourth, Sixth, Seventeenth and Second Armies and held a sector from the Belgian coast to just north of St Quentin. The army group commanded by the German Crown Prince was made up of the Eighteenth, Seventh, First and Third Armies and its line stretched from St Quentin to just south of Reims.

Like every other commander on the Western Front, Ludendorff had learned, at great cost to his troops, one important lesson from the war. As Sir Basil Liddell Hart puts it, the depth of advance before the momentum of an offensive was lost equalled roughly half the frontage attacked. In other words, if the attack was made along a front of 16 miles, the attacking troops could expect to penetrate to a depth of eight miles. Not only was it rarely possible to exceed this, but the loss of life involved became more and more disproportionate to any gains made. Thus the battle on which Ludendorff had now launched his men was not to be a single offensive, but rather a whole series each abandoned when the consolidation of enemy resistance made the going too hard. Nevertheless each, in terms of men and materiel involved, was vast enough, even if compared with other big battles of the war.

First in one place, then in another, the armies struck. In the initial assault, on 21 March on the Somme, British casualties exceeded 100,000 and 500 guns were lost while the Third and Fifth Armies were pulled back by their commanders with as much speed as was possible. Never, in the whole war, was terrain ceded in such large areas as it was during this series of offensives.

Next the battle moved to Flanders with the crucial Channel ports as the objective. At one point the attackers were outside Hazebrouck, whose fall would endanger the entire British communications network.

Further south Arras, Péronne, St Quentin, Amiens and La Fère were all threatened or taken. Beyond them the Chemin des Dames, Soissons, Fismes and Reims were each on the front line and soon to be behind it.

The French, by this time themselves involved, began to fear for Paris. Pétain, their Commander in Chief, convinced that under pressure the British would make for the Channel ports and, in all probability, embark, disposed his forces as a semicircular shield around the capital. By doing so without consultation he made it very difficult for his allies to maintain continuity of line.

By April his fears seemed about to be realized. The Channel ports were no longer in jeopardy, but with the fall of Château-Thierry Paris was only 30 miles away.

Left: Artillery bogged down in mud during the German advance in March 1918.

Below: German storm troops march through what is left of the village of Messines during the Battle of Kemmel.

Far left: French soldiers find cover in a quarry at Ribécourt on the Oise in April 1918.

Already the city had been subjected to shelling from 'Big Bertha,' the enormous cannon which the Germans had emplaced at Laon, 75 miles away.

The sense of urgency and impending disaster which gripped the city was comparable only with those early weeks of the war until the First Battle of the Marne broke the Germans apparently inexorable advance. Everyone who could began leaving for less exposed regions of the country and the Prime Minister, Georges Clemenceau, must if anything have fuelled this panic by his statement to the Chamber of Deputies, 'I fight before Paris, I fight in Paris, I fight behind Paris.'

May, June and July all saw further German gains in one place or another along the line. Nor can it be said that there was a substantial abatement in July. As late as 2 August Ludendorff was still nursing further offensive plans. Yet Ludendorff completely lost his nerve shortly afterward.

To trace the origins of the 'Black Day' one must go back a month to 4 July. It was on that day that an Australian division recaptured Hamel and Vaire Woods, south of the Somme. This was accomplished by infantry and the new weapon – tanks. They worked in close cooperation and with the infantry and were present in large numbers, not

in the 'penny packets' so derided by Liddell-Hart. It was by no means the first time tanks had been so used during the series of actions which began on 21 March. Indeed, as early as 24 April there had actually been, as harbinger of what was to come 22 years later, a purely tank battle with 13 British engaging 13 German ones.

On 18 July the French general Charles Mangin had used the fast Renault tanks to considerable effect on the Marne. The Germans, including Ludendorff, admitted that they were totally taken by surprise and attributed their failure to withstand the attack very largely to this. Rawlinson, who had replaced Gough as commander of the British Fourth Army, was eager to see tanks used as a weapon in a major offensive to replace the artillery barrage which, by this nature, gave the enemy preliminary warning of what he could expect.

Another reason for the sudden reversal of German fortunes was Allied reorganization. On 26 March, largely as a result of appeals by Haig, who saw the need for total coordination, particularly now the large American armies were beginning to arrive, General Ferdinand Foch was made supreme commander of all the Allied forces. For the first time in the war there was unified direction. One imme-

Left: German heavy artillery in action during August 1918.

Right: Men of the 10th Australian Battalion occupy a trench near the Bois de Crepy on 10 August 1918.

Far left: Georges Clemenceau, the French Prime Minister in 1918.

Below: An Australian Field Artillery unit which took part in the Allied offensive on 8 August 1918, at Villers-Brettoneux.

diate result was that reinforcements, drawn from any national army, could be sent to the assistance of any other. This was quickly put to use in Flanders where French troops were sent to support the hard-pressed British units.

Foch was the apostle of '*l'attaque*,' the overzealous application of which in the early days of the war had proved so costly and disastrous. His belief in attack was undiminished, but he had learned much from experience and had acquired a marvellous intuition about battles and the moment to strike.

At a conference on 24 July attended by the British, French and American commanders, the question of a counterstroke was considered and Haig drew attention to Rawlinson's proposal. Foch saw its potential. If the stroke were to be delivered east of Amiens this might free the Paris-Amiens railroad, not actually in German hands but within such easy reach of their guns that it was unusable. This, in turn, would open up the entire lateral communica-

tions network. He therefore ordered the French First Army on the right of the British Fourth to participate and put it under Haig's orders, though he was to use only its two left-hand corps on the first day of the attack. To the south of Amiens, the German line bulged out in a salient which embraced the recently captured towns of Moreuil and Montdidier. Foch accordingly ordered the French Third Army to the south side of this salient to attack in concert with the First. This was not the end of his intervention. The offensive was scheduled to start on 10 August. He had it moved forward two days – one of the very few times such a thing had happened. More often offensives were postponed.

Since the essence of tank attack was surprise, this had to be safeguarded at all costs. Every conceivable subterfuge was adopted. No two conferences were held in the same place. Reconnaissance was carried out in the most elaborate secrecy. Divisional commanders were not even told of the attack until 31 July. The troops themselves were told only

36 hours before.

All troops and other movements were made at night. As guns were slipped into place they registered on target by joining in each day's regular bombardment of the enemy, while other guns, already in place, remained silent. It was hoped the enemy would not realize that the batteries were being increased. In this way 1000 extra guns were brought in. During the course of about a week, up to D-Day, the ranks of Fourth Army were virtually doubled. There were six fresh infantry divisions, as well as two of cavalry. The tank force numbered 600, of which about 420 were combat ones. The British air force had amassed about 374 planes and the French had an even bigger force, though it was not to be used until the 9th.

Such was the secrecy that not even the War Cabinet in London were told. The story is related of how William Morris Hughes, the Australian premier, who had come to London with the express purpose of demanding that his

Right: The American entry into World War I was decisive. The Germans were demoralized further at the prospect of facing fresh troops.

Below: On the trail of the Hun by W J Aylward.

Left: General Sir Herbert Plumer, the commander of the British Second Army.

Far left: General Hubert Gough was one of those blamed for the German breakthrough in 1918.

Below: An Australian 18-pounder is rushed into action near Merricourt on the Somme in August 1918.

own country's troops should be taken out of line, was in the full flow of rhetoric when the news came that they were at that moment advancing upon the enemy.

The Australian Corps, under General Sir John Monash, certainly one of the war's finest commanders, was on the left of the Canadian Corps who were to strike the main blow. It was also part of the secrecy that, since they were known as shock troops, they were kept out of the line until a few hours before zero hour.

The British contribution included the III Corps and the Cavalry Corps, plus a reserve division. The United States 33rd Division was in reserve to III Corps. The French First Army were providing three corps and were also to use tanks, but as these were all light it was decided that they should be employed for exploitation rather than for the initial shock. Altogether there were 21 divisions, British, French and American, with another four in reserve. They faced 14 German ones of the Eighteenth and Second Armies.

Surprise was total. The 8 August was a morning of dense fog, 'rendered,' as Ludendorff puts it, 'still thicker by artificial means,' and it was out of this that 456 tanks, rumbling forward along a 14-mile frontage, rolled down on the German trenches. The six divisions holding those trenches were barely more than skeletons thanks to casualties in the previous weeks of battle, and averaged about 3000 men each. An attack was so unexpected that none of the usual meticulous German defensive preparations had been made.

Coincident with the tank advance, the guns opened up and the infantry surged forward. South of the Somme were the Canadians, next the Australians and north of the river the III Corps. It was only here that there was any check, partly because the British troops had fewer tanks in order to maximize the strength of the main punch and partly because the trench works and rusting barbed wire of the old Somme battlefields checked the advance. Reserves which had been set in motion as soon as the attack began arrived shortly afterward.

No less effective than the tanks were the armored cars which chased up the roads, penetrating far behind the German lines. One of them even reached a staff headquarters where its members were taken by surprise over breakfast.

One may perhaps take up the account from the German point of view. Ludendorff tells us that six or seven divisions, thought to be battle worthy, were completely broken. Whole bodies of men gave themselves up to a single enemy soldier. Retiring units, encountering those going up the line, shouted abuse at them, 'Blacklegs,' 'You're prolonging the war.' Officers lost their influence. A crack alpine corps broke down into parties of men of all ranks, who, according to its official history 'wandered wildly about, but soon for the most part finding their way to the rear.'

Of course attempts were made to hold the advancing enemy, reserves were hurried from the north, thus depleting the forces of Prince Rupprecht. Troops, rushed in trucks, often had to fight as they scrambled off their tailboards. There was an inevitable confusion of units. The

Bottom right: The wreckage of enemy transports on the road to Abancourt in August 1918.

Below right: The bodies of German soldiers on the road to Chipilly during the Allied advance in August.

Right: A soldier of the London Irish Rifles fires at a sniper during a patrol in Albert, August 1918.

There was, naturally enough, jubilation among the Allies. This was caused not so much by the seizure of ground, for the war had seen too much of this kind of victory, as by the evidence of sharply declining enemy morale. During the advance a number of important documents were captured. These plainly showed that the Germans were reaching the end of their manpower reserves.

It was only to be expected that the German press should seek to reduce its significance and turn it into a purely local victory of no strategic value. Such was their success in playing down every Allied victory in the coming weeks that the German people were left stunned and unbelieving when they learned in November that an Armistice was being sought. This accounts for much of the confusion and the sense of betrayal which was felt after the war.

A great deal of hard fighting remained before that day was reached. There is no room for doubt, however, that the 8 August 1918 saw the beginning of the process. It is debatable how much of the credit is due to Haig.

Sir Basil Liddell Hart quotes an exchange of letters between Foch and Haig which started on 12 July, a time when the Germans were still in the ascendant. It proposed that the British offensive then being planned should be in the north round the Lille industrial area, a place of enormous value to the French. The objective was to be the freeing of

drain on precious reserves was enormous.

So far as the attackers were concerned the only major resistance was encountered in villages which could offer some kind of cover for the defenders. The pace of the first day could not be maintained on the 9th. The Germans were enormously reinforced with something like 14 divisions. The day saw the beginning of the attacks by the French Third Army south of the salient, but they were late – the Germans were already withdrawing.

By the 12th, the struggle was largely over, though with sporadic fighting occurring up and down the line. Haig's reaction was to bring it to an end and launch his Third and First Armies southeastward to strike the enemy in flank and reduce pressure on the Fourth and French First Armies. Foch, on the other hand, was demanding that the advance on the present line should continue. After a fierce quarrel Haig agreed to the extent of ordering localized probing attacks, but Rawlinson, the Fourth Army commander, and Sir Arthur Currie, commanding the Canadians, were so strongly opposed to this that they actually countermanded orders, once leaving the French in a bad spot. Foch was forced to concede, as he was always prepared to do once convinced.

The struggle on 8 August – 'The Black Day' – had produced a famous victory. More important still in a war distinguished by its extravagance with human life, it had been extremely economical. British losses during the four days were 22,000, and the French were about 20,000. German losses, never made official, have been estimated at something like double these combined figures, though this is likely to be exaggeration. What is certain is that the British and French together took some 30,000 prisoners.

the Bruay mines and the protection of the communication center of Estaires. This was not at all to Haig's liking, as he made plain in his answer of the 17th. He saw 'no advantage in an advance over a flat marshy region.' His counter-proposal was to push forward the Allied line to the southeast and east of Amiens to safeguard the town and railroad. This would be a combined operation with 'the French attacking south of Moreuil and the British north of the Luce.' He added that to 'realize this object I am preparing plans

secretly for an offensive north of the Luce, direction east. . . . In liaison with this project the French forces should, in my opinion, carry out an operation between Moreuil and Montdidier.' This was, of course, the plan which was subsequently followed.

However the fundamental tactical idea, that of using tanks in mass came from Rawlinson after witnessing the success of the attack at Hamel on 4 July. Thus there is some justification for claiming that this was a British concept.

Left: An artillery convoy moves to the front, a watercolor by Georges Scott.

Far left: The result of the German offensive in April 1918, painted by François Flameng.

Below: Large areas of northern France were left totally devastated by four years' fighting.

On the other hand, Haig never pretended to be solely responsible for the strategic plan which brought such a gratifying victory. The claim was made on his behalf by the British press, all too eager to show that a general of their own country could actually win a battle decisively. It was then taken over by historians writing shortly after the war.

However, in one respect Haig's philosophy of the war had been justified. This was in his theory of 'the last reserves.' He had held consistently to the view that in the final analysis the Entente must always win, simply because they had greater human resources. This view has been the subject of bitter parody and in the process his actual opinions have been distorted. He was not saying the war should be conducted without consideration for human life because the Entente possessed a huge reserve of manpower, as some detractors have made it appear. He was simply stating, in times when the entire battlescape looked its blackest, that there were still some grounds for optimism. The enemy simply could not win because the mathematics were against him.

When first enunciated, this doctrine had been based on

the fact that Russia with its seemingly endless numbers was in the struggle. Though they had fallen out, they had been replaced by another, and far more significant ally — the United States.

Through the spring and summer, Ludendorff's troops kept running into groups of American soldiers. At first they were simply small groups, fitted out with a hotch-potch of British and French equipment and hurried into position to aid their allies. Although they were brave, often suicidally so, they were no match for the cunning German veterans. Ludendorff dismisses them with contempt (he never had a good word to say for a brave opponent).

However by June they were becoming a force to be reckoned with. On the first day of that month a machine-gun battalion of the 3rd Division showed its mettle in the defense of Château-Thierry. On 6 June the 2nd Division launched an attack which won a village and part of Belleau Wood. By July, the time of the Second Battle of the Marne which set a limit upon the enemy advance, there were 25 divisions in France. They played a significant part in that battle as they did at Amiens on 8 August. By the second half of the month, their Commander in Chief, Pershing, was able to gather all his units together into one cohesive whole which was to be increasingly important over the coming months.

There was another element in the victory: the tanks which came out of the fog upon the ill-prepared German trenches. At their inception tanks were named, very accurately, 'land-ships.' Haig, like Kitchener, the British War Minister, had been a late convert to the tank. In Haig's case, this was only to be expected from a cavalryman.

In the end, Haig was if anything rather overpersuaded of their value and allowed their use first at the Somme in 1916 and later at Cambrai in ways which were in direct breach of their designers' principles. Colonel Swinton had declared they should be deployed in large numbers, sweeping suddenly down upon an enemy and wiping out his defenses. At the Somme, only 60 out of the 150 machines ordered reached France and for mostly technical reasons only 32 actually got to the start line. Nine accompanied the infantry, nine were overtaken by the foot soldiers, nine broke down and five ended up in battlefield craters. In this way the shock to the enemy which could have come from a massed attack was frittered away. He was warned of the existence of a new weapon and actually given the idea of making it himself. Luckily, the German General Staff was, if anything, even more purblind than the British. Had they not been the story of the March offensive might well have been quite different. However Rawlinson's proposal to employ tanks to spearhead the 8 August attack was not original. He was simply reverting to the principles of Swinton.

The view of a German general, Zwehl, quoted by Liddell Hart, is instructive, 'It was not the genius of Marshal Foch that beat us, but "General Tank." ' Another German general corroborates, 'The arrival of tanks on the scene had a most shattering effect on the men. They felt quite powerless against these monsters which crawled along the top of the

Right: General Douglas Haig sits next to Arthur James Balfour, then Foreign Secretary, at the Trianon Palace.

Below left: After the Black Day the Allied troops advanced rapidly. German prisoners are rounded up near Bellicourt, 29 September 1918.

trench enfilading it with continuous machine-gun fire and closely followed by small parties of infantry who threw hand grenades at the survivors.'

The tank was one element in German disintegration and, if important, still only one. There was besides a supreme war weariness, made worse by the hardships imposed on them through the Allied blockade. The German government took no steps either to control the money supply through taxation or to introduce a fair system of rationing. It was *sauve qui peut* on the Home Front with appalling suffering imposed on the poorer sections of the community. This made them a breeding ground for discontent.

If German morale was cracking, so too was that of its Chief of Staff. Ludendorff, in the late summer of 1918, seemed to be in a disturbed state of mind. On the one hand, he failed to apprehend the fundamental truth — that his country had lost the war and its only hope lay in making peace. On the other, at the first signs of disaffection he was thrown into a state of hysteria. One might feel some pity for his condition were it not that of all the generals of all the belligerents he is the one least able to excite such reactions. Even the stolid Hindenburg is redeemed by a certain generosity of spirit which could lead him to commiserate with a beaten foe. All Ludendorff could do in the same circumstances was gloat.

Least of all does one find in Ludendorff's memoirs, as one frequently finds in Hindenburg's praise of the skill of an opposing general. In one sense this is history's loss for nothing is more useful in trying to assess the merits of a commander than what his opponents say about him. Thus, in the case of Foch, Zwehl's dismissal of him forces us to reassess his contribution to the victory.

The resonance of Foch's reputation, one which finally brought him to be Commander in Chief, was based on his supposed success at the First Marne. Liddell Hart has shown how relatively unimportant, indeed hazardous to the enterprise as a whole, his conduct actually was. However one has to recognize that he brought special qualities of character to the office of Generalissimo. Of these, the greatest was his open-mindedness. He could quarrel with a fellow general, as he did with Haig, but finally admit his antagonist had been right. What was more he could continue to work with him thereafter without rancor. It was from this magnanimity that there sprang his ability to understand, as no other French general and few British had, the need to act in strict cooperation with allies. He gave Haig command of French units when this seemed desirable and sent French troops to reinforce the British ones (and was criticized for it) when he saw the necessity.

His other gift was that already referred to — of divining intuitively the state of the war. Thus in July 1918 while others could see only German victories he was declaring 'the edifice is beginning to crack.' He was right, of course. This is not just second sight, like Rommel's famous '*Spitzenfingergefühl*' or feeling at the fingertips. A commanding general has access to an enormous number of sources of information, among them the results of the interrogation of prisoners. These plainly indicated that the German spirit was breaking.

If we lack an appraisal of Foch from the other side of no man's land, we do have one of Haig. Like Ludendorff a change had come over the British Commander in Chief during the last months of the war. The change in him, however, was precisely the opposite one. It made him, as one enemy commentator put it, 'the master of the field.' Foch provided the authority, the aura of confidence, the essential coordinating skill. Haig, in the last weeks of the war, was the strategist.

The question which presents itself is this: would the war not have been a very different thing had Foch been Commander in Chief of all the Allied Forces and Haig his Chief of Staff from its earliest days. Haig may not have been the only figure behind 8 August. He was certainly no Marlborough, Wellington or Moltke. On the other hand, it is hard to see how victory on the 'Black Day' or in the days and weeks which followed could have come about in his absence.

GUDERIAN AT THE MEUSE 1940

Heinz (Schneller) Guderian became interested in tanks and armor during World War I and elaborated his own doctrines thereafter. During the invasion of France, in May 1940, he was able to put to the test, at a pivotal point of the battle of France, his basic *Achtung! Panzer!* doctrine which finally made his reputation.

Guderian was the rather typical descendant of a Junker family from the Warthegau, his father being the first military man of this rather austere and poverty-stricken family. Born on 17 June 1888 to Lieutenant Friedrich and Clara Guderian he was taken all over Germany by his parents who were posted to obscure garrison towns of the Wilhelmian Reich. While the parents were stationed at St Avold (Lorraine) Heinz went to cadet schools, at first at Baden, and then in Berlin. He liked military life and even enjoyed the rigid obedience and discipline, but he also exhibited intellectual independence in argumentation, an exceptional quality in a young Junker bent on a military career.

In 1907 he graduated from the war school at Metz (Lorraine), which he had found rather tedious and was posted to serve in his father's regiment. As a serving officer he showed rather catholic cultural tastes: he enjoyed hunting, was keen on shooting and at the same time was keenly interested in architecture and countryside – paysage. Once again his intellectual independence was discernible in a healthy criticism of his surroundings. It was noted that he found it difficult to make friends, especially with his elders – this was to mark him for the rest of his life. It would always be easier for him to make friends and inspire his juniors. However, with seniors, be they his brother officers or politicians, he somehow failed to communicate.

In 1912 Guderian was engaged to a young girl, Margarete Goerne, whom he married the following year, just before going to the War Academy in Berlin. The marriage brought him in contact with brother officers Wilhelm Keitel, Erich von Manstein and Colonel Count Rüdiger von der Goltz. Both Keitel and von der Goltz were to exercise a profound influence on his life and career. As it happened Guderian never finished his war course; it was dissolved when World War I broke out in August 1914, and Guderian went back to his previous posting (shortly before going to the War Academy he had been on a radio course), the Heavy Radio Station No 3, part of the 5th Cavalry division. He was 26 years of age, specializing in signals, full of patriotism and determined to win the war for Germany. Instead the war proved his *Wanderjahre*: he was to become familiar with tanks and acquire the experience necessary to combat them.

His first combat experience taught him that without good signals bravery was useless. His I Cavalry Corps under General von Richthofen was given the task of cutting off the French Second Army by radio, but the French had broken the German code and were prepared for this drive. When despite this the corps actually performed the task and found itself north of Soissons in the enemy's rear the army superiors were unaware of this brave achievement and it went to waste as the German cavalry unprotected against enemy fire could not press home its advantage. Later Guderian insisted on having radio receivers in each individual tank – the protected cavalry could press home an advantage. While his experience was varied – he fought in initial battles, flew as an observer in aircraft, became a staff officer – he never had to face tanks directly, but heard of the French and British use of the tanks, as a terror weapon at Cambrai, Amiens and elsewhere. When the massed French tanks reversed the German breakthrough on the Marne he was, for the first and last time, involved in the

Guderian was never far from the action during the Blitzkrieg 1940.

mobile defense of the area of the Marne and Vesle. These experiences marked him for life.

Just before the armistice Guderian was sent to Italy on a liaison mission, and had to escape back to Germany to avoid capture. He witnessed the collapse of the German Reich in Munich, but then made his way up to Berlin where he was appointed to the Eastern Frontiers' Protection Service to keep an eye on the Poles and the Russian Bolsheviks. After a spell with the Iron Division in the Baltic lands, he was finally sent to the Inspectorate of Transport Troops in 1922. This in fact meant that he was back to his hobbyhorse, mechanized formations. Furthermore he developed his ideas theoretically by writing articles for the *Militär-Wochenblatt*: he came to advocate the *Stosskraft* (dynamic punch) as the latest combat method. In 1914 the new combat methods had been mobile artillery and infantry machine guns – with technological changes the tanks (armor) became the new method. In 1927 Guderian was promoted to major and henceforth devoted all his military efforts to the theory and practice of armored warfare.

As early as 1928 Major Guderian founded a tactical center for tanks and their cooperation with other arms. Then he went to Sweden to drive the tanks in person – by the Treaty of Versailles Germany was not allowed to manufacture armor – and he also made a technical study of them. Back in Germany Colonel Guderian insisted on improvements in communications, not only with the tanks but also with field telephones and teleprinters. In fact he was obsessed with the formation of a new command, a sort of army within an army, incorporating elements from each arm. However both the new political leaders – the Nazis had come to power in 1933 – and the pro-Nazi military leaders, Blomberg and Reichenau, did not care for Guderian's ideas for the moment. It is true that so far Guderian had only produced halfbaked ideas and semidigested inno-

vations. For example, at this stage, he saw the future Panzer divisions as weapons of defense. He knew that the Germans had helped the Russians to develop the tank and he intended to use the German armor in defense of the Eastern Frontiers. However all this changed in 1934 when the new Commander in Chief, General von Fritsch, created the *Panzertruppe* and Colonel Guderian became the Chief of Staff of this new branch.

With Guderian's official appointment the theoretical justification of his belief in technological advance and armor finally came. Already a year before he had Captain Liddell Hart's articles on deep penetration by armored troops translated into German and the following year he published an article on another favorite subject: tactically, tank commanders needed to ride ahead of their squadrons controlling them by means of individual radios. While Guderian's book, *Achtung! Panzer!*, contained all the tactical innovations gained from long practical experience, the basic strategic ideas were in a sense the military response to Hitler's innovatory ideas on the war, and in particular to his concept of the Blitzkrieg, which was the main reason why this book attracted so much attention in 1935 when it came out.

Learning the lesson of the last war Guderian thought that the remedy of the Allied tank failure lay in the fully mechanized (Panzer) division moving into battle at equal speed: medium 'breakthrough' tanks armed with machine guns and cannon up to 75mm; antitank guns and motorized infantry following closely behind; tactical air forces delaying defenders' reserves and airborne troops capturing important enemy points in the rear. Guderian also spelled out his strategic doctrine, 'concentrated blow applied with surprise on the decisive point of the front, to form the arrow head so deep that we need have no worry about the flank.' As he seriously thought of applying these doctrines Guderian was suddenly replaced as Chief of Staff by Friedrich Paulus, and as a result the Panzers were split up as in all the European armies. Guderian's influence with the upper echelons and Hitler seemed to have vanished.

Guderian was most disconcerted by this development and at one stage lost his nerve, walked up to his old colleague Fritsch and blamed him for ignoring his advice on armored forces. Before Guderian could be punished Fritsch and Blomberg were suddenly dismissed by Hitler and he was appointed general officer commanding the XVI Corps and was detailed by Hitler to perform special duties involving the Panzers. Thus on 12 March 1938 Guderian led the Panzers into Austria and subsequently had to remedy the many breakdowns that occurred on that march.

Although an established armor theoretician and practitioner Guderian did not have it all his way. On the contrary top army echelons proved consistently hostile, especially after the adverse reports on the armored troops from Spain. Guderian had to counter criticism of himself in print. He praised strategic speed, 'the tanks had to keep moving despite enemy's defensive fire, thus making it harder for the enemy to build up fresh defensive positions.' In 1938, when military exercises had gone disastrously wrong, Hitler forced General Beck's resignation, and at long last showed a personal predilection for Guderian. Their dialogues became very close and personal but this in turn provoked

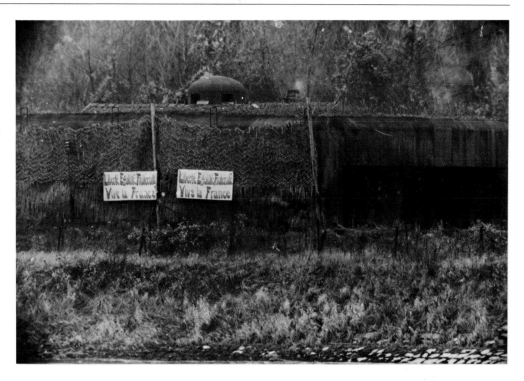

Left: Winston Churchill, General Gamelin and General Gort in France on 8 January 1940. This was during the Sitzkrieg when the Allies and Germans faced each other over the Maginot Line.

Right: During the *Drôle de Guerre* phase the soldiers indulged in propaganda exercises. They put up slogans on their lines to demoralize the enemy.

personal hostility from other senior officers. Thus Hitler sent Guderian's XVI Corps to occupy the Sudetenland and subsequently enabled him to visit Britain to do a little more research in British armor progress. Hitler used Guderian to divide top army officers, but though he thus obviously favored him, he made no headway with his obsessive armor warfare because of army obstruction. It took the Polish campaign to vindicate Guderian's theories.

In August 1939 Guderian, who late in 1938 was appointed general in command of Mobile Troops, conducted last-minute exercises with the 3000 tanks at his disposal and came to the conclusion that they could be put to good use in the coming Polish campaign, since the communication systems had been completed and supplies had been improved considerably since the disasters in the previous year. Thus according to him six Panzer divisions and four light divisions, aided by massive air intervention, would achieve a complete defeat of Poland in a few days, a feat that would have taken the remaining 45 German Army formations weeks to accomplish. Although his new XIX Corps exhibited certain shortcomings it in fact accomplished its tasks in a few days with perfection so that when Hitler visited the battlefield Guderian proudly showed him round proving to him the effectiveness of armor. As far as Hitler was concerned Guderian was preaching to the converted and Hitler sent him to Brest-Litovsk, to finish off Poland which gave him the opportunity to put into practice the strategic envelopment, from north to south by massed Panzers. The 4th Panzer Division, badly used, had taken a hammering and the German army had failed to take Warsaw from the south. Because of lack of command the operations had become confused, but ultimately Guderian's personality carried the day. On 13 September the 18th Polish Division surrendered and the following day Brest-Litovsk was taken after hard fighting. Guderian's Corps suffered only four percent casualties in the campaign, accomplished all its tasks and only half of the Panzers needed major overhaul. Although the generals minimized

the effect of the tanks (and Guderian) on the campaign, because of 'enemy impotence,' Hitler became convinced that the new weapon would win him the war. Guderian became his key to the victory and he was to be proved right in the near future.

Hitler was already planning the war in the West and on 28 September 1939 the German General Staff set to work on plans for the invasion of France. Both the Commander in Chief, General Walther von Brauchitsch, and the Chief of Staff, General Franz Halder had very little time to plan the operation, and even less confidence in its success. According to them the Maginot Line had to be outflanked and the *Schwerpunkt* of the whole operation was to be north of the difficult terrain of the Ardennes, in the general direction of Namur. On the right wing, Holland was to be subdued and simultaneously on the left wing, a relatively strong force would be sent through the Ardennes to reach the river Meuse between Givet and Sedan. No one seems to have liked this plan of 'improvisation'; its execution was several times postponed and after 10 January 1940, when a staff officer with the details of the plan made a forced landing in Belgium, it was abandoned.

Long before its abandonment the plan was criticized by Hitler, and Generals von Manstein and von Rundstedt. Hitler suggested that the drive through the Ardennes be enlarged and be aimed as the main attack across the Meuse toward Amiens and the Channel coast, thus cutting off the northern enemy wing. Manstein wanted a complete destruction of the northern enemy wing through a strategic encirclement similar to that of the elder Moltke, which the younger Moltke failed to carry out in 1914, and which Manstein and Rundstedt had successfully achieved in Poland only recently. Rundstedt sent the General Staff his suggestions which were remarkably similar to those of Hitler but with military meat in them (Hitler's were based on intuition and dreams).

Inevitably Guderian was brought in as the foremost Panzer expert. Early in November 1939 General Wilhelm

Keitel called him in for consultations. He explained that the fear of bad weather which would cause the immobility of the armor was the reason for the delay in the war against France, and he wanted to know if a strong tank force could pass through the Ardennes. Guderian was in a doubly strong position: he knew the terrain in 1914 and 1918 and from this knowledge he derived the certainty that Panzer divisions could pass through the difficult area. However after this general consultation Guderian was told that his XIX Corps would lead the drive on Sedan and he immediately considered his two Panzer divisions and one motorized division as insufficient and requested seven divisions as a minimum to ensure success. Needless to say this request was made when the Meuse operation was still subsidiary to that of Namur.

In January 1940 the war games were held by Rundstedt and they demonstrated the feasibility of the main attack against Sedan. However, Guderian's insistence on the armor spearheading the attack through the Ardennes, executing the crossing of the river Meuse and then advancing deep into France, was treated with scorn. General Halder thought Guderian's ideas senseless and Rundstedt supported him in this opinion. Nonetheless Guderian had

the courage to contradict them both and insisted on his suggestions: a surprise drive *en masse* would drive a wedge so deep and wide in the enemy's front so that the Germans would not need to worry about their flanks. Some generals were prepared to support Guderian in his stand and among them Manstein tipped the balance in Guderian's favor. On 17 February 1940 Manstein saw Hitler and described to him Guderian's plan, infecting him with his own enthusiasm. Next day Hitler saw Brauchitsch and Halder, told them that Guderian's plan was in fact his: that was the way France would be attacked and destroyed.

Thus on 24 February 1940 *Plan Gelb* (invasion of France) was revised and became *Plan Sichelschnitt*. Guderian's concept of the breakthrough in the Ardennes became the *Schwerpunkt*; in addition he personally was going to execute this new plan. Army Groups A, B and C under Generals von Rundstedt, Fedor von Bock and Wilhelm von Leeb remained responsible for the previous sectors, but Army Group B's role was relegated to become, in Captain Liddell Hart's words, a matador's cloak, while Army Group A with its Fourth (General Kluge), Twelfth (General List) and Sixteenth Army (General Busch) came to occupy the pivotal point of the *Sichelschnitt*. General Wilhelm List created a special Panzer Group under the command of General Ewald von Kleist, who in turn had under him General Reinhardt's XXXXI Corps, Guderian's XIX Corps and General von Wietersheim's XIV Corps. The center of both the strategic blow and the tactical fighting was Guderian with the 1st, 2nd and 10th Panzer Divisions and the crack motorized SS regiment, Grossdeutschland. The Kleist group, with some 1260 tanks (out of the overall 2800) was given priority of air support, while advancing, and massed bombing while actually crossing the Meuse. This arrangement made heavy artillery redundant, as otherwise the operation would have been greatly retarded; the narrow and bad roads in the Ardennes would have made it impossible for the artillery to follow up closely on the tanks – shell supplies would also be delayed. In March 1940 Hitler finally asked Guderian what he proposed to do

Left: A German soldier keeps a careful eye on activities behind the Maginot Line.

Below left: German troops take cover as shell bursts beside them.

Right: A propaganda picture showing a storm boat being used in an amphibious attack.

Below: Another posed picture demonstrating the usefulness of rubber boats. These boats were used during the crossing of the Meuse.

after the crossing of the Meuse, to which Guderian replied that he would have made a dash for Amiens or Paris, or the best optimal option, for the Channel coast. Hitler fell silent refusing to divulge his final objective, that is the destruction of France. However, Guderian's tactical victories implied in all three options would inevitably lead to the final objectives.

In the meantime Guderian concentrated on hard training. Tank crews practiced in the Eifel mountains under their general's personal supervision. There were map reading exercises, but the tanks could not fire their guns, because of shortage of ammunition. Infantry and engineers practiced river crossing, ferrying tanks across and then pontoon building. The river Moselle was almost identical with the river Meuse. During these two months of preparation all the ranks came to know their general personally; he inspired confidence and even enthusiasm. Many survivors speak of his fairness, paternal care and the personal share of the bustling general in the hardships of the exercises and combat itself. While his men had complete faith in his plans, Guderian's superiors, and occasionally even himself, were full of doubts. Guderian had no confidence in Brauchitsch and Halder, for although they were belated converts to his plans, they continued to vacillate. List wanted infantry to lead the assault across the Meuse. Rundstedt, like Hitler, refused to consider deep penetration after the Meuse. Kleist had no experience of armor. Busch never thought that Guderian would get across the Meuse, while Bock, whose

Army Group was relegated to a secondary role, thought the whole operation was crazy, 'You will be creeping along, 10 miles from the Maginot Line for your breakthrough, hoping that the French will watch inactive. You are massing all those tanks on the narrow roads in the Ardennes as if there was no such thing as air force. You then hope to operate as far as the coast with an open flank, some 200 miles long, with the French army letting you through.' However Guderian, after all the planning and practical exercises, became totally confident. He felt sure that if he were allowed to execute his plans, total victory would be his. Between 8 and 10 May 1940 the tanks of XIV, XXXXI and XIX Corps, stretching some 100 miles from head to tail, began to move into their border positions with Sedan as their principal axis of movement. Guderian together with 1st Panzer Division passed through Luxembourg and was ready on the Belgian-French border for the attack through the Ardennes. On the day of assault Kleist suddenly deflected the 10th Panzers from Sedan to Longwy much to Guderian's annoyance. After long arguments the 10th Panzers did not go to Longwy, but changed their axis of advance causing the 1st, 2nd and 6th Panzers to become entangled. Fortunately the French and British Air Forces made no attack on these confused columns and Guderian was able to sort out the confusion. However, everywhere else the schedules were kept and the advance was smooth. Halder described it as 'a very good marching achievement.'

The first battle on the frontier river Semois was decided

before the bulk of XIX Corps arrived in the area. The elements of the 1st Panzers forced the French 5th DLC to retire voluntarily toward the Meuse and at night Guderian took up quarters in the Hotel Panorama at Neufchateau, where he luckily escaped injury after a shell hit the hotel. On the following day Guderian again narrowly escaped injury after an air attack at Bouillon. Still with his 2nd Panzers lagging slightly behind Guderian took advantage of the French withdrawal and pushed his 1st Panzers toward Sedan, where its forward tanks arrived in the evening of 12 May. By nightfall the 10th Panzers also reached the Meuse at Bazeilles, but the 2nd Panzers were nowhere and Guderian flew to Kleist's headquarters for further orders. He found out that General Rommel's 7th Panzers had also reached the Meuse at Dinant and that the Kleist Group would attack generally across the Meuse in the afternoon of the following day. On the flight back Guderian's pilot lost his way and almost landed behind French lines.

On 13 May the Meuse was crossed by infantry and motorcyclists on either side of Sedan. The crossing was preceded by air bombing lasting five hours which demoralized the second-rate French troops facing the Germans. All through the night the Germans were constructing tank ferries and pontoons under Guderian's personal supervision. After the infantry had established bridgeheads on the other side of the Meuse, Guderian paddled across the river to meet his old friend, Colonel Balck, who greeted him with a joke 'about joyriding in a canoe on the Meuse' and the news that the bridgehead, three miles wide and six miles deep, was secure. The first tanks would begin the crossing at dawn. The French had no idea that the crossing would be attempted only one day after the German arrival and on the whole held their fire to save ammunition until the time when the real assault occurred. They were badly let down

Top left: German motorcyclists press into France.

Above left: Crossing the Meuse in Belgium on 13 May 1940.

Top right: A German bicycle squad cross the Meuse-Scheldt canal in Belgium on 13 May 1940.

Above right: The remains of a French column in Sedan wood, 14 May 1940.

Right: The Blitzkrieg left a trail of destruction in its wake as witnessed from this picture of a Channel town.

by the air forces, which because of the lack of communication between the French and the British commands, failed to support them. The Germans had to do some hard fighting to dislodge the French from their bunkers and defensive lines. However, once they had achieved it the French High Command panicked; General Corap, commanding the Ninth Army ordered general retreat.

However, on the French side it was not all panic and confusion, despite the fact that General Lafontaine had under his command only reservists. General Grandsard in command of the Meuse sector, at first thought that nothing was lost, but then he heard reports that German tanks were in the La Marfée area. The reports were incorrect, but they panicked two of his colonels into issuing withdrawal orders. General panic spread and Colonel Pourcelet committed suicide. While Lafontaine withdrew his headquarters to Chémery, Grandsard sent two tank battalions and two infantry regiments to counterattack. Behind them General Joseph Georges, who had dismissed Corap and replaced him by General Henri Giraud, was sending up to Sedan the powerful units of the Third Army and 3rd Motorized Division. Lafontaine ordered a two-pronged attack at dawn, but the units were not ready in time for the counterattack, which started at 0700 hours after the German tanks had already crossed the river in force. To plug the hole on the Meuse, between Dinant and Sedan, the French command ordered its 1st, 2nd and 3rd Armored Divisions into counterattack. However, the 1st Division found itself without fuel and was subsequently annihilated and the 2nd entrained and was cut into two at Hirson. Only the 3rd actually went into battle against Guderian, but from the beginning proved rather static, went into battle piecemeal and was chopped up not even by German armor but mainly by the *Sturmpionierbatallion*. Initially the situation looked rather ugly for the Germans, but after they had put out of action about one half of the French

tanks, the French turned round and withdrew. During the battle Guderian went back to La Chapelle to prepare orders for the following, decisive day of the battle. After the French counterattack the bulk of the French 55th and 71st Divisions had ceased to exist, fleeing in disorder. The contagion of fear and panic also spread to Grandsard's X Corps boding ill for the French armies still resisting the German assault. By the 14th Guderian's bridgehead was 30 miles wide and 15 miles deep and some 85 Blenheim bombers had been shot down over the German pontoons.

On the 14th Guderian's 1st Panzers moved resolutely against Chémery and the 10th Panzers supported by the SS Grossdeutschland pushed onto the high ground of Bois Mont Dieu, both effectively preventing the French XXI Corps from assembling for a counterattack, though hard fighting went on for the rest of the day at the key village of Stonne. Guderian was presented with a gap of 12 miles through which he could drive his 1st Panzers in order to break toward the west and the Channel thus fulfilling his wildest hopes and executing Plan *Sichelschnitt* to perfection. At noon Guderian reported to Rundstedt on the state of the battle, 'in the very middle of the bridge, while air raids were in progress.' Then he issued new orders to his men: they were to cross the Ardennes canal and head west. This was a risky decision for the Second and Ninth French Armies were still counterattacking and far from routed. The southern flank at Stonne was only guarded by the battered Grossdeutschland and 10th Panzers, while there was a

Left and below: Pz Kw 38(t) tanks in action in May 1940. These were Czech tanks which were redesignated to serve with the Wehrmacht. They equipped the 7th and 8th Panzer Divisions.

Bottom: Another French town is engulfed by flames.

Far left: The destruction of the Maginot Line.

Below left: German soldiers pick off snipers in a small town in Lorraine.

possibility of the Allied air forces succeeding in destroying his pontoon bridges. Guderian therefore moved forward his AA batteries to ring off the bridges: they brought down some 112 aircraft and Guderian's armor went on crossing the Meuse. By nightfall Colonel Balck had reached his objective at Singy and the French Generals Flavigny and Huntziger caused confusion by issuing frequent and contra- dictory orders. The greatest battle that Guderian had to fight on that day was with his superior, General Kleist: the latter insisted that Guderian consolidate his southern line before pushing westward to Rethel. Guderian was both furious and bitter, as he saw himself deprived of the fruit of his tactical victories. In the end Guderian won the argument, for the generals on his flanks, Hoth and Rein-

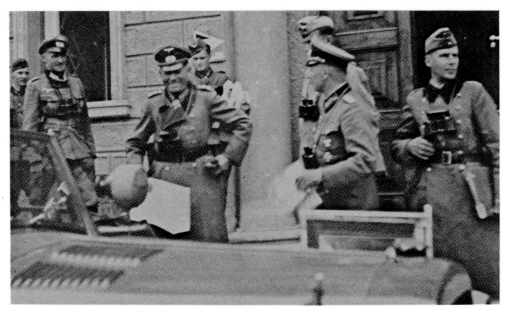

Above: Panzer Mark IIIs (background) of Guderian's Panzer Corps cross the cornfields of northern France.

Left: General Heinz Guderian leaves a meeting. Note the censor has whited out his briefcase.

Top: French forces surrender to the Germans in Lille, 29 May 1940.

Top left: The retreating British blew up this bridge over the Meuse in Belgium, 22 May 1940.

Opposite top: Guderian plans the advance of his Panzer Group at Langres, June 1940.

hardt, were also on the point of breaking through.

Some French historians speak of 15 May as the day France lost the war, but for Guderian it was a day of miracles: considering the nature of the terrain it seemed miraculous that his Panzers succeeded in breaking through. French counterattacks were constantly delayed for technical reasons and the Germans were able to deploy antitank guns and rush up reinforcements. However, the progress of 1st and 2nd Panzers on that day was not impressive as they had to smash through tough French defense not yet confused and demoralized by superiors' orders. General Brocard was dismissed, but the French armor was nevertheless routed by all three German generals, Guderian, Hoth and Reinhardt. Nonetheless Guderian once again had a verbal battle with Kleist who ordered him in the evening to stop advancing. Some lively shouting on the telephone won Guderian 24 hours of freedom to advance: at dawn he arrived at Bouvellemont where the 14th French Division, after fighting hard all day under the future Maréchal de France de Lattre de Tassigny, had just withdrawn from the combat. There and then Guderian personally briefed the commanders for the operation ahead and instead of resting the troops set out immediately.

On 16 May Guderian thrust forward only with his 1st and 2nd Panzers, leaving the 10th Panzers and SS Grossdeutschland on his southern flank as insurance, and in deference to Kleist. By the end of the day they were 40 miles west, at Dercy on the Serre, while XXXXI Corps reached Guise on the Oise. Guderian then issued orders by radio for the following day: advance was to continue. However, he did not reckon with Kleist whose orders he was disobeying. Kleist's HQ monitored Guderian's orders and issued counterorders. Kleist also asked Guderian to report to him the following morning. When they met, on 17 May 1940, the exchanges were acrimonious as both men were on edge and their nerves were rapidly giving up from excitement. Kleist accused Guderian of deliberately disobeying his orders and Guderian offered his resignation on the spot. When Rundstedt heard of it he immediately ordered Guderian to remain in charge and sent General List to act as mediator. Once again Guderian won the day: his HQ remained on the spot, but his troops were permitted their reconnaissance in force. Guderian just lay his communication wires and dashed away from his HQ to join his advancing tanks. At the end of that day his vanguard passed Montcornet and Laon. However, on that very day Hitler joined Brauchitsch and Halder and the rest of the generals in their fear of French counterattacks from the south: thus the disputes continued, while the Panzers rolled on gathering speed as they went. The very speed of their advance made it impossible for the French armies to react.

Guderian's 2nd Panzers reached St Quentin on the 19th and Abbeville on the following day. At long last the French command ordered counterattacks, but because of the changes in the personnel the offensive was disrupted and never materialized.

On 21 May, near Amiens, British 4th and 7th Tank Regiments and the French 3rd Mechanized Division unexpectedly turned on General Rommel's 7th Panzers and caused a lot of anxiety, but Guderian would have dealt

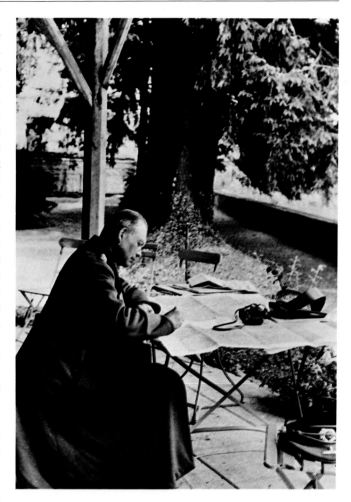

with the threat as efficiently as he did at Montcornet, when de Gaulle's 4th Armored Division counterattacked. Though Guderian was ultimately halted for four days (24–27 May) which saved Dunkirk for the British Expeditionary Force, his tanks took Boulogne and Calais thus cutting Allied armies into two. On 28 May Hitler put him in command of a special Panzer group which then transferred to the east and which during the three weeks of June 1940 cut across eastern France from Châlons sur Marne to Pontarlier and Belfort. France was defeated and on 22 June signed an armistice.

Even with hindsight it is thought by military experts that the battle of France, had it been fought along the lines of Plan Gelb, would have ended in a deadlock. It can be said without exaggeration that Guderian's tactical and strategic ideas embodied in Plan *Sichelschnitt* virtually decided the issue. The factors of surprise and the psychological blow that the French command and armies suffered after the Germans emerged from an impenetrable area and effected their main breakthrough were decisive for this battle of France. In the execution of his ideas Guderian acted resolutely having absolute faith in them, while his political and military superiors and masters dithered.

At this stage of World War II he was years ahead scientifically and technologically of his friends and foes and his achievements on the battlefield fully vindicated his theories and doctrines. Thus for Guderian the battle of the Meuse, which really meant the battle of France, was a perfect victory, never to be repeated again so clearly by any other warlord.

ROMMEL AT TOBRUK 1942

Even before the beginning of World War II the great desert wastes of North Africa captured imaginations in Europe and America, and once the Desert War began in earnest, much of the romance formerly engendered by the French Foreign Legion became attached to the new desert warriors. The Afrika Korps, the Long Range Desert Groups, the spies sipping gin in the clubs of Cairo and the British Tommies sweltering in their tanks – all have won a place in modern mythology.

The campaign in North Africa fascinated the British, especially Churchill, to the extent that soon its strategic considerations became almost overshadowed by the psychological need to win a great victory over the Afrika Korps and its legendary leader, General Erwin Rommel, the Desert Fox.

Churchill described Rommel as a master of war. Troops on both sides called him, half-affectionately, 'that bastard Rommel.' During the desert campaign he was to become the best-known and – even in Britain and America – practically the most popular figure in the Middle East owing to his brilliance, his courage, his skill at tactical maneuver (often when gravely outnumbered), and his old-school, chivalrous attitude toward his opponents. To the British soldier he came to be the personification of the bold feint, the surprise attack, the wild chase. 'Rommel is coming!' would race through the troops with the speed and destructive force of a forest fire. In fact, General Sir Claude Auchinleck, Commander in Chief of the British forces in the Middle East, found it necessary to issue an extraordinary Order of the Day, begging his senior officers to 'make every effort to destroy the concept that Rommel is anything more than an ordinary German general,' adding that, 'this matter is of great psychological significance.'

Thus Tobruk, a Libyan port not far from the Egyptian frontier, soon assumed an importance far beyond its already vital strategic position. The British captured it from the Italians early in the desert campaign in January 1941. In the spring of 1941 the stubborn Australians who held out for some nine months against Rommel's siege became the heroes of the Empire. When the fortress fell to the Afrika Korps a year later it was a crushing blow to the British public and Rommel's reputation was not so much made, as confirmed.

Erwin Johannes Eugen Rommel was born in Heidenheim, near Wurtemburg, on 15 November 1891. He was one of five children, and his sister describes him as a gentle, amiable, dreamy child. He was small for his age, and had little interest in books or sports. In his teens, however, he suddenly woke up and developed a keen interest in physical fitness, spending every spare minute on his bicycle or on skis in winter. The dreamer became a hard-headed, practical youth who did well in school and studied aircraft design as a hobby.

In June 1910 Rommel joined the army. Since the family had no military connections (his father and grandfather were both schoolteachers and mathematicians), he joined the 124th Infantry Regiment at Weingarten as an 'officer cadet' – which meant he had to serve in the ranks before going on to a *Kriegsschule* (War Academy). He was promoted to corporal in October, made sergeant by the end of December, and was posted to the Kriegsschule at Danzig in March 1911.

As a young officer he was good at drill and was found to be especially effective in training recruits. Like the young Montgomery he showed an unusual interest in the smallest details of military organization – but unlike Monty, he was never argumentative, usually preferring to listen rather than talk.

During World War I Rommel showed the boldness, independence, and understanding of the value of surprise that he would use to such advantage almost 30 years later. He stood out almost immediately as a perfect fighter. He was cold, cunning, ruthless and untiring – quick to make decisions and incredibly brave. Before the year was out he was transferred to a mountain battalion where his remarkable eye for country and his ability to ignore physical discomfort were invaluable. By the end of the war he had been wounded twice and had been awarded not only the Iron Cross Classes I and II, but also Germany's highest decoration, the *Pour le Mérite* (corresponding to Britain's Victoria Cross or the United States' Medal of Honor).

His comrades from this period invariably describe him as having *Fingerspitzengefühl* – a sixth sense, or intuition in his fingertips. To a man they credit his tactical genius – and remark that he was often disliked by his fellow officers, from whom he expected as much as he did from himself.

At the end of the war Captain Rommel turned to peacetime soldiering, ending up in November 1939 a colonel in command of the Kriegsschule at Wiener Neustadt. He lived a quiet life with his wife and son. He did not smoke, drank little and did not care much about food or parties. He was good with his hands, and could make or fix almost anything.

Like the majority of his fellow countrymen, Rommel considered the Nazis upstarts but saw Hitler as an idealistic patriot who had a chance to pull the country together and oust the Communists. This attitude may have come more easily since he was not part of the snobbish Prussian clique that included so many regular army officers. He was never close to Hitler, which perhaps is one reason why his admiration took so long to wear off, but through their brief encounters in the early days of the war the Führer developed a liking for him. Rommel, for his part, admired Hitler's magnetic personality, his amazing memory for technical detail and his physical courage.

At the outbreak of World War II he was commander of the Nazi headquarters in Poland, but by June 1940 Hitler had given him a fighting command, at the head of the 7th Panzer Division of the 15th Armored Corps (the 'ghost division' that took part in the stunning German advance through France).

On 15 February 1941 Rommel – now a newly appointed lieutenant general – was given command of 'the German troops in Libya.' His mission was to assist the Italians and help prevent a British breakthrough to Tripoli. In two months General Sir Archibald Wavell's small force of three British divisions – 31,000 men, 120 guns and 275 tanks – had chased 10 Italian divisions totalling over 200,000 men across 650 miles. Though Hitler still could not bring himself to take North Africa all that seriously, he had finally realized that if something were not done quickly Britain

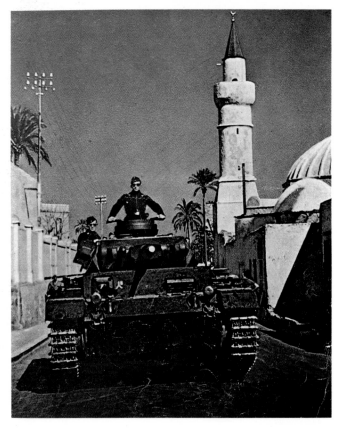

itself the Afrika Korps.

For the next two years they would be fighting over a featureless wasteland of gravel and scrub, dotted with ancient wells and the tombs of sheiks. The battlefield stretched almost 400 miles, from Dernia in the east to El Alamein in the west. The only road followed the coast and the only dominant physical feature was a 500-foot escarpment that faced north to the coastal plain, descending from the limestone plateau where the armies maneuvered. With no natural obstacles and few civilians or settled areas except along the coast, the campaign over the vast spaces of the desert bore more resemblance to a naval war than to a traditional European land conflict. Rommel was the first to really appreciate the fact and fully exploit the freedom of movement it gave him.

In addition to their human adversaries, the soldiers fought the desert. Temperatures rose to 120 degrees in summer, with the stones and sand remaining burning hot until late at night. The sand got everywhere, in hair, underclothes and machinery. Insects and sand fleas viciously bit everyone, general and enlisted man alike, and dysentery was rife. The men grew lean and tanned, with skins like leather. The infantry prepared their positions, the sappers laid their mines and the tank crews sweated in their tanks, all in a climate which many would have considered impossible for Europeans to work in at all.

The existence of a common enemy – the desert – may have been one reason why the North African campaign was, by and large, a 'gentleman's war.' Neither the Afrika Korps nor the British abused prisoners. In fact the former, according to Rommel's biographer Desmond Young, treated enemy prisoners of war with, 'almost old-world courtesy.' Compliments were traded sincerely: Rommel often described General Wavell as a 'military genius' and commander of the highest order, while for his part Wavell sent Frau Rommel a copy of his lectures on generalship inscribed 'to the memory of a brave, chivalrous, and skillful opponent.'

Much of the credit on the German side must go to Rommel himself, who had strong feelings about correct behavior and observance of the 'soldier's code' – feelings that were shared by most officers in the regular German Army (with a few notable exceptions). He was also lucky not to have any SS troops attached to his command and to be a continent away from headquarters.

Perhaps because of their early successes in the hostile desert environment most people believed that the Afrika Korps was an elite volunteer unit, specially trained in desert warfare. On the contrary, the men of the Afrika Korps had, for the most part, been plucked out of the Balkans and set down in Tripoli with no preparation at all. They were typical German soldiers – strong, brave, well-trained and disciplined. They were not well-suited to the desert. Many, especially the very young, the very blond and the older veterans of World War I, could not adapt to the new, rigorous conditions as well as did the British colonial troops or even the British regular troops. Few had ever been out of Europe before and they lacked the British experience with foreign lands. It was difficult, for example, to teach the troops not to drink untreated water. German doctors knew less than their British counterparts about

would gain control of the entire southern shore of the Mediterranean, leaving Europe's 'soft underbelly' dangerously exposed.

Rommel built up his army and eventually had at his disposal two Panzer divisions (the 15th and the 21st), an Italian armored division (the Ariete), a German infantry division (the 90th Light), a 'frontier group,' two Italian motorized divisions and four Italian infantry divisions. They formed Panzer Army Africa but the German section called

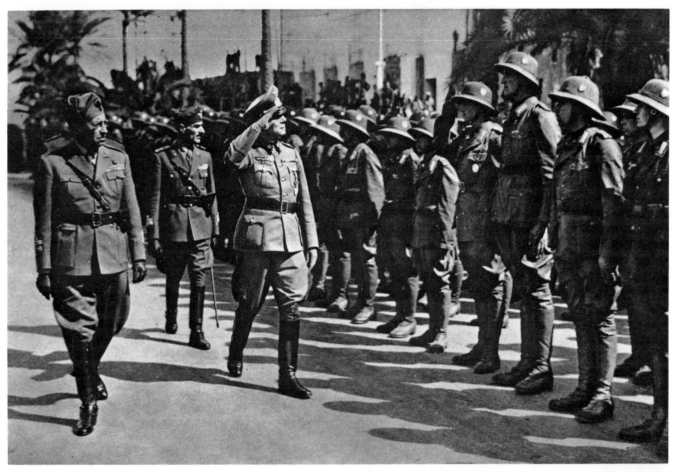

Left: Rommel and General Gariboldi on a tour of inspection in Tripoli, February 1941. This was shortly after Rommel arrived in North Africa.

Far left: General Sir Archibald Wavell was Commander in Chief, Middle East until July 1941.

Far left below: German tank passes through a Libyan town.

Below: General Rommel and General Cavallero inspect Italian troops in Tripoli.

tropical medicine and German field hospitals were far inferior. Sickness, especially dysentery and jaundice, took a heavy toll in the early days of the campaign.

The Afrika Korps had some definite advantages as well. Though they had less transport, their weapons outclassed those of the British, especially in the beginning, and they understood more about using them effectively. The men had better prospects of leave and received more news from home (even publishing their own paper, *Oase*) — all of which improved morale. In addition, they were a homo-geneous group, in distinct contrast to the Eighth Army, which was a mixture of divisions from every part of the far-flung British Empire.

With all this it was Rommel who, by sheer force of personality, turned the Afrika Korps into a tough, resiliant and self-confident fighting unit. He taught each man to give 150 percent and never to admit defeat, so that even as they were marching down to the prisoner-of-war ships in 1943 they were able to hold their heads high.

Life in the desert was unfamiliar and rigorous, but

Right: Destroyed British tanks, knocked out during Rommel's whirlwind advance through North Africa in 1941.

Right below: Following the fighting at Ras el Madauar on 30 April 1941, the first British prisoners to be taken outside Tobruk are marched into captivity.

Below: Rommel decided to bypass Tobruk and push forward into Egypt but the city remained a thorn in his side. Rommel looks at the front following the failure of the British Battleaxe operation, 19 June 1941.

Rommel found it no problem becoming 'desert-worthy' (a British term that came to be applied to anyone and anything that functioned effectively in the desert). Though no longer young, he was in fine physical condition, with a Spartan streak that made him take pride in the stoic acceptance of discomfort and fatigue. As one of his officers put it later, 'he had the strength of a horse . . . he could wear out men 20 and 30 years younger.'

He did not need much sleep nor did he care much about what he ate. He insisted on getting the same rations as his men, which were not too good (the food that arrived on the supply ships was usually much too heavy for the desert and did not include fresh fruit or vegetables). He was appalled when he discovered that there were three 'classes' of rations in the Italian army — for officers, noncommissioned officers and enlisted men. His reading was limited to newspapers or books about military topics. Though he did have a mild interest in North African history, the story that he was an avid classical scholar and archeologist was fabricated by the German propaganda machine.

Most days he was awake by 0600 hours, and by 0630 hours — always shaved and in uniform — would be off on his daily round of the positions. Sometimes he took to the air, piloting his own Stuka, but more often he drove himself around the desert in his Volkswagen. He would arrive at the most isolated post without warning — and it was an unlucky senior officer who was caught in bed after 0700 hours. Nor were the visits mere formalities. He missed nothing, from a badly positioned machine gun to an inadequately camouflaged minefield. At the end of the day he would eat dinner in about 20 minutes, listen to the news on the radio and write his daily letter to his wife. Official papers or letters to the survivors of his World War I battalion (with whom he was a faithful correspondent) took up the rest of the evening.

Rommel was fond of young people and was very definitely a 'front-line type' so it is not surprising that the men of the Afrika Korps idolized him. The younger officers admired him especially, for his concern with their problems, his tactical ideas and his skill in navigating the desert. General von Esebeck has said, 'He had a smile and a joke for everyone who seemed to be doing his job . . . he had a very warm heart and more charm than anyone I have ever known.'

His charm and sensitivity, however, were not always so apparent to senior officers, with whom he could be impatient and, on occasion, brutal. He was in the habit of giving orders directly to subordinates instead of following the chain of command and would fly into a rage if his orders were questioned. He also tended to rely on his own judgment much more than his superiors would have wished — and the fact that he was so often right probably did not make the pill any easier to swallow. His relationship with his nominal Italian superiors was difficult, while he made no secret of the fact that he considered Halder and many others on the German General Staff fools who had no practical experience of war. Even Hitler, who liked him personally, would become angry at his 'veiled' reports to headquarters.

One of his most distressing habits was that of dashing around the battlefield, often taking his Chief of Staff with him and leaving no one with authority at headquarters. While his officers fretted in the rear, Rommel would be racing around the front.

In fact, his system of command was not haphazard. He and his commanders did not lead attacks from the front line out of a love for histrionic heroism, but because of their

Left: A German *Kübelwagen* seems to have got stuck in the sand.

Far left: Rommel and his Chief of Staff, Fritz Bayerlein, walking through the Libyan Desert.

Far left below: Rommel and other German officers relax.

Below: Unloading precious supplies for the Afrika Korps from a Ju 52.

knowledge of armor tactics and troop psychology. Time and again a tank crew who had halted their vehicle would hear a loud knocking on the side. Opening the turret they would discover Rommel's aide, Lieutenant Freiherr von Schlippenbach using a crowbar as a knocker, while the General, standing up in his car, shouted, 'On your way! Attacks don't succeed by standing still!' Though he took great personal risks, his uncanny instinct for what the enemy was going to do saved his life on several occasions.

His admirers will point out that this personal command was one of the main reasons why the Germans were consistently ahead in the speed of decision making and velocity of movement. Even his harshest critics will admit that he was extraordinarily brave, wonderful with his men, generous with praise and willing to admit when he was wrong. In sum, he was the best possible commander for the desert war at that time.

Since he was frequently outnumbered Rommel's main strategy was to keep his troops concentrated in the open and to use the vast desert for wide maneuvers to strike at the flanks or rear of the enemy, dividing their forces so that they could be more easily disposed of. The British frequently appeared to be cooperating with this strategy. As he commented to one captured brigadier near the end of Operation Crusader, 'What difference does it make if you have two tanks to my one when you spread them out and let me smash them in detail? You presented me with three brigades in succession.'

His main contribution to tank tactics was the use of a screen of self-propelled antitank guns to shield his Panzers as they advanced, withdrew or refuelled. Although he had several 105mm guns with tapered barrels that were highly effective against tanks, his most valuable weapon was the 80mm gun with high-velocity, armor-piercing shells that could inflict serious damage on both tanks and aircraft. Wherever possible artillery, rather than tanks, was used for defense, to help keep tank losses down. The tanks themselves – 22-ton Mark IIIs with 75mm guns – were superior to Allied tanks. German tank recovery operations, too,

were much better organized than those of the British.

Rommel used every ruse he could think of to deceive the enemy or keep them off balance. The first order he issued upon landing in Tripoli was for the construction of dummy tanks. Transport trucks – some with airplane engines mounted on the back – were often used to raise dust and create the illusion of a major army on the move. Captured vehicles were used not only for extra transport, but also to confuse the British.

Another innovation was the formation of 'combat groups.' These were about the size of a battalion and consisted of a tank company, a mixed company of antitank artillery and flak (75mm guns, 50 and 37mm antitank guns and 20mm flak) and a column of armored reconnaissance trucks and radio cars. These groups proved to be the ideal fighting unit for the desert and Rommel had several under his personal command, constantly flinging them into the hottest parts of the battle.

Mines were a major weapon for both sides. Probably in no other theater did they play such an important role. Air support was important too, for it could seriously damage the enemy's supplies and communications lines. However in the desert it had limited effectiveness against front-line

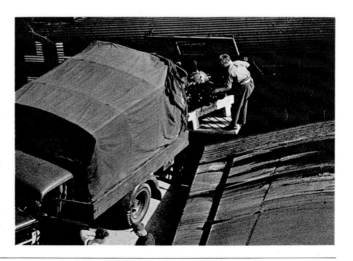

Far right: German soldiers climb aboard a tank during a lull in the fighting, 1941.

Bottom: The main square in Tobruk after it had fallen to the Germans, 21 June 1942.

Below: Rommel observes the fighting from a safe distance during the Crusader Battles at Sidi Azeiz, December 1941.

strength. It could hamper enemy movements but it could not check an advance on the ground.

The real battle in the desert war was for vital supplies, especially gasoline and water. The drivers of the supply trucks on both sides are the, largely unsung, heroes of the campaign. Doggedly they drove their three-ton trucks across burning sands when tires burst like balloons, through freezing nights and through sandstorms, where visibility was reduced to about a yard and lookouts had to lie along the front fender clinging to the radiator, to shout directions to the driver. In the Afrika Korps the motor-cyclist was the jack-of-all-trades, fetching ammunition, directing the artillery and carrying the wounded to dressing stations – all with a vehicle that could not have been more inappropriate for the terrain.

During 1941 and 1942 the campaigns in North Africa were inconclusive. In January 1941 the British took Tobruk, along with the rest of Cyrenaica, from the Italians. On 31 March Rommel, who had been told to submit plans for a counteroffensive by 20 April, sent out a reconnaissance raid in force. The British front collapsed in front of him and within 12 days, to everyone's surprise, he had recaptured Bardia, only a few miles from the Egyptian frontier.

He had recovered all the territory the Italians had lost except Tobruk, which he had under siege, and which the British were determined to hold at all costs. The British were embarrassed. Their prestige sank to a new low in the United States and the Soviet Union, and their future seemed dark indeed. More important, they found themselves with a very precarious hold on the eastern end of the Mediterranean, and it became obvious that now they were going to pay for their neglect of tanks and tank warfare between the wars. The British tanks were too slow and their guns too weak to compete with the German equipment.

While Rommel turned his energies to asking Hitler – in vain – for four more Panzer divisions, Churchill had no such reservations. North Africa was no sideshow to the British; in fact, it was to become the focus for the greatest single military effort of the Empire. On 12 May a large convoy survived the risky journey across the Mediterranean and delivered 238 tanks to General Wavell. Wavell, knowing that Rommel was short of supplies and fuel, launched an immediate offensive (Operation Brevity) to relieve Tobruk. However, instead of retreating, Rommel counterattacked and chased the Eighth Army back into Egypt.

With his tanks outnumbered four to one, Rommel had to come up with a way to keep the British off the coast road to Tobruk. He deployed his small forces to create a bottleneck where they could stall the next offensive until he had time to bring up his reserves. Meanwhile, he joined Admiral Raeder in pressing for a decisive offensive against Egypt and Suez – a concept which Hitler did not even begin to understand. The Führer continued to give Barbarossa (the campaign against the Soviet Union) top priority – one of his greatest blunders of the entire war.

The British offensive, Operation Battleaxe, came on 14 June. It was Wavell's last chance if he wanted to hang on to his Middle East command – and it failed. By the end of the day he had lost almost half his tanks in Rommel's trap.

True to form, the Germans counterattacked on 15 June. The result was another stalemate.

Churchill immediately removed Wavell and sent General Sir Claude Auchinleck as his replacement, giving him everything he had denied his predecessor – men, materiel, and time to prepare. By the time Auchinleck launched Operation Crusader on 18 November 1941 he had an unprecedented superiority in men and equipment – almost three times as many planes, twice as many tanks and tens of thousands more men. The British neutralized their numerical superiority by dividing their force up into several attack groups for speed and flexibility – which the wily Rommel simply dealt with one at a time.

The result was another draw. Though Rommel could blunt Crusader with his skillful flanking movements and unexpected counteroffensives, he was not strong enough to defeat it. With no prospect of reinforcements in the near future, he decided to conserve his forces and withdraw to safety in Tripolitania. The siege of Tobruk was abandoned on 7 December and the Axis forces moved back across Cyrenaica, their withdrawal punctuated by a series of sharp, savage battles that took a heavy toll among the (mostly Italian) infantry units.

On paper it looked like a major victory for the British. However they were exhausted and their supply lines were long and weak, while Rommel was sitting at his home base in strong, well-prepared defensive positions. At about the same time the Germans belatedly realized that Malta was the key to the North African supply routes and began immediate steps to neutralize it. In August 1941 some 35

Right: A Messerschmitt Bf 110 prepares for take off. The Bf 110 could not compete with Spitfires and Hurricanes and was used in the 'safer' theaters in North Africa, the Balkans and Russia.

Below: Sand is raised during shelling.

percent of Rommel's supplies and reinforcements had ended up on the ocean floor. In October about 63 percent had been lost and by November the flow was down to a trickle. However, in January 1942, after a concentrated effort by the Luftwaffe, not a single ton of supplies was lost.

Rommel had no thought of remaining on the defensive a moment longer than necessary, and the arrival of several dozen tanks on 5 January was enough to start him planning the next offensive – over the strenuous objections of his nominal superiors. Near the end of the month the worst weather in many years – alternating sandstorms and heavy rains – offered the perfect cover for a surprise attack. The Panzer Army Africa emerged from its defensive positions in one of Rommel's most brilliant displays of opportunism and agility.

Benghazi, with its large supply of fuel and ammunition, fell on 25 January but by 8 February the Axis impetus was

spent. Rommel was brought to a standstill at a line stretching from the coast just west of Gazala, south to the British-held oasis at Bir Hacheim. As both sides settled down to build up their resources, activity dwindled to a series of harassing operations as the British long-range desert groups and German frontier patrols stabbed at each other's lines.

Thus, in spring 1942, little had changed since the beginning of the year. The Eastern Front was still static after the long winter. In the Pacific the Japanese continued their string of victories – and continued to ignore Hitler's request for a strike against India. In North Africa Axis and Allied forces still faced each other at the Gazala Line, some 50 miles west of Tobruk.

The Gazala Line was a 40-mile-long stretch of minefields from the coast to Bir Hacheim. Minefields alone cannot stop tanks for long, so Auchinleck and Ritchie had studded the line with a series of static field dispositions, called 'boxes.' These strongpoints stood alone, like medieval castles. They were usually circular barbed-wire entanglements about two miles in diameter, enclosing a minefield with listening posts, machinegun nests and gaps covered by artillery. The garrison, about the size of a brigade, was supplied for long-term defense and had two jobs: to guard the minefield so that the enemy could not clear a path through it at leisure and, in the event of a breakthrough, to form pockets of resistance to harass his flanks, rear and communication supply lines. The armored and motorized units ranged around behind the boxes, ready to fall on the enemy forces while they were tied up at the strongpoints.

On paper it was a brilliant defense system, but it made the same mistake as Crusader, splitting up the forces into small groups. Rommel, by consolidating his forces, was able to trample through the defenses in one great sweep before the superior British numbers and newly arrived American Grant tanks began taking their toll.

For his Tobruk offensive Rommel fielded 561 tanks, though the only really effective ones were 280 German medium tanks – the 228 Italian 'sardine tins' and the German light tanks hardly counted. The British Eighth Army had some 850 tanks, including 167 Grants, with 75mm guns that out-shot everything on the battlefield except Rommel's 19 Mark III Specials. Rommel's 50mm, 75mm and 88mm artillery pieces were far superior to the little British two-pounders. In the air the German Luftflotte 2, with 542 aircraft, opposed the 604 planes of the Desert Air Force.

On 26 May Rommel made his move. At the unusual time of 1400 hours, General Crüwell led a magnificently staged feint on the Gazala Line. In the center was the 361st Regiment of the 90th Light Division (hot-headed, hard-fighting ex-Legionaries), on the flanks were Italian infantry divisions and behind them all raced the motorized units, recovery vehicles – anything with wheels – throwing up enough sand for two entire Panzer armies. Behind all this activity, at 2030 hours, Rommel gave the code word 'Venezia,' and five divisions moved due south, navigating by the stars, toward Bir Hacheim.

As dawn broke the Italian Ariete Division (20th) split off to engage the Free French garrison at Bir Hacheim, while the rest of the force – the two Afrika Korps armored divisions (15th and 21st, with the 90th Light and reconnaissance units on the left) – moved up behind the Gazala defenses toward the coast. Soon they encountered the 3rd Indian Motor Brigade Group, newly arrived from Egypt, and within minutes an alarmed report was speeding to Headquarters, 7th Armored Division, 'We have the whole bloody Afrika Korps in front of us!'

By midday on the 27th Rommel had good reason to congratulate himself. His force was making considerable progress against various British armored units, in fulfillment of his first principle of desert warfare: concentrate your own forces and split the enemy's, destroying them at different times. Later, led astray by faulty intelligence, he decided that he had disposed of the British armor and could safely attack the rear of the enemy infantry positions. It was a costly error. His divisional commanders, throwing caution to the winds, flung themselves into the attack without adequate artillery support. Suddenly they were attacked on all sides by British armored units – including the new Grants and American six-pounder guns. By late afternoon the armored units were encircled in the north and the 90th Light immobilized in the east, both cut off from their supplies and transport. Tactical cohesion broke down and the attack foundered in the desert south of Knightsbridge. By nightfall the 15th Panzers were completely out of gasoline and the 21st was only slightly better off.

All through the 28th Rommel worked desperately to get supplies up to his strike force, which was continually being harassed by British tanks and all the British air power in the area. Typically, he never once thought of withdrawal. During the night General Crüwell was ordered to try to break through the main Gazala Line to help, but before the operation could begin his plane was shot down and he was captured. The day was only saved from total failure by the Italians. The Ariete abandoned their attack on Bir Hacheim and made their way up to Bar el Harmat where they set up an effective antitank screen to cover the supply columns. Meanwhile, the Trieste and Pavia divisions had managed to clear preliminary gaps in the minefields from the west, where they were crossed by the Trigh el Abd and Trigh Capuzzo caravan routes. Unfortunately both gaps were covered by the 150th Brigade Group box at Got el Ualeb – of which Rommel was not yet aware.

Rommel spent all day on the 29th snaking supplies to his stranded armor, while the delayed attack on the main Gazala Line failed to break through the South African and 50th Division positions. The tank action that day around Knightsbridge, in blazing heat and blinding dust storms, was some of the fiercest so far in the campaign. At sundown both sides fell back exhausted and Rommel pulled his forces into a close defensive formation between the Sidra and Aslagh ridges – the area that came to be known as 'the Cauldron.'

On 30 May the General decided that his only hope lay in breaching the British minefields from the east, to regain contact with his main supply bases. Thus, on the 31st, he massed his artillery to protect the minefield gaps. Ritchie, thinking the strategic withdrawal was a retreat, cabled Cairo: 'Rommel is on the run!'

Rommel was not retreating but consolidating. For the next two days he tried in vain to knock out the 150th Brigade box. If the British had mounted a decisive armor attack immediately they would have had the Afrika Korps virtually at their mercy. Instead, they softened up the air offensive and launched a series of ill-coordinated jabs at Rommel's antitank guns. Those guns had been set up on the ridges in accordance with Rommel's second principle: everything possible must be done to protect one's own supply lines and to upset, or better still, cut the enemy's. Ariete and 21st Panzer were well dug in and resisted all attacks. By the time a major attack was launched on 5 June, it was too late. Got el Ualeb had been overrun, almost before Ritchie realized what was happening.

Rommel's brilliant improvisation had turned a near-fatal encirclement into a wedge driven deep into British territory – and once again the British had been defeated by their inability to move their forces rapidly, as a unit.

Next, Rommel turned his attention to Bir Hacheim – the southern key to the whole Gazala Line, and a serious

Left: Italian artillery shells the retreating British columns after the fall of Tobruk.

Right: Those who surrendered at Tobruk are taken into captivity, 22 June 1942.

threat to his flanks and rear. That battle lasted a week, and turned out to be the hardest fought so far in the campaign. While it was still going on, the tank commanders of the Afrika Korps in the north — by now used to Rommel's tactics — reacted to the British attack against the Ariete at Got el Ualeb on 5 June with a fierce counteroffensive on 6 June and another on the 7th. Though both these attacks were repelled, the British suffered heavy losses and it was clear that the balance was shifting in Rommel's favor.

Finally, on 10 June, the Free French outpost fell. It was an important event: not only could Rommel's supplies now move freely, but a large number of tanks, artillery pieces and planes were released for the next move — to Tobruk itself.

Immediately he gathered most of his force for the move north. On 13 June Ritchie sent a force to the southwest for an attack on the Axis flank, but Rommel, concentrating his heavy artillery, lured the British forces into an ambush. In the heaviest blow struck so far by either side, about 300 British tanks were lost, compared to about 70 for the Axis. The engagement marked the final turning point in the battle. By 15 June Rommel had cut the coast road just west of Tobruk, and the British were forced back to their third defensive line near El Adem and Rezegh. This stand did not last long: both El Adem and Rezegh were abandoned by 18 June.

In 1941 the Australians had held Tobruk for nine months, until Rommel's withdrawal to the west. That winter the Middle East Command in Cairo had decided that without naval support it would be impossible for the fortress ever to be held again in isolation. London had been informed and had — they thought — agreed, but on 15 June Auchinleck received a telegram from the Prime Minister, 'Leave as many troops in Tobruk as are necessary to hold the place for certain.' At length a compromise was reached. Tobruk was to be 'temporarily' invested while a new strike force was built up near the frontier.

The main part of the garrison was to be formed by the 1st South African Division with General Klopper — a major general of one month's standing — named commander of the stronghold. The port's physical defenses, while not in good shape, were hardly weaker than they had been in April 1941. The barbed wire, tank traps and well-placed gun emplacements were still there. Equipment was, if anything, a bit better. There were two partial medium-artillery regiments and the garrison was strong in field artillery. Although there were no antitank regiments, there were about 70 antitank guns, including 18 six-pounders. In antiaircraft guns — 18 37mms and a number of Bofors — the strength was about the same, and there were about 55 tanks. The strength of the garrison was also about the same — some 35,000 men. There was one important difference — and it was one which Klopper, none too sure of himself or his position, was ill-equipped to deal with. This time the defending troops were exhausted, their morale was low, and the camp was filled with a feeling of insecurity and impermanence.

As Tobruk prepared for battle the South Africans took up their positions along the northern coast and the western and southern perimeter from the sea to the El Adem road. East from there were the 2nd Camerons, 2/5th Mahrattas and 2/7th Gurkhas. Near the Palestrino Ridge in the center were the 201st Brigade headquarters, the 3rd Coldsteam, and the Sherwood Foresters. Meanwhile, the rest of the Eighth Army made their way toward the defenses at the Egyptian frontier.

As usual, Rommel had devised a ruse for capturing Tobruk. Only his infantry approached the western perimeter, while his mobile forces swept on past, to give the impression that he was heading straight for the border as he had done the year before — and sending messages in clear to reinforce the illusion. Just before Bardia he and the 90th Light Division turned back to join the Afrika Korps assault divisions and the XX Italian Motorized Corps, who had been waiting southeast of the city. He was using the same plan he had intended for 23 November 1941.

Rommel's zero hour was 0520 on 20 June. As the first rays of sunlight began to creep over the desert the long black lines of tanks, trucks and infantry slowly started to move forward. From far away there came a faint drone. As it grew louder small black dots appeared on the horizon which, as they drew nearer, resolved themselves into a wave of Stukas and Ju 88s. Every airworthy Axis plane in North Africa had been pressed into service for the battle. As the heavy artillery began to fire, the planes released their bombs and quickly got out of the way of the next wave, operating a shuttle service between the defense perimeter and El Adem airfield, 10 miles away. They pounded open a gap 600 yards wide. Behind them, under cover of the artillery barrage and half-hidden by smoke and dust, German and Italian sappers raced forward to lift the mines and bridge the tank traps, and tanks and infantry raced through the gaps. As they moved forward they lit red, green and purple flares and the Stukas dropped their bombs just ahead of the advancing, multicolored smoke screen while the other planes and the artillery blasted the enemy's rear with bombs and shells.

The timing of the entire operation was perfect. Panzer Army Africa might well have been on maneuvers. The first shock troops broke into the fortress from the southeast. A second group breached the defenses in the south, along the El Adem road, soon after. As tanks poured into the city they fanned out and headed for the harbor, while para-chutists were dropped behind the lines to disorganize the defenses and protect the supply dumps from demolition.

Inside Tobruk the situation was chaotic. General Klopper — his headquarters bombed out, his radio and telephone wrecked and his code book destroyed, lost the last vestige of control. Disconsolately he and his staff watched the Panzers race past their headquarters on their way to capture the fuel dumps in the harbor. Some British troops broke out to the east. Others fought grimly on, while still others, like the South Africans in the west and south-west, hardly realized anything was happening until the 90th Light came up on their rear.

By dawn on 21 June Tobruk was a pile of ruins. The streets were a maze of rubble and in the harbor the masts and funnels of sunken ships rose pathetically from the water. General Klopper gave his compass and staff car to seven young men from the South African 6th Brigade who were determined to escape, saying, 'I wish I was coming with you.'

A few hours later a small party of officers set off in a truck, a little white flag fluttering over the hood, and at 0940 on the Via Balbo Klopper officially turned the city over to Rommel. Soon after, a large white flag was hoisted over 6th Brigade Headquarters by South African native drivers.

The signal to surrender created even more confusion. Some units never got it. Others, like the 3rd Coldstream, decided to ignore it and try to escape. The Cameron Highlanders, along with the remnants of some of the Indian brigades, held out for more than 24 hours — surrendering only after being told that if they did not the Germans would concentrate every piece of artillery in Tobruk on their

Left: British prepare to reenter the city following the German withdrawal after the Battle of El Alamein.

Left center: Tobruk harbor in flames.

Below: Rommel with General Bismarck in the summer of 1942.

Far left bottom: British prisoners waiting to go into camps after the fall of Tobruk.

position. Finally giving in, they marched down to the prisoner of war cage in parade formation, with the pipes skirling 'The March of the Cameron Men.' As they approached every man along the way – prisoner and German sentry alike – snapped to attention.

After two years in British hands Tobruk had fallen in two days – and despite Rommel's anger at the extent of the destruction effected by British demolition squads on vehicle parks and fuel dumps, he still had captured enough to carry him on his drive to Egypt. The fall of Tobruk came as a shattering blow to the British public (as Churchill had known it would), as well as to the Australians and South Africans. General Klopper came in for most of the criticism, but he was not entirely to blame. The decision to invest Tobruk at all had been, in General Bayerlein's phrase, 'a fatal decision.' Though a more experienced general might have made more progress toward pulling the garrison into shape in time, there was also confusion among the British High Command. For example, Auchinleck realized full well that Rommel was almost certain to stick to his original plan and attack from the southeast. When Ritchie flew into Tobruk on 16 June to confer with the defenders, he warned Klopper to pay special attention to the western perimeter.

On the Axis side there was great enthusiasm. Mussolini, hitherto anxious to move slowly and consolidate positions, flew to North Africa with a white horse to ride when he entered Cairo at the head of his troops. Hitler was ecstatic, calling the victory an 'historic turning point' of 'decisive import' for the whole war. On 22 June Rommel received a message from the Führer informing him that at the age of 49 he had just been appointed Germany's youngest Field Marshal. He celebrated that night with canned pineapple and a small glass of whisky, but after dinner he wrote his wife, 'Hitler has made me a Field Marshal. I would much rather he had given me one more division.' Still, he was in unusually good spirits – it was the high point of his career as well as for the North African campaign.

Typically, he saw it not as an end, but as the springboard to a new Egyptian campaign. True to his cardinal rule – never give the enemy a breathing space – he did not celebrate too long. The next day his Order of the Day read, 'Soldiers of the Panzer Army Africa! Now we must utterly destroy the enemy! During the coming days I shall be making great demands upon you once more, so that we may reach our goal.' Gathering the tired but triumphant Afrika Korps together he set off in pursuit of the Eighth Army and that ultimate goal – the Nile.

He would never get there. Hitler, by discontinuing the attack on Malta and refusing to send Rommel adequate supplies, would make defeat in the desert inevitable. Later, the Field Marshal would find himself presiding over another fiasco – the defense of Normandy – and still later would come involvement in the plot against Hitler and, eventually, suicide.

All this was in the future; in June 1942 the Desert Fox was as he is still best remembered – dashing, resourceful and brave, racing across the desert with the tanks of the Afrika Korps, heading for the pyramids of Egypt.

MONTGOMERY
AT ALAMEIN 1942

In the last week of June 1942 the entire British position in the Middle East seemed to be on the verge of collapse. The battered Eighth Army was in retreat, racing for the Egyptian frontier before, beside, and sometimes even behind Rommel's victorious *Panzerarmee Afrika*. The loss of some 80,000 men since 26 May and the wreckage of two armored corps testified to the triumph of German professionalism over superior numbers. The victory seemed so complete that Rommel, even though he had orders to halt on the frontier and await the capture of Malta, was given the go ahead to continue the chase and take advantage of the panic and resulting disorganization of the British Army.

On 25 June the Commander in Chief for the Middle East, General Sir Claude Auchinleck, flew to Mersa Matruh from Cairo to take over personal command of the Eighth Army from General Ritchie and begin a planned, more orderly withdrawal to the defenses at El Alamein. By 30 June this had been accomplished and the two armies had begun arranging themselves, with Auchinleck hurriedly organizing the defensive positions for a last-ditch stand while Rommel pulled his exhausted troops together for another major effort. If the seemingly indestructible Afrika Korps could overcome this obstacle there would be little to stand in their way as they drove toward the Nile and the Suez Canal. Less than a hundred miles away, in Alexandria, papers were destroyed and government offices evacuated with a speed the Desert Fox himself would have envied, while the Royal Navy hurriedly sailed out of the harbor.

Waiting in the wings was another actor − a complex, often abrasive character who would soon achieve a reputation in the desert that would equal Rommel's and receive the impressive title, Field Marshal the Viscount Montgomery of Alamein, KG. In July 1942, of course, he was simply Major General Bernard Law Montgomery, a largely unknown career soldier in the Home Army, with more than a month to go before his first appearance on the desert stage.

Montgomery came from a large family (the fourth of nine children) that had no military tradition. Born in 1887 in Moville, County Donegal where his father was an Anglican bishop, he lived in Ireland for two years before the family was moved to Tasmania, Australia. From all accounts, including his own, he had a very unhappy childhood which he describes as 'a series of fierce battles, from which my mother invariably emerged the victor.' He was, again in his own words, 'a dreadful little boy' − a loner, in constant rebellion against an unusually strict, methodical mother, given to rudeness, bullying and hysterics.

In 1902 the Montgomerys returned to England, and young Bernard became a day pupil at St Paul's School where he asked to be enrolled in the 'army class.' This involved no commitment to the military; the 'army class' was simply designed for those more inclined to practical than academic pursuits. His mother's overreaction to the news decided him − from that moment on he was determined to be a soldier. At home he remained surly and morose, but at school he was energetic, good at cricket and other games (where his agility and stamina earned him the nickname 'Monkey'), and a confident, effective leader. He had no hobbies, no intellectual interests, and very little scholastic ability but he did have a driving ambition.

General Bernard Law Montgomery with on his right General Brian Horrocks.

At the age of 19 − in January 1907 − he entered the Royal Military College at Sandhurst. The year began well and after six weeks he was among the few outstanding cadets promoted to lance corporal. The honor gave him an overinflated sense of power and he soon became the ringleader of a gang that persecuted other cadets. Following an unfortunate episode in which Montgomery set fire to someone's shirt tails, resulting in severe burns, he was demoted to gentleman cadet (the lowest possible rank) and was not allowed to graduate with the rest of his class. This reverse finally gave him the impetus he needed to settle down and work and for the first time he began to demonstrate the concentration on and devotion to minutiae, the passion for precise detail, that was to play such a large part in his future professional life.

On leaving Sandhurst he joined the Warwickshires − primarily because they had a good reputation but also because he liked their cap badge. He was anything but a typical officer − he was not good on a horse, had no military connections or social graces, and showed only intermittent respect for authority.

In 1913 back in England after a tour of duty in India, the young officer began for the first time a systematic study of the art of war. However, within three weeks after World War I began he was in France learning about war on a much more practical level, at the first battle of Ypres. Badly wounded in this, his first major action, he was sent back to England, promoted to captain, and awarded the DSO − one of the highest honors the British Army can bestow (usually reserved for majors and above) for sustained gallantry in the face of the enemy. For a subaltern to win it was very rare, and generally meant that he had just missed the Victoria Cross.

During the 1920s and 1930s he began to stand out as a radical crusader for military efficiency − a quality badly needed in the British Army at the time. In 1927 he married Betty Carver, a widow with two sons. The next year their son David was born and Montgomery's life was completely changed. He and his wife were inseparable and she used affection and gentle mockery to soften his rough edges. Her death, only ten years later, 'utterly defeated' him for the first time in his life. From that time he built a wall around himself which was impenetrable and he began living only for his work.

By 1938 he was established in his first command, with the 8th Infantry Division in Palestine, where the flood of Jews fleeing Nazi persecution in Europe had led to a state of emergency among the native Arab inhabitants. This grounding in Palestine was useful. He was noted for his insistence on methodical operations from a firm base (though he was fighting guerrillas), his egotistical view of his troops and their operations, and his ability to make sure that 'his' achievements were known and recognized in the proper quarters. He was also ruthless with the incompetent or inefficient.

When World War II began Montgomery went to France with the British Expeditionary Force, in command of the 3rd Division. With his usual energy he immediately began strenuously training his men, instilling a professional attitude toward war that helped immeasurably in maintaining order during the British retreat to and evacuation from Dunkirk. At this time too he made a great impression on his corps commander, Alan Brooke – which was to be of great value to him in his future career.

After Dunkirk he was stationed in England, climbing the ladder of promotion fairly rapidly, despite his abrasive personality and his unfortunate habit of displaying an insolence that approached insubordination toward officers he did not respect (a group which included General Auchinleck). By 1941 he was a Lieutenant General in charge of the South Eastern Army – England's main anti-invasion force, the post he still had at the beginning of July 1942.

Meanwhile, in Egypt, Auchinleck and the Eighth Army were racing against time to prepare for Rommel's arrival. The area chosen for their final defense was a narrow neck of land, about 40 miles wide, between El Alamein on the Mediterranean and the Qattara Depression in the south. The northern half of the passage was featureless, so much so that almost imperceptible rises in the ground were to assume great tactical significance in the months that followed. South of the long, low rise called the Miteirya Ridge and the rocky, austere Ruweisat Ridge came the smooth swelling of Alam Nayil, with the Alam Halfa ridge some 14 miles to the east. These were followed by a series of abrupt escarpments. Further south the going got even worse as the rocks disappeared in a stretch of eroded channels and soft sand – 'devil's country' that continued to the edge of the great Qattara Depression and the steep cone of Mt Himeimat, which rose to almost 700 feet, dominating the landscape like a great pyramid.

Auchinleck had chosen well. If they were properly disposed, there was no way the defenders' flanks could be turned in that narrow passage, especially since the rough going in the south would drastically hinder the movement of Rommel's armor. It was just as well, for the British had their backs against the wall. With such a small area for maneuver, the loss of even a little territory could be vital in the defense of Egypt. Rommel, on the other hand, could afford to lose much more ground without really damaging his position. Similarly, in the race for supplies and reinforcements, gaining a slight advantage would not materially affect Britain's position. Even if they could push Rommel back to the border and ease some of the pressure on Alexandria, it would not be enough for them to destroy him

altogether. For the Axis, though, even a small increase in men and materiel might be enough to allow Rommel to make a temporary breakthrough, which could be all he needed to clear the way for his dash to the Nile.

So, Auchinleck threw everything he could muster into the breach at El Alamein. It was just enough. Time and again during July Rommel sent his tired troops against the British line only to see them thrown back. The balance of forces was too even to allow either side to launch a successful counteroffensive.

Meanwhile, behind the lines, the race for supplies went on. Britain had by far the longer and more dangerous supply route, but thanks to President Roosevelt a stream of men and equipment – including American tanks and planes – flowed steadily into Alexandria. Rommel, for his part, could obtain little from a country already strained to its limits by the demands of the Russian campaign. In air power, he could not match the Desert Air Force, now supplemented by American forces. Though possession of the port of Tobruk helped ease his supply lines it was attacked almost nightly. His convoys, too, were under constant bombardment by planes and submarines, as German strength was diverted from Malta to the Eastern Front.

Once again, the attitudes of the Axis and Allies toward the North African campaign were to be the deciding factor. Hitler never really appreciated its significance, always putting it second to his Napoleonic dreams of conquest in Europe. Even before Italy entered the war in June 1940, the Mediterranean and the Balkans had played a major role in British strategic planning. After America entered the conflict in December 1941, it was agreed at the Acadia Conference that one of the Allies' primary aims must be to 'tighten the ring' around Germany – and the southern section of that ring ran along the North African coast.

Thus, Auchinleck was under considerable pressure to do more than fight a holding action. Churchill, not the most patient man at the best of times, was having political difficulties at home and was anxious for a spectacular victory to bolster his fading popularity. In addition 'the Auk,' as the Commander in Chief for the entire Middle East, could not give his full attention to affairs in Egypt, and was frequently distracted by developments in Iraq, Syria and elsewhere. In short, his command was too large and complex and there was too much expected of him in too short a time – a fact Churchill subsequently admitted when it was too late.

There were, however, some severe problems within the Eighth Army, and Churchill fastened on them eagerly. There were indications that Auchinleck's command organization was not working harmoniously or effectively, and he seemed reluctant to change it in any way. Furthermore, morale was at a new low. The ups and downs of the desert war had sapped the battle-hardened veterans' confidence in their ability to finally defeat the Afrika Korps. The uneasy stalemate in July, with its frequent orders for attacks that turned out to be futile, accompanied by unfortunate, if necessary, precautionary plans for withdrawal, further weakened morale.

Churchill decided that only a drastic change could restore the Eighth Army's confidence. Early in August he visited Cairo with General Sir Alan Brooke (now Chief of the Imperial General Staff) and after a whirlwind tour of several Eighth Army units the two concluded that 'a new start and vehement action were needed to animate the vast but baffled and somewhat unhinged organization.' The Prime Minister's temper was not improved on this visit by Auchinleck who, lacking Montgomery's facility for public relations, made few provisions for his comfort or entertainment and left him more or less to his own devices.

Churchill's plan embodied changes in both organization and personnel. On the organizational side, Persia and Iraq would retain the name 'Middle East Command' while Libya, Egypt, East Africa, Palestine, and Syria would be detached to form the 'Near East Command.'

Within this new organization, he proposed, Auchinleck would take over the Middle East, with communication lines running back to India. For the Near East he had a new team: General Sir Harold Alexander would be installed as Commander in Chief, headquartered in Cairo; Brigadier 'Strafer' Gott would take over as commander of the Eighth Army (though Gott himself felt that he was too tired and lacking in new ideas to handle the job effectively); and Brooke's protégé, Montgomery, would be named British Task Force Commander for Operation Torch (the Allied landing in North Africa, scheduled for early November). The day after the decision was made, the plane in which Gott was returning to Cairo was shot down and the general

killed. Thus two unknown Luftwaffe fighter pilots can take credit for bringing together what was to become the winning British command team. Montgomery was given Gott's job as Commander, Eighth Army, while Lieutenant General Kenneth Anderson took his place with General Eisenhower.

Alexander – considered by many to be the best strategical brain in the Empire – was the ideal man for the labyrinthine politico-military atmosphere of wartime Cairo. He had a wealth of battle experience, having participated in most of the major battles of World War I and in many minor operations from the Baltic to India's Northwest Frontier; from this he had developed not only sound military judgment, but also a real knowledge of British and Indian soldiers that helped him avoid psychological mistakes when dealing with them. Above all, he was an ideal supervisor – good at decentralization and knowing not only how much freedom to give his subordinates, but also when and how to step in if things were going wrong. He was a perfect superior officer for Montgomery – who was a strong, demanding and extraordinarily difficult subordinate.

The new commander of the Eighth Army stood out in

From left to right: Mr Anthony Eden, General Brooke, Air Chief Marshal Tedder, Admiral Cunningham, General Alexander, General Marshall, General Eisenhower and Montgomery with Winston Churchill in the center.

god-like figure. In addition, many of his superiors considered him to be a first-class leader who took no risks and was the epitome of the dedicated professional. This professionalism was one of his best qualities – along with his ability to instill it in the men under his command. He had the great gift of being able to explain the most complicated plan so that it appeared simple and when he had finished a briefing everyone present knew exactly what he had to do – and more importantly why he had to do it and how his job fitted into the overall operation. In fact, Montgomery had more flair than the rather diffident Alexander when it came to talking to men and officers in public. His high-pitched rasping voice could hold an audience spellbound.

In his work, Montgomery was devoted to precision, caution and control. His plans – which usually relied more on overwhelming force than on skillful maneuvering – left nothing to chance. Most of his experience had been gained in the staff room rather than on the battlefield, and where Alexander deplored useless loss of life for humanitarian reasons, Montgomery hated it because it reflected poor organization.

Though he could with justice claim that he never lost a battle, he often made disastrous miscalculations. Some of these stemmed from his naturally unpredictable, eccentric state of mind, but also especially since the death of his wife, the world outside his work had become shadowy and unreal. This narrow view often hampered his decision-making capability. As will be seen later, the battle of Alamein is a good example of a certain victory that was very nearly turned into defeat.

Upon their arrival, the new command team faced three major challenges: to improve the Eighth Army's morale; defeat Rommel's next attack, which intelligence sources predicted for 26 August; and prepare their own offensive (codenamed Operation Lightfoot), which was to be co-ordinated with Operation Torch.

Montgomery immediately plunged into the work of training and reorganizing the worn-out army, directing all his energies toward making it an efficient, professional and

distinct contrast to his urbane superior officer. He was not a likeable character – still less the sort of 'decent chap' so highly prized by the upper echelons of the British army. His conspicuous lack of some of the more civilized virtues led many of his contemporaries to see him as a vain, opinionated showoff, an overrated general and a thoroughly unpleasant human being; even Churchill once referred to him as 'a little man on the make.'

To many of the men who served in the ranks in the desert or, later, in the Normandy landings he was an almost

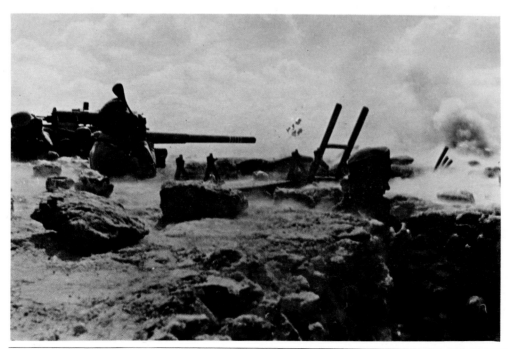

Above left: English prisoners of war near El Alamein, 18 June 1942.

Left: A German 88mm antiaircraft gun bombarding British tanks. The 88mm gun ended the Desert supremacy of the Matilda tank.

Above right: German soldiers move forward to El Alamein in July 1942.

Right: Members of the Afrika Korps eat their meager rations during the summer of 1942.

above all tidy organization. His first move was to establish communications with all levels of the army, so that when the time came each of the tens of thousands of soldiers would not only know what to do, but would have the incentive to do it.

He was the first British general consciously to project an 'image' to his public. Every unit was visited, and as the general's cold gaze balefully fell on the idle or incompetent, as the rasping voice explained, questioned, or ordered, he was striving to leave an impression on every man's mind. Even his studied informality of dress and his famous hats (an Australian slouch hat carrying all the 9th Australian Division badges or a black Tank Corps beret) were carefully calculated to make the 'new boy' part of the desert world as soon as possible. Pressmen and photographers appeared in unprecedented numbers and the Army public relations staff began working overtime.

In addition to his famous 'no bellyaching' order, Montgomery stressed in his talks to the troops that there were to be no plans for withdrawal, and that in the future there would be fewer risks, no short cuts and – most important – no more failure. The organizational changes he announced included training the X Corps, under General Lumsden, as a mobile 'corps de chasse' to rival the Afrika Korps, and the relocation of Eighth Army Headquarters from the eastern end of Ruweisat Ridge to the seashore at Burg el Arab – for closer cooperation with the Desert Air Force and for greater comfort. This firm line was well received. Some of the men were too disillusioned to accept this unknown general, who had just arrived from England with his 'knees still pink,' at face value, but most were at least content to give him the benefit of the doubt.

The next problem, preparing for Rommel's expected attack in August, was easier to solve. Soon after his arrival Montgomery had several conversations with Auchinleck himself, with General Ramsden (commander of the XXX Corps), and with Brigadier de Guingand (Auchinleck's Brigadier General Staff) – all of whom described their plans for the defense of the British position. In talks with Churchill and Brooke on 19 August, these became Montgomery's plans – but in fact the prelude to Alamein, the battle of Alam Halfa, was eventually to be fought on a plan constructed by General Dorman-Smith (first Auchinleck's principal Operations Officer and then, until Montgomery's arrival, Deputy Chief of Staff) and approved and initiated by Auchinleck, and utilizing fixed defenses which had for the most part been dug before he ever left England.

By the end of August Rommel was still at a disadvantage, despite the reinforcements that had arrived earlier in the month. He still had only 200 German tanks with guns, and was so short of fuel that, though he still planned to sweep around the southern flank, he had to then use a much shorter turning radius than he would have liked. The British, by contrast, had 713 tanks in the forward area (including 164 heavy Grants). All infantry and artillery divisions now had 6-pounder antitank guns, and the Desert Air Force had achieved complete control of the skies over Alamein. In addition, Rommel was so ill that he could not get out of his truck. He was not only under constant medical supervision but had a replacement ready on the spot at all times. Gause, his Chief of Staff, was also sick – none of which helped morale in Axis army.

Nevertheless, after nightfall on 30 August, Rommel's four veteran divisions – the Afrika Korps and the Italian XX Corps – began to work their way through the British minefields. The barriers were thicker than they had expected, so that as dawn broke on 31 August they were only just emerging instead of being already in position in front of Alam Halfa Ridge.

Almost from the beginning it was obvious to Rommel that the offensive would not succeed. In fact, he considered a withdrawal at 0800 hours on 31 August but he allowed himself to be dissuaded by General Bayerlein. The only doubt in Montgomery's mind was whether Axis troops really were committed to an attack from the south. By 1100 hours it was clear that this was the case, and British forces were rearranged accordingly. At 1300 the Panzer Army stopped to refuel and then, instead of swinging out to the center and eastern end of Alam Halfa in an encircling movement, they turned sharply north and drove straight for the heavily defended western end – a move dictated by the shortage of fuel and the time they had lost in the minefields.

The attack stalled and that evening Allied aircraft inflicted heavy damage on both equipment and personnel (for the first time US pilots in Liberators, Mitchells, and Kittyhawks were flying alongside the RAF). The next night, 1–2 September, saw more of the same. By dawn – battered and almost completely out of fuel – the Afrika Korps began to edge away to the west.

At this point Montgomery, by launching a counter-offensive across Rommel's communication lines, could probably have encircled all the Axis armor and finished the Battle of Alamein before it ever began. With his usual desire to avoid any risk of failure and his unwillingness to deviate from a set schedule, he declined pressing the issue. By the night of 3–4 September the opportunity had passed and the Panzer Army was executing another of its skillful withdrawals. On 6 September they were out of danger, and in addition had established a bridgehead on the eastern edge of the British minefields, astride Mt Hememat.

In later years Montgomery was to claim credit for devising the defensive tactics that prevented British armor from being destroyed piecemeal as in previous engagements. However, according to General Renton, Gott (ordered before his death to prepare a detailed defense against the

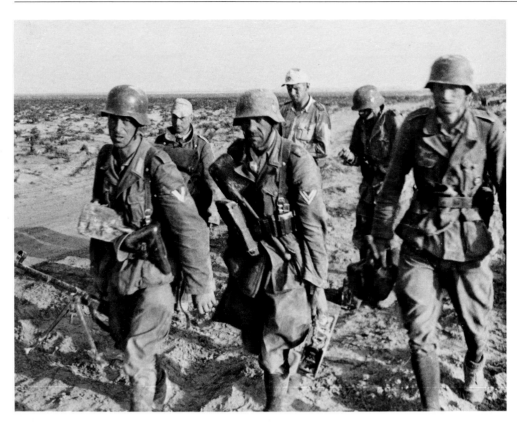

Left: Soldiers of the Afrika Korps advance during the first Battle of El Alamein.

Left below: Members of the Afrika Korps fry some eggs, which they probably made up from captured British rations.

Left bottom: An early morning wash.

Far left below: Grant tanks of the 22nd Armored Brigade advance to the front line in column, south of El Alamein.

German attack) had never intended 'unleashing the armor.' Despite this, and despite the missed opportunity, Alam Halfa was a model defensive battle that reflects great credit on both the planners and the field generals (Montgomery and Gott's replacement, Horrocks) who executed those plans.

Characteristically, Churchill wanted to follow up Alam Halfa with an immediate offensive in mid-September. Equally characteristically, Montgomery refused, determined to do nothing until the odds were overwhelmingly in his favor. Eventually the Prime Minister gave in, but he did so with bad grace. He insisted that the Eighth Army must have a decisive victory over Rommel before Operation Torch was launched on 8 November.

Much has been written about whether or not the battle of Alamein was really necessary. From a strictly military point of view, it probably need not have been fought at all. Rommel would have had to withdraw as soon as Operation Torch began, and would have found himself sandwiched between two forces almost immediately. There were several political reasons for a strong British offensive: to dispel any feeling in the United States that American boys were being killed to salvage British prestige in an obscure colonial backwater; to influence the ambiguous French population in Morocco and Algeria; and to help Churchill quell the atmosphere of distrust that marked his dealings with Stalin.

Thus, throughout September and October, Allied naval and merchant vessels delivered supplies and reinforcements to Egypt. Workshops hummed, supply depots swelled and spread and camps were crowded with pale-skinned soldiers.

Rommel knew that a major attack was imminent, but did not have enough transport to withdraw to a better position at Fuka. All he could do was dig in and make his positions as strong as possible. In the weeks before he went on sick leave his Italian and German sappers laid half a million mines across the entire front, in a honeycomb pattern. Within the cells of the pattern they planted 'Devil's Gardens' — patches of mines and any other booby traps they could evise, such as harmless-looking wooden poles attached to huge charges of explosives. They employed other tricks too — like burying metal rods which would register on metal detectors, to camouflage the gaps in the minefields. One group actually followed a British sweeping squad, laying mines behind them, so that the

reconnaissance group that came later found a nasty surprise waiting. Another group crept into British minefields and removed detonators, then reburied the harmless mines. (Needless to say, the British sappers were engaged in many similar activities.)

German and Italian infantry units were strung out all along this line. The biggest problem to be faced, however, was deployment of the armor. There was no way Rommel could obey his own cardinal principle and consolidate the armor because he did not have enough fuel to then move it effectively. In addition it was too vulnerable to Allied air attack when it was on the move. Out of necessity, then, he placed his 15th Panzer and Littorio Divisions in the north, where they formed into three mixed groups; 21st Panzer and Ariete did the same in the south. His only reserves, 90th Light and Trieste, guarded the coast at El Daba against an amphibious landing. On 22 September, having done all he could to secure his position, Rommel finally left for Germany to have his swollen liver and constantly inflamed throat seen to.

By the end of September 1942 Montgomery had 195,000 men to Rommel's 54,000 Italians and 50,000 Germans.

A British 25-pounder fires at enemy positions near El Alamein in the early morning, September 1942.

He had 1029 medium tanks to the Germans' 496, 1451 antitank guns as opposed to 800 (of which some 85 were the impressive 88s) and 908 pieces of field and medium artillery against the Panzer Army's 500. All this was in addition to virtually unlimited supplies of ammunition, fuel and other stores.

Most welcome of all the new weapons were 300 Sherman tanks – products of American tank expertise combined with

British battle experience. With their powerful 75mm guns, they were a match for anything the Germans could field. Almost as valuable were the 'Priests' – 105mm self-propelled guns, on Grant tank chasses, with a flashless charge to make them harder to locate. British antitank guns – the 6-pounders – were good weapons, but had one defect. Most of them were carried on Austin trucks, called 'portees,' with high, bulky silhouettes that made them horribly conspicuous against the desert horizon.

For their part, in addition to the Panzer Mark IIIs and IVs, the Axis forces had the most formidable piece of artillery in the desert – the famous 88, with its 21-pound armor-piercing shot that could kill an enemy tank at 3000 yards. One of these guns could hold off an entire tank squadron for some time. The German infantry was armed with the Spandau, described as a 'vicious' machine gun with an intimidating sound like a racing car revving up.

Throughout September and the beginning of October, Montgomery collected more supplies, trained his army and laid his plans with his usual supreme confidence. Starting with Auchinleck's general concept of a breakthrough in the northern sector of the line (previously both sides had always swung first south, then north toward the coast in an attempt to encircle and trap their opponents), he developed his own system of organization and tactics. His would be a methodical, controlled operation; he still did not have enough confidence in the level of training throughout the army to give his forces much independence. In this he was probably justified. During their years in the desert the veterans of the Panzer Army had come to understand each other so well that they fought as a team almost by instinct. The British army, on the other hand, had always been a much more unwieldy, less homogeneous group and could not achieve that instinctive cooperation.

Just two weeks before Operation Lightfoot was scheduled to begin, Montgomery radically changed his plan of attack. Contrary to all the tenets of desert warfare, which held that armor should be destroyed first (at which the infantry would collapse almost of its own accord) he decided to have his armored divisions simply hold off the Axis tanks while the British infantry units destroyed their opponents in the main defensive system.

Four infantry divisions of the XXX Corps were to open two gaps through the German minefields: one in the north toward Kidney Ridge and another in the south over Miteirya Ridge. Right behind them would come the three armored divisions of X Corps, who would pass through the gaps and establish Report Line 'Pierson,' some two miles beyond the infantry's goal, 'Oxalic.' There they would set up defensive positions until the Axis infantry had crumbled, then chase and cut off the remnants of the Panzer Army. If the infantry had not reached Oxalic by dawn of the first day, the tanks would have to fight their own way out to Pierson.

Meanwhile, XIII Corps and 7th Armored Division would mount a diversionary attack in the south to pin down the 21st Panzer/Ariete groups. Other features of the long, elaborate campaign to deceive the Axis about the real focus of the attack included fake radio traffic and troop movements, and the building of a dummy pipeline. Even though General Stumme (who had assumed command on Rommel's departure) incorrectly believed that the attack would take place in the south, he was never in any doubt about the actual timing of the offensive, despite all the British efforts to hint at a late-November date.

As D-Day drew nearer, confidence in the British command – which had been noticeably shaky – began to improve. Their unprecedented superiority in men and materiel, their complete control of the air, and the efficiency of their intelligence operations made the outcome apparently certain.

By contrast the axis forces were in an unhappy position – short of food, water, fuel and supplies. To make matters worse, the German High Command appeared to have no conception of the gravity of the situation. On 23 October – D-Day – a visiting staff officer told Stumme that in OKW's opinion there was no danger of a British offensive in the near future.

But that evening, as the full moon rose, 882 guns opened fire, in Montgomery's words, 'like one battery' along the 38-mile front. The German guns, under orders to conserve ammunition, remained silent. Twenty minutes later the barrage lifted and more than 70,000 British soldiers and 600 tanks moved out toward the 12,000 men

Left: German troops in full retreat following the defeat at El Alamein, November 1942.

Below: Italian infantry during the battle at El Alamein in November 1942.

Below left: A 5.5 Range gun is fired raising a cloud of dust round the gunners' feet at El Alamein in November 1942.

of the Italian Trento and German 164th Infantry divisions.

Most of the carefully laid traps in the Devil's Gardens had been destroyed by the artillery barrage. Getting through the gaps should have been a simple process. However there were too many men and too much equipment packed into the narrow lanes. The infantry, with no room to fight, could not get to the western edge of the minefields. The sappers could not clear lanes for the armor and the tanks piled behind everyone where they attracted a good deal of enemy fire. Soon the area looked to General Carver like a 'badly organized car park at an immense race meeting held in a dust bowl' and into the immobile mass deadly and accurate fire continued to pour from the Axis guns. The cumbersome crowding together of infantry and armor had turned out to be a major blunder.

The problem was accentuated by the gulf of sectional pride and professional suspicion that traditionally separated infantry and armored forces in the British army. The German services achieved close cooperation naturally; their similar training and all their experience were geared toward establishing a harmonious working relationship. As Corelli Barnett has pointed out, asking the British services to do the same was, 'like asking an estranged man and wife to make love.'

All through the 24th the attack continued. The Littorio and 15th Panzer Division had moved in to form a containing line which, by fighting desperately, they managed to hold through the thunder of the artillery and the rain of Allied bombs. The X Corps (Montgomery's *corps de chasse*), with orders to fight its way through if necessary, was still 1000 yards from its objective at the western end of the northern gap. At the southern gap, the armor commanders (Gatehouse and Lumsden) were understandably reluctant to send their tanks over the crest of Miteirya Ridge and down through uncharted minefields under heavy German fire. Montgomery, however, insisted that the objectives must be met. One regiment, the Staffordshire Yeomanry, tried to get through — and lost all but 15 of its tanks. Finally, at dawn on the 25th, the British armor had

either to withdraw back behind the ridge or risk being caught without cover within range of the powerful 88s. In the southern sector of the front the diversionary attack had gone astray, leaving the 7th Armored Division and 44th Division stranded in the German minefields. Already the offensive seemed poised on the brink of failure.

Early on the 25th Rommel was recalled from his sick bed and boarded a plane at Wiener Neustadt. That evening he landed at El Daba and immediately set off for the front. The report he received next morning from General Ritter von Thoma was anything but encouraging, despite the fact that his men were still managing to hold the British off. General Stumme – a courageous soldier, but one who lacked Rommel's desert experience, instinct and luck – had been killed in the front line. Most of the Devil's Gardens had been destroyed by artillery fire. The men were becoming demoralized and much equipment had been lost as the result of bombing and strafing by Allied planes, which were flying virtually uncontested missions. The 15th Panzer had only 31 tanks still in working order and no new supplies of fuel or ammunition could be expected.

Rommel's only hope lay not in withdrawal at this point,

Left: An Italian antiaircraft emplacement on the Alamein front.

Right: German wounded are tended to after the Battle at El Alamein.

but in a swift, violent counterattack. He immediately issued orders to mass all mobile forces in the northern sector. For a time he was afraid to bring 21st Panzer and Ariete up from the south, but it soon became evident that Montgomery was himself moving troops north. Rommel gambled, and on the 27th pulled 21st Panzer and half the artillery up to help with the attack. He also brought the 90th Light and Trieste forward from El Daba to reinforce the coastal positions.

Montgomery, meanwhile, had spent most of 26 and 27 October in seclusion, rearranging his own plans and dispositions to create a force that could break the stalemate. The 7th Armored Division was to be moved north into reserve where it would join the New Zealanders, the 10th Armored Division, and the 9th Armored Brigade. The 1st Armored Division would continue to press westward around Kidney Ridge, and the Australians would begin a move on the coast road.

On 27 October Rommel launched his offensive – but this time the British stood their ground and the attack was beaten off. On the 28th he tried again. The offensive was broken up by Allied air strikes before it ever got off the ground. The Axis forces braced themselves for the British counteroffensive – but nothing happened. Montgomery was still reorganizing his troop dispositions and would not move until the last man was in position.

The stalemate continued for some days. Though the fighting was fierce – often getting down to hand-to-hand combat in the German artillery positions – the British could make no real progress. Still, it was obvious to both Montgomery and Rommel that no amount of skill or courage could change the final outcome in view of the Allies superiority in manpower and materiel.

Montgomery hoped to launch his great breakthrough, Operation Supercharge, on the night of 31 October–1 November; but when the time came, X and XXX Corps were still too disorganized, and the main event had to be postponed for 24 hours. General Morshead and the Australians did mount a preliminary attack on the Axis coastal positions to 'keep Rommel occupied,' and managed to trap part of the 164th Division against the sea for a time, before

they were beaten off by a violent counterattack from the 90th Light and a battle group from the 21st Panzer.

As night fell on 1 November, most of Rommel's men had been in action for nine days without a break. The northern front, which had been gradually pushed back until all his minefields were in British hands, had been broken in many places. The new front was being desperately defended with too few guns, too little armor and the remains of decimated divisions.

That evening Montgomery followed his well-established pattern. There was a three-hour artillery barrage, followed by carpet bombing by the RAF and an infantry attack. At 0100 on 2 November, 400 tanks rushed through the gap (there were 400 more still in reserve) to meet Rommel's 90 German and Italian 'battlewagons.' Supercharge appeared to be going well in the beginning but amazingly, as the last great tank battle of the desert war developed on 2 November around Tell el Aqqaqir, the attack stalled. The Desert Fox was fighting one of the best tank actions of his career. In fact, at one point his counterattacks almost broke through the British salient. Behind the German lines, however, the infantry units had begun slipping away toward Fuka, while von Thoma prepared to continue the delaying action – with less than a third of his men and only 35 tanks remaining to face the reserves which Montgomery now threw into the breach.

All through 3 November the British X and XXX Corps attacked over and over again. It seemed that the Afrika Korps would never break. While the veterans of the German and Italian armored divisions were carrying out their phenomenal defense, held together by loyalty and the force of Rommel's personality, the rest of the Panzer Army was continuing its withdrawal. It was a difficult day for Rommel, but when he saw that, 'the enemy was operating with . . . astonishing hesitancy and caution,' he considered that he had a good chance of pulling through.

On 3 November, however, in response (he thought) to a message he had sent Hitler regarding the withdrawal, Rommel received a personal telegram from the Führer – containing one of his famous 'stand fast . . . victory or death' exhortations. Rommel hesitated, but eventually decided that he, who had always insisted on unqualified obedience from his own men, could not depart from that principle himself. All orders for withdrawal were cancelled. Montgomery had received help from an unexpected source.

At 0800 on 4 November Montgomery threw 200 tanks against the northern sector of the line, held by the 90th Light and the remaining 22 Afrika Korps tanks. Shortly before noon von Thoma was captured. In the center another 100 tanks descended upon the battered, badly equipped survivors of the Italian Tank Corps who, though outflanked, fought until their last tank was destroyed. At 1730 Rommel finally decided to pull his men out against orders. As it happened, it was a decision Hitler was happy to accept; his original message had been the result of a mix up at headquarters, but he had been reluctant to cancel it for fear of losing face.

The battle of El Alamein was over and the chase, which would finally end in Tunisia, had begun. On 5 November an exuberant Montgomery held a press conference to announce his 'complete and absolute victory.' Victory it was, but the fruits of that victory, which Clausewitz has said must be gathered in vigorous pursuit, were not to be forthcoming. Again, Montgomery had a chance to destroy the Panzer Army – but again he chose a cautious, methodical approach that kept the huge British war machine lumbering along one step behind Rommel. Of course, he had laid plans for a pursuit, but adequate provision had not been made for the problem of getting several divisions, under two different corps commands who were not on the best of terms, through the narrow salient. In addition, the men were physically exhausted after 12 days of hard fighting, and were disinclined to snatch the initiative even if Montgomery had ordered it. His staff were mentally fatigued and simply not up to coordinating operations.

By the time Montgomery could mount a full-scale chase, Rommel and the Afrika Korps already had a day's head start. Worn out and pounded down to less than 5000 men, some 11 tanks and about 25 antitank guns, they were still the masters of desert warfare – and proved it as they conducted their skillful, fighting retreat. Bringing up the rear, as usual, were the sappers – blowing up roads, laying mines, and setting booby traps almost under the Eighth Army's noses, eventually leading Radio Cairo to report that, 'the advance of the Eighth Army is meeting little resistance, but is seriously hampered by the . . . engineers.' With no transport, much of the German and Italian infantry had been overrun. Tens of thousands were captured, but others made it back – like the Ramcke Parachute Brigade, which managed to hijack a complete British transport column and join Rommel at Mersa Matruh in high style.

Four times Montgomery sent his pursuing troops on tight turns toward the coast, hoping to trap the Axis forces – only to find that they had already gone. On 7 November the heavens opened, and heavy rains turned the sands around Mersa Matruh into an impassable bog. Later Montgomery was to claim that it was the rain that gave Rommel his chance to escape – apparently forgetting that it fell equally on both armies, and that Rommel had already left before the Eighth Army appeared.

After Mersa Matruh the two forces settled down to a 1500-mile march across the desert, with Rommel in the lead and the Eighth Army slowly and methodically bring-

ing up the rear. The British commanders begged to be allowed to race ahead and force Rommel into a battle where he would surely be destroyed. They pleaded in vain. Montgomery was not only obsessed with order and method; to a large extent he had fallen under Rommel's spell as completely as the men of both armies. The set-piece battle was his area of expertise and the open desert was Rommel's country. Who knew what unexpected things he might do, even with only 10 tanks and no gasoline? It was much safer to stay behind, knowing that approaching from the opposite direction were 80,000 American and 25,000 British soldiers who would close the mighty pincers on the doomed Panzer Army.

The British victory at Alamein, coming as it did after a year of defeat, was greeted by ringing church bells, banner headlines and an outpouring of public adulation for Montgomery that continued, almost unabated, throughout his subsequent career as Field Marshal, leader of the British troops during the Normandy landings and commander of the British forces in Western Europe.

No reasonable person would deny that Montgomery was the victor at Alamein nor that Rommel was defeated. There is no need, on the other hand, to depict him as a savior who appeared out of the blue to singlehandedly snatch a defeated army from the jaws of disaster and disgrace. At the time he assumed command, the Eighth Army was anything but defeated. It had just stopped Rommel in his tracks and paved the way for a major offensive which, as Montgomery himself saw most clearly, they were at the time too weak to begin. As we have seen, many of the innovations at Alamein were based on planning done by Auchinleck and his staff, while many of Montgomery's own plans led to chaos and confusion. Time and again his inability to improvise and his unwillingness to take chances gave Rommel the breathing space he needed to regroup and prolong the action.

The fight that the Panzer Army put up in the face of impossible odds is one of the great actions of World War II – and therein lies the only real basis for naming Montgomery the victor. For despite Britain's overwhelming numerical superiority in men and arms, it required one man with Montgomery's self-confidence, determination and rapport with the ranks to elicit the dogged, unremitting effort that eventually resulted in the British victory.

PATTON AT THE BULGE 1944

The Battle of the Bulge, often known as the Ardennes Offensive, has been called – by no less an authority than Winston Churchill – the greatest American battle of World War II. Adolf Hitler, reacting to a situation in Germany that had been steadily worsening since the Allied landings in June and the abortive 20 July bomb plot, had developed a bold, imaginative plan to recapture the initiative in the west. As a result, in one month, from mid-December 1944 to mid-January 1945, the American army lost some 80,000 men and an enormous amount of equipment opposing this last great German offensive of the war.

There were many heroes at the Bulge – most of them unsung – but of them all one name stands out above the rest, that of General George Smith Patton. Flamboyant, swaggering and controversial, he was a man of contrasts: deeply religious and fiercely profane; a hot-tempered, ruthless fighter with a kind heart; a fiery tank commander and a learned military theoretician. With the Battle of the Bulge he hit the apex of his career, amply justifying the German High Command's opinion, expressed in an analysis of Allied generals, that he was 'the most dangerous man on all fronts.'

George Patton probably never considered anything other than a military career. This was perhaps because there was a strong soldiering tradition in his family. In June 1909 Patton graduated from West Point a year behind the rest of his class, owing to his problems with mathematics. During the 1930s he devoured military studies by Erwin Rommel and Heinz Guderian, Basil Liddell Hart and John Fuller, on infantry and armor tactics and strategy. However, in his own reports he had to be very cautious as by this time he had made some highly placed enemies. He felt it necessary to make his points obliquely, while still paying lip service to traditional concepts.

In 1938 General George Catlett Marshall was appointed Deputy Chief of Staff, and fortune finally turned in Patton's favor. Marshall, an astute judge of character, was not put off by Patton's flamboyant eccentricity. Furthermore, he was himself convinced of the importance of armor in the new army and had read enough between the lines of Patton's reports to recognize the latter's preferences.

Patton would never have agreed that 'war is hell.' He saw it as the only area in which he could excel. In 1940, when the German blitzkrieg rumbled through the Low Countries, France and Poland, he was tremendously excited – not only by war itself, but by the thrill of seeing the armor tactics he had been studying for 20 years actually being put into practice. Immediately he began hounding Marshall for a job nearer the action and at the same time tried to obtain a commission in the Canadian army.

In July Marshall came through. The first two American armored divisions were established and Patton was sent to Fort Benning, Georgia to organize one of the brigades, comprising 2nd Armored Division. He was promoted to Brigadier General and he soon took over command of the division, and began to turn it into a polished, dashing outfit. Meanwhile, his own extraordinary personality was doing much to publicize the new service and he was rapidly gaining a reputation as America's top tank expert.

However Patton was never just a tank specialist. His extensive reading and study had given him a broad view of war that enabled him to see parallels that many others missed. He was greatly interested in weapons and tactics used by the other services, and in fact held strong views on almost every aspect of the conduct of war. His insistence on military discipline was well-known – to the extent that an especially snappy salute was often called a 'georgepatton.' Discipline, he believed, saved lives, and as for the outward manifestations, 'If you can't get them to salute when they should salute and wear the clothes you tell them to wear, how are you going to get them to die for their country?' His opinions even extended to the placement of military cemeteries. This interest in minutiae and the ability to fit them in a broader context were traits he shared with another great field commander, Erwin Rommel. The two tank men had other things in common, for instance their habit of roaming the front lines during battles.

Thus beneath the flamboyance, the emotionalism and the 'goddamming,' the discerning eye could spot Patton's dedication to his profession. One of his superiors who recognized that professionalism was Marshall, another was Dwight David Eisenhower. The two were old friends who had served together in the tank corps during World War I. However Ike's support during the next war, often against considerable opposition, was not solely based on friendship. He saw Patton as a 'master of pursuit' – the sort of general, like Napoleon or Grant, who could spur his men on to chase the enemy even when they were dropping from fatigue. For his part, Patton had early predicted that Eisenhower would one day be his superior officer. 'Ike,' he said, 'You will be the Lee of the next war and I will be your Jackson.'

In 1942 Patton was given command of the Western Task Force for Operation Torch, the Allied landings in North Africa. Although the responsibilities of the post gave him less direct contact with the armor than he would have liked, both he and his men profited greatly from their experience in Africa, learning lessons that would be put to good use later in France. Later, at the head of Seventh Army in the dust and heat of Sicily, he demonstrated his talent for pursuit to the full. He also showed his quick temper and after hitting a soldier in public was demoted. Finally, in January 1944, he was called to England and placed in charge of Third Army.

Operations in the European Theater were controlled by Supreme Headquarters, Allied Expeditionary Forces (SHAEF) and the Supreme Commander, General Eisenhower. Under him were two army groups. The British 21st Army Group, under General Montgomery, consisted of the British Second Army and the Canadian First Army. General Omar Bradley was in charge of the US 12th Army Group – US First Army, commanded by General Hodges, and Patton's Third Army. In the Normandy landings, the First Army would hit the beaches at Cherbourg; the very existence of Third Army would be kept secret until at least D-Day+10, when they would land south of the First Army positions and execute Patton's favorite type of operation – a breakthrough followed by an advance clear across France to Germany.

The choice of commanders shows that Marshall, as much as he appreciated Patton, was not blind to his faults.

Although on the face of it Patton was best qualified to lead the invasion, his impetuousness, Marshall knew, would be a grave handicap in that intricate political/military situation: Patton 'needs a brake to slow him down . . . someone just above him and that is why I am giving the command to Bradley.' That Patton recognized his own limitations is shown by the fact that he accepted the news of his former subordinate's promotion with good humor. He had always considered himself more of a tactician than a stratigist; in any event, he much preferred commanding at the field army level where there was more personal contact with the men.

The Third Army's embarkation from Southampton was delayed; it was 5 July – almost a month after Operation Overlord – before they finally slipped ashore in France and dug in near Néhou, some 15 miles south of Cherbourg. While Patton champed at the bit, the transporting of men, equipment, and supplies took its deliberate course, and it was not until 26 July that Cobra was ready to strike.

Following a mammoth aerial and artillery bombardment by the First Army, the Third Army took off, racing through the gap at St Lô, past Avranches on the 30th, and on through France in an extraordinary sweep that brought them to the outskirts of Paris by 21 August.

The Third Army could easily have entered the French capital, but instead Patton was instructed to bypass the city to the north and south and continue his advance toward Germany – an order that did not sit well with the men of Third Army, who objected strongly to the news that Montgomery, with his British troops and the US First Army, were parading the streets as liberators.

Their tempers were not improved by the sudden realization that their supplies were being drastically reduced. Montgomery, whose forces were some 100 miles behind Patton's, had been arguing for some time that instead of advancing on a broad front, there should be one decisive thrust – in his northern sector. Thus most of the supplies should be diverted north, while the troops in the south fought a holding action. Near the end of August Eisenhower had arrived at a compromise: Montgomery's push into Belgium would be given priority until he had taken Antwerp. Then the offensive would revert back to the 'broad front' advance.

Furious with Eisenhower, whom he felt had sacrificed an early victory to Montgomery's 'insatiable appetite,' Patton ordered his advance units to keep moving until their gas tanks ran dry – and then to get out and walk. Third Army took Verdun, surrounded Metz, and reached the Moselle River (where they linked up with the Franco-American Seventh Army under General Alexander Patch). There – about 30 miles from the great industrial complex in the Saar valley and less than 100 miles from the Rhine – they finally came to a halt at the beginning of September.

The dash across France was a triumph for both Patton and his staff – which was, at his insistence, the fastest, most efficient, and most professional in Europe. Ever since landing in Europe his orders had been to 'advance and keep on advancing' and that is exactly what his army had done – repeatedly bypassing areas where the Germans tried to make a stand, never giving the enemy time to stop and organize a counterattack. But though the attacks were

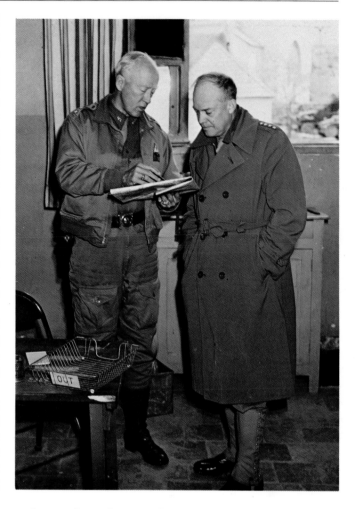

violent and unrelenting, they were never wild or uncontrolled; staff planning was always at least two operations ahead of the one in progress so that the army advanced with great speed, but never in haste.

The support between Patton and his Third Army staff was mutual and wholehearted, whether the battle was being waged with the Germans, 12th Army Group Headquarters, or even SHAEF. When the gas crisis was nearing its height, Patton received a bitter complaint that Third Army officers, disguised as First Army men, had stolen quite a lot of fuel. With a straight face, he replied, 'I'm very sorry to hear First Army lost some of its gas. But I know none of my officers would masquerade as First Army officers. They wouldn't stoop to that, not even to get gas SHAEF stole from us.' The merit promotions that several young officers in the Quartermasters Corps received shortly thereafter were probably coincidental.

Antwerp was finally taken on 4 September, and Third Army's supplies began arriving again. But in the meantime the German High Command had taken advantage of the 'miraculous' – if to them incomprehensible – respite to reinforce the area. Though Patton was able to force the Moselle in several places, he had to scrap his plans for a lightning offensive and settle down to a hard, set-piece battle.

Nancy, the old capital of Lorraine, fell to Third Army on 15 September. A few days later Patton received word that he was to stop and assume the defensive while Montgomery and the 21st Army Group made another concentrated assault, north of the Ardennes. If there was one thing Patton hated, it was defensive warfare; he considered it not only a waste of lives, but even un-American. His method of defense, therefore, was to maintain a continuous series of local actions with units small enough to escape Group Headquarter's notice. If questioned about his actions he would reply that he was only 'rectifying the line.'

As winter drew near the weather became almost as bitter an enemy as the Germans. The Third Army was receiving minimal supplies, not only of fuel and ammunition but also of other essentials like raincoats, sleeping bags and winter clothing. Despite the efforts of the Quartermaster Corps, who commissioned what they could from local suppliers and improvised the rest, sickness (especially trench foot) began to increase alarmingly. At one point the sickness rate equalled the battle casualty rate.

Patton spent most of October hounding headquarters for permission to attack, while Bradley and Montgomery argued the merits of a single attack in the north against the Ruhr versus a two-pronged assault against both the Ruhr and the Saar Basin. Eventually Bradley won his point, and Patton was called to Group Headquarters to receive the good news that the winter campaign would involve a series of assaults along the entire front with an attack on the Saar as one of the two main efforts.

Little planning was necessary since they had been working on a Saar offensive for over a month, but the precarious supply situation had to be taken into account. There were also some new troop dispositions. For this offensive, the VIII Corps would stay in the Ardennes under the control of the First Army. The Third Army would get the III Corps in its place, along with two divisions presently en route from the States, the 10th Armored and 95th Infantry Divisions. On 3 November Bradley reported that Montgomery had not yet set a starting date for his half of

the attack, but would probably not be ready before 1 December. Patton, however, could go whenever he was ready.

The Third Army attacked on 8 November. Metz was under Patton's control by the 19th (though the last of its forts held out for another month). Mud and slush hindered the offensive and it became more and more difficult to maintain momentum. However, after six weeks of fighting, the Third Army had reached the Siegfried Line along most of its front and in one place had driven a wedge some 30 miles beyond it. Overall, they had advanced approximately 50 miles. Meanwhile, the northern offensive had been stopped in an attempt to take the Roer River dams and in the south the Seventh Army had reached the Rhine and turned to join up with Patton's right flank.

Although the Allies' headlong advance had been slowed down and their initial complacency dispelled to some extent by the Germans' stubborn resistance, it was obvious

Top: A German assault gun is hidden in a farmyard as part of the preparations for the Ardennes Offensive.

Left: The Siegfried Line is breached by the 39th Infantry, 9th Division, 3rd Armored Division on 15 September 1944.

Far left above: Generals Eisenhower and Patton consult a map in North Africa in March 1943.

that they would come out the winners in a battle of attrition. However, as early as September Hitler had conceived an audacious plan. In one last, gigantic offensive, he would strike westward, penetrate between the First and Third Armies to Antwerp (thus depriving the Allies of their main supply port), and mop up the British and Canadian Armies along the Belgian-Dutch border. The attack would be mounted through the Ardennes, where he had made his great breakthrough in 1940. He knew that this area was thinly held by only four infantry divisions. Field Marshal Gerd von Rundstedt was called out of retirement to lead the offensive (code named Operation Autumn Fog), and the task of quietly collecting an attack force began.

In November a few high-ranking German staff and army officers were informed of the plan. The generals were astounded. They pointed out that Germany was much weaker than it had been in 1940 and furthermore was facing a much stronger enemy. Together von Rundstedt, Field Marshal Walther Model (Commander of Army Group B) and the three field commanders – SS General Sepp Dietrich (Sixth SS Panzer Army), General Hasso von Manteuffel (Fifth Panzer Army) and General Erich Brandenburger (Seventh Army) – concocted an alternative plan with more limited objectives. Hitler remained adamant. He was convinced that he could shatter the 'unnatural' Allied union with one blow – and the generals were too intimidated after the purges that had followed the July Plot assassination attempt to put up much of an argument.

On the evening of 12 December several senior German

field commanders were taken to a secret rendezvous at Hitler's bunker near Frankfurt where many of them learned for the first time of the great offensive, scheduled to begin in only four days. Over 250,000 men – 28 divisions, nine of them Panzer units – had been assembled, along with some 2500 tanks and field guns. It was a puny force compared to the resources Rundstedt had controlled on the same front in 1940, but the Germans were not without some advantages.

Although the men themselves were not as fit or well-trained as the previous strike force, their ranks were stiffened by the addition of several fanatical, well-equipped SS units. In addition, the Germans still had superiority in some important weapons. The Mark V Panthers and Mark VI Tigers, for example, had thicker armor and wider tracks than the new Shermans and were armed with the more powerful 88mm guns, compared to the Sherman's 76mm.

There were also some desperate problems. Allied bombing raids had left the German transportation network a shambles and there was a grave fuel shortage. Hitler was counting on his last, most important weapon to help overcome these difficulties – the advantage of surprise. Despite the lesson of 1940, Allied planners persisted in viewing the Ardennes, with its heavily wooded hills cut by deep valleys where tank advances could easily be stopped, as unsuitable for a large-scale armor action. From the German point of view, however, the forest was a natural blind for concentrations of ground forces, while the drier high ground gave the tanks more maneuverability.

The night of 15 December was cold and a thick mist covered the German troops as they moved into position along their 70-mile front between Monschau and Echternach. Bad weather had been forecast for the next several days and was essential to the success of the operation, to protect the German supply columns from Allied air strikes. On the 16th they moved out. In the north, the main strike

Left: German troops captured by the 82nd Airborne Division are lined up on a road near Hierlot, Belgium.

Far left above: A Marder III with a 75mm gun in December 1944.

Far left: A knocked out American half-track near Malmédy, 16

December 1944.

Top: A German soldier examines an American half-track, which has been converted into an ambulance.

Top left: Soldiers of the Adolf Hitler Division on the road between Malmedy and St Vith, 17 December 1944.

force, Dietrich's Sixth Panzer Army had orders to advance northwest, past Liège to Antwerp. Manteuffel and the Fifth Panzer Army, in the center, were to push through the Ardennes and then turn north to the Meuse and, eventually, to Antwerp.

The offensive came as a complete surprise to the Allies — and unnecessarily so. Third Army advance units had been keeping a faithful eye on the German troop dispositions ahead of them. As early as 4 December Patton's G-2 (Intelligence) staff had sent a Special Estimate to Group Headquarters that concluded, 'A large build up of troops and supplies is clearly in progress opposite the southern (Ardennes) flank of First Army.' Allied planners were blinded by overconfidence. Montgomery and Bradley were both convinced that Hitler lacked the resources for a major offensive, and that he would be forced to throw everything

he had into stopping their drive toward the Rhine. An unofficial rebuff was the only reply to the Third Army's communique, and on 15 December Montgomery issued his own assessment of the situation, 'The enemy is at present fighting a defensive campaign . . . he cannot stage major offensive operations. . . . He has not the transport or

A German tank passes some of the many US prisoners taken during the first days of the Ardennes Offensive. 17 December 1944.

the petrol . . . nor could his tanks compete with ours in a mobile battle.'

He could not have been further from the mark. In the north, where Sepp Dietrich (a good fighter, but one with little understanding of armored warfare) was in command of the attack, the Allied line buckled, but held at several key points. In the center, however, the brilliant tank commander Manteuffel led the Fifth Panzer Army in a rapid advance that recalled the days of the first blitzkrieg. Despite the terrible weather, the delays in bringing up fuel supplies and occasional pockets of American resistance, it was more than 48 hours before his headlong rush was stopped, not far from Bastogne, by the US 10th Armored Division's desperate delaying action.

Manteuffel was assisted by the confusion in the American ranks sown by Operation Greif. This consisted of about 40 jeep loads of English-speaking German commandos in American uniforms, led by the famed Otto Skorzeny, whose mission was to infiltrate the American lines and turn signposts, cut communication wires, kill messengers and do anything else they could think of to create confusion. One captured commando started the rumor that a unit was on its way to kill Eisenhower with the result that the Supreme Commander was virtually immobilized in his Paris headquarters for some days, to his extreme annoyance. In the attempt to weed out the infiltrators, soldiers in the battle area were frequently required to identify themselves by correctly answering questions like 'Who won the World Series in 1938?' Bradley had to spend some time convincing a zealous sentry that Springfield, not Chicago, is the capital of Illinois.

As the German attack began on 16 December the Third Army was preparing for its own offensive, an elaborate assault on the Siegfried Line. On the 17th, when they finally got a clear idea of what was happening, several staff members were optimistic, thinking that the action to the north would take some of the pressure off their own operation. Patton, however, was less sanguine. Realizing that he would probably have to postpone his own plans, he set the staff working to prepare three contingency plans, in case they were asked to move north and help.

This proved to be a wise precaution. The next day he was ordered to Luxembourg to confer with Bradley, and by the 19 December he was attending a meeting of senior American commanders called by Eisenhower at Verdun. Ike decided that the First and Ninth Armies, in the north, should be temporarily placed under Montgomery's command – a plan that greatly displeased Bradley. All were agreed that the Allies' first move should be a counterattack by the Third Army from the south, against the underbelly of the Bulge. There were only two problems. First, how far north could General Jacob Devers stretch his 6th Army

Group to cover Patton's territory (eventually he moved up to a point between Saarlautern and Saarbrücken), and second, how to time the attack. As far as Patton was concerned, he could begin immediately and be in position to attack by 21 December. This was no idle boast. His staff had completed their plans and were simply waiting for him to telephone a code word, telling them which of the three to put into operation.

It was eventually decided that Middleton's VIII Corps would be returned to the Third Army. Most of it was already engaged in and around Bastogne, but the remainder would be launched on the left against the nose of the German salient, toward St Hubert. The XII Corps would attack on the right, toward Echternach. In the center would be Milliken's III Corps — 80th and 26th Infantry and the 4th Armored Divisions — with their main objective the liberation of Bastogne (by now surrounded and under siege). This was a calculated risk, for it meant leaving the 50-mile north-south front, including the Saarlautern salient, in the hands of just XX Corps (two infantry and one armored division) and a Cavalry Group. Though too weak to withstand an attack in force, they were in a position to fight a strong delaying action — as well as prevent a surprise attack through that sector.

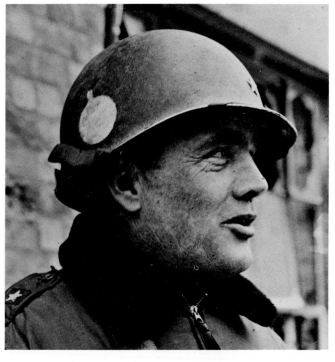

General 'Nuts' McAuliffe, commander of 101st Airborne Division.

Members of the 101st Airborne Division leave Bastogne to relieve a neighboring village, which has been under attack for 10 days, 29 December 1944.

Returning to his own headquarters, Patton found his staff under a considerable amount of tension, which he characteristically dispelled as soon as possible. Standing in front of the room, he glared into the tense faces before him and after a few moments announced impressively, 'This will get the bastards out of their holes so we can kill all of them. Now go to work!'

And work they did, racing against time to shift a three-corps, north-south battle line to a four-corps line running east-west in the Ardennes and north-south in the Saar. Hundreds of units had to be moved quickly and efficiently. At Patton's orders they disregarded all blackout regulations and drove north with headlights blazing and throttles wide open. Thousands of miles of telephone wire had to be laid and an entire communications network, capable of remaining operational despite both cold and enemy attack, had to be established. A new supply system had to be set up, and thousands of tons of supplies shifted for distribution or storage in new depots and dumps. Hospitals had to be organized and stocked, maps and orders distributed, and hundreds of other details taken care of. During those busy days Patton worked as hard as anyone else, but neither then nor later would he claim credit for the gigantic effort. His staff, he said, had performed a miracle. (He was willing, however, to take credit for being the unofficial 'ray of sunshine and backslapper' for both his men and his superiors.) At 0600 on 22 December, right on schedule, III Corps attacked.

Meanwhile, the 'Battered Bastards of the Bastion of Bastogne' – the 101st Airborne Division along with remnants of the 10th Armored Division, the 705th Destroyer Tank Battalion and several other units, all under the command of General McAuliffe – had been grimly hanging on under the German barrage. Although it was a tiny town with a population of about 3500, Bastogne was the junction of seven major paved roads, and the key to the defense of both the Ardennes and the Meuse beyond. Theoretically the Germans could have bypassed it on secondary roads, but these were in such bad condition that during bad weather they were practically impassable for military vehicles.

On 18 December, when Manteuffel's spearheads had advanced to within 15 miles of Bastogne, there were few American troops in Bastogne. However, by that evening, when his main force arrived, the town was already occupied by the 101st Airborne. Starting the previous evening from Reims, over 100 miles away, the 'Screaming Eagles' had beaten the Germans in a decisive race. Eventually, and with some difficulty, Manteuffel got his divisions around Bastogne, but he was forced to leave a substantial force behind to deal with the junction. In addition, the delay had given the Americans time to bring up more reserves, and Manteuffel was getting no support from Dietrich's army (which had been cornered by the US First Army near Stavelot on 19 December). Although an advance guard would eventually reach the Meuse at Dinant on the 24th, they would soon be cut off and forced to withdraw.

In effect, the German advance was stalled at Bastogne where, as an anonymous GI put it, 'They've got us surrounded, the poor bastards.' On the 22nd General Heinrich von Lüttwitz, commander of the German XLVII Armored Corps, sent a message to McAuliffe demanding he surrender the city. McAuliffe's reply, 'Nuts!' is probably unequalled in the annals of military history, both for its brevity and the amount of confusion it caused in the enemy camp before it was deciphered.

The III Corps began their attack first, in the worst possible weather conditions. They were hampered by fog, a howling blizzard and below-freezing temperatures. Their winter equipment still had not arrived. They had no snow-camouflage material, parkas, hoods or fur gloves. Blankets were cut up for shoe liners, and yards of white cloth purchased from the French were run up into camouflage suits by the Quartermaster Corps. Along with their improvised equipment the men carried a prayer for good weather,

Left: The 101st Airborne Division held out in Bastogne from the 19 to 26 December when the 4th Armored Division relieved the 'Battered Bastards of the 101st.'

Right: German prisoners of war are marched into captivity.

Right center: Soldiers of a Volks Grenadier Regiment are taken behind the lines. Some 14,279 prisoners were taken during the first days of the counterattack by Allied troops.

Right bottom: More German prisoners.

Far right: Members of the 101st Airborne who held out in Bastogne.

composed some days before (for the Saar offensive) by Chaplain James H O'Neill.

On the east of III Corp's front, the 80th Division was attacking toward Ettelbruck and the Sûre River, while in the center the 26th Infantry Division was aiming for Wiltz. The terrain these two divisions were moving through was some of the worst in the entire Ardennes. On the left was 4th Armored Division which had orders to 'drive like hell' straight for Bastogne. The division was divided into three units, or combat commands. Combat Command A (CCA) went north along the Arlon-Bastogne road. Combat Command B (CCB) took secondary roads through the hilly, wooded countryside from Hubay-la-Neuve (about 5 miles west). Their orders called for them to gradually move closer to each other until they were advancing on parallel paths about two miles apart. Combat Command Reserve was held back; they were rarely committed to action.

The two 4th Armored units made good progress at first, but Combat Command A was slowed down by an American minefield originally laid to stop the German Seventh Army. In the afternoon they ran into a German rifle company guarding the demolished bridges at Martelange, and were held up until about 0300 on the 23rd. Combat Command B met little resistance on the back roads, and by noon had advanced nearly 12 miles – to within 7 miles of the center of Bastogne. They too, however, were stopped cold until the small hours of the morning, this time by a German company holding a blown bridge at Burnon.

The next morning, 23 December, was crisp and cold with clear, sunny skies. As the air filled with the sound of Allied aircraft, a jubilant Patton shouted at one of his staff officers, 'Hot damn! That O'Neill sure did some potent praying! Get him up here, I want to pin a medal on him!' For the next five days pilots of the XIX Tactical Air Command (TAC) flew until they were out of ammunition, touched down to

reload and refuel, and took off again. As darkness fell a Night Fighter (P-61) Squadron took over.

Patton called Milliken and ordered the 4th Armored to 'stop piddling around' and get on toward Bastogne, by-passing centers of resistance and mopping them up later. Combat Command A followed orders. At midday they tried to go around the village of Warnach. However, the Germans put up a desperate defense of the area, and Combat Command A was not able to either take Warnach or bypass it for 24 hours. Thus by noon on 24 December they were still several miles behind the point Combat Command B had reached 48 hours earlier.

Combat Command B fared little better. At noon on the 23rd they took Chaumont, which had been under heavy aerial assault all morning, but the sun thawed the open ground, and the Shermans became thoroughly bogged down. When the Germans realized what was happening they moved an assault-gun brigade onto the hills above the village, knocked out every tank they could see, and retook the town, inflicting heavy losses on the Americans. By the end of the day Combat Command B had managed to struggle only as far as Hompre – a distance of just over five miles. They were still three miles from the Bastogne perimeter.

Patton fought the Battle of the Bulge in his own fashion – tearing around the front lines in his open jeep, which was specially equipped with a loud horn and blazoned with huge red stars. One of his cardinal rules was that 'Commanders (and their staffs) should be seen physically by as many individuals of their command as possible, certainly by all combat soldiers.' Patton, in his worn field overcoat, visited battle lines and unit headquarters, showing up at every critical point. No one saw him moving backward. He always flew to the rear, to save time and avoid the possibility of lowering morale.

On the day before Christmas the Bastogne defenders received the message from Patton, 'Christmas Eve present coming up. Hold on.' It was not to be. Though the attack had picked up somewhat once the planes were in the air, the tanks and infantry still moved slowly over the winding, icy mountain roads, battling fiercely for every foot of ground. This did not conform to Patton's theory of warfare, and he called Eisenhower several times to apologize for the delay.

Despite its initial success the offensive, in von Rundstedt's and Model's view, was a failure by 22 December. The field commander, Manteuffel, came to the same conclusion on Christmas Eve. He knew he could not hold the narrow salient much longer. On 25 December he pulled troops from the eastward advance and turned them toward Third Army. In the east, in VIII Corps' sector, he launched power-

ful Panzer attacks against St Hubert, Rochefort, and Hotton; another series of heavy assaults hit Bastogne itself. In addition, in the west, General Brandenburger initiated several violent battles in the Saarlautern region.

Combat Command A and Combat Command B had each been strengthened with a battalion of infantry, and even Combat Command Reserve had been thrown into the fighting, on a line parallelling the Neufchateau-Bastogne road. Again, they could not make a decisive breakthrough. Patton's temper on Christmas night was precarious, and it was not improved when Bradley relayed Montgomery's suggestion that Patton fall back to the Moselle and 'regroup' (as Montgomery himself was doing). Patton's reaction was that it was a 'disgusting' idea.

The 26 December was an important day in the battle. Manteuffel finally received official permission to establish defensive positions, though Hitler was still convinced that Germany could ultimately take Bastogne, drive through on the Northern Front and capture Antwerp. That same day, Bastogne was relieved. In the afternoon, advance elements of the 4th Armored Division's Combat Command B made contact with the 101st Airborne Division's outposts on the perimeter, and that evening five tanks from Combat Command Reserve entered the city itself. In the afternoon Combat Command Reserve's two battalion commanders, Lieutenant Colonels Creighton Abrams and George Jacques had decided to ignore the battle plan for the day and drive straight through Assenois to Bastogne. While most of their forces engaged the Germans at Assenois, the five tanks plus an infantry half-track slipped away from the battle and into the beleaguered town. The first exchange between Captain William Dwight and General McAuliffe was typical of the American command style that Germans, and other Europeans, found so difficult to understand. 'How are you General?' asked Dwight. 'Gee, I'm mighty glad to see you,' replied McAuliffe. The latter's first message to Patton was typical of the Bastogne defenders' attitude throughout the conflict, 'Losses Light. Morale high. Await-

Right: A scene from the Ardennes
Offensive: German soldiers go
through the possessions of dead
American soldiers. The US boots
have been removed as they were
much better than standard
German issue.

Far right: Troops of the 82nd
Airborne Division march German
prisoners to the rear on 29
January 1945.

Below right: The outskirts of
Bastogne.

Below: US trucks bring supplies
into Bastogne after it was relieved,
22 January 1945.

ing orders to continue the counteroffensive.'

Bastogne, of course, was still an island in hostile territory, though it now had a thin, tenuous lifeline to Third Army — whose first priority had to be widening and protecting it. The Germans, who rallied with their usual speed and efficiency. launched two heavy attacks on the narrow corridor that night. Two convoys loaded with food, ammunition, medicine and other supplies were ready to go on the 27th, but the journey was still too hazardous. Instead, Patton, after much haranguing of headquarters, arranged for an airlift to drop as many supplies as possible. Though SHAEF air mission to evacuate the wounded had to be scrubbed, XIX TAC improvised their own lift. A small squad of L-5s, with P-47 fighter support, dropped several teams of medics into the town. By the evening of the 27th the corridor, though still dangerous, was passable. The siege of Bastogne was over; the battle was just beginning.

On 28 December the weather closed in again and the Germans began their next attack on Bastogne in a heavy snowstorm. In addition to the reinforcements from the west, Manteuffel had been able to call on German units in the northern sector, where Montgomery was still refitting his four armies. Within a few days, at the height of the battle, Third Army would be facing elements of 12 German divisions in the Bastogne area alone. Seven other divisions would be thrown against the newly-reinforced VIII Corps in the west and XII Corps in the east.

The German attacks were held off on all fronts. This success was due in large part both to XIX TAC, which managed to keep its planes up almost all day despite the weather, and to the artillery units. The new proximity fuze had given an added boost to the artillery, which proved to be indispensable in the days ahead. Still Hitler would not consider a German withdrawal. Despite Manteuffel's pleas that he be allowed to pull out while he still had a chance to save his army and despite Guderian's warning that the Eastern Front was a 'house of cards,' the Fuhrer — in a harangue lasting several hours — ordered the western offensive resumed.

For the next eight days, from 28 December to 5 January, it was attack and counterattack, as Germans and Americans engaged in a series of murderous battles. On the 28th Patton launched a three-corps offensive toward St Vith, Houffalize and Echternach. The Germans quickly countered with their own series of attacks. On 30 December Manteuffel threw five divisions against the Bastogne corridor but the weather cleared for a few hours and they were beaten off with help from XIX TAC. On 1 January the Luftwaffe launched a well-coordinated attack on Allied airfields. Although they inflicted some damage, they also lost about 300 of their own planes. That same day there were seven attacks on Bastogne, and a force of eight German divisions moved against the Saar. None succeeded.

On 3 January there was another heavy attack against Bastogne, by two German corps (nine divisions). While all German eyes were on Third Army, First Army was allowed to finally make its move in the north. By the 5th it was obvious, even to Hitler, that the great Ardennes Offensive had failed. There were still some weeks of hard fighting left, but from then on the outcome was never in doubt. The Germans executed a skillful withdrawal. Operating behind

Right: A US soldier examines the slogan written on a wall in Trois Vierges, north of Clervaux. It reads 'Behind the last battle of this war lies our victory.'

Far right: Mark V Panthers were the best German tanks of the war and took part in the Ardennes Offensive.

Below: German prisoners en route to the rear following their capture by troops of the 102nd Division.

infantry attacks, armored groups moved at night to avoid the worst of the air assaults and fought from prepared positions during the day. The German experience in Russia proved to be of great value; Hitler's forces were much better than the Americans at travelling through the deep snow and over the icy roads. The withdrawal was accelerated on 12 January when the Russians launched their mammoth winter offensive.

Finally, on 16 January, First and Third Armies linked up at Houffalize. It was an especially satisfying meeting for Patton, since First Army was represented on this historic occasion by a task force from his old unit, 2nd Armored Division. Now there was only mopping up to be done. On 23 January St Vith was retaken. The Battle of the Bulge was over.

Hitler had gambled and lost – and in losing, had not only sealed the fate of his armies in the west, but had also made defeat in the east inevitable. Overall, Germany lost more than 120,000 men (killed, captured and wounded) during the Battle of the Bulge, along with some 800 tanks and guns, 1600 planes and 6000 vehicles. American losses included about 80,000 men and over 700 tanks and guns. The Allies could replace their men and equipment, while Hitler had staked everything on this last throw.

There were three basic reasons for the failure of the German offensive. First, Hitler grossly overestimated his own capabilities vis-à-vis the Allies. Not only did he discount the effect of superior Allied numbers of men and equipment, but he also had little regard for the American soldiers' fighting ability. He was misled, as were many in the German High Command, by the Americans' generally casual approach to military discipline and appearance. The second reason for the failure was the Allies' overwhelming superiority in the air – and the five days of clear weather

(23–27 December) that enabled it to be used to such effect. Last, but not least, was Third Army's unexpectedly quick assault on the southern flank of the Bulge. The Germans never dreamed that Patton could turn and strike so hard in such a short time.

This chapter has looked at just one aspect of one engagement in Europe, but it is one which Patton described as 'one of the greatest exploits of military history . . . executed under the most difficult and trying conditions and against tremendous odds . . . and also without any help from anyone.' He was not praising himself, but was speaking, quite sincerely, about his army. Characteristically, he always maintained that he had had 'Damned little to do' with the victory. Speaking of himself in the third person, he emphatically told the press, 'All he did was to give the orders. It was the staff of his headquarters and the troops in the line that performed this matchless feat.' During his

last staff briefing in Europe he told his men, 'There is probably no commander in Europe who did less work than I did. You did it all.'

Patton was not indulging in a show of false modesty, he believed every word he said. What he did not say, however, was that in addition to giving the orders, it had been he who turned Third Army into an efficient, well-knit team capable of carrying them out, and who kept that team functioning at peak performance under extremely difficult conditions. Though his reputation was made as a tank commander, his army's success at the Bulge depended far less on spectacular tank battles than on the superb coordination of armored, infantry, artillery, air and support forces. The arguments, the political gaffes, the eccentricities, aside, Dwight D Eisenhower has summed him up best, 'George Patton was, if nothing else, a man who knew his business.'

ZHUKOV
AT BERLIN 1945

Soviet military leaders during World War II were in a more difficult position than their Western counterparts in so far as the formulation of strategy was concerned, because their warlord, Josef Stalin, insisted on formulating it himself, giving them an even smaller leverage in executing it than Western generals had. It is true that in the case of Marshal Zhukov he was always consulted and much of his advice was accepted by Stalin. However, Zhukov could never be sure of anything. Like Hitler, Stalin insisted on controlling even tactical maneuvers of the various armies under Zhukov's command. The result was that all the strategic planning had to be done through Stalin and the credit for it had to go to him. Much of the tactical execution went to Stalin who not only controlled reserves, but also frequently altered the lines of attack by groups of armies (fronts), armies, corps and even armored units. Thus only within these narrow limits could Soviet generals establish their reputations and claim credit for the battles of Stalingrad, Leningrad, Kiev or Berlin.

Together with Marshal Vasilievsky, Zhukov was in a particularly privileged military situation, for from the very beginning of the war he was Stalin's most intimate adviser on strategy and his personal 'executor' on the spot, at the battles. Thus, for example, Zhukov had to inspect the battle ground at Stalingrad long before Stalin finally decided on the strategy of that battle. Zhukov reported his findings to his master and advanced his suggestions. Together with other commanders, who were only allowed to comment on their partial tasks, Zhukov often forced on Stalin his military decisions. However equally often Stalin, who had additional sources of information (the NKVD channel, for example) and his own finger on the strategic reserves button, made his decisions contrary to the military advice proferred. However, Zhukov had an additional privilege; that of commanding the groups of armies — especially toward the end of the war — in the execution of Stalin's

strategies which he had helped to formulate. Naturally in the latter capacity Zhukov had a greater scope for initiative and decision making, but even then his powers were limited by Stalin's frequent checks and especially, famous telephone calls, which usually resulted in changes of tactical plans and operations. Thus, with all these reservations in mind, we can now consider Zhukov's role in the Battle for Berlin.

Stalin earmarked his favorite general, Zhukov, for the final Battle of Berlin in October 1944. Zhukov himself says that this was exactly one day after he had persuaded Stalin to halt the Warsaw offensive, whose objectives were unclear to him, and which was draining Soviet military resources quite disproportionately to its significance. Zhukov had only just returned from Bulgaria and was inspecting the Warsaw front: the 1st Byelorussian and 1st Ukrainian Fronts came to a halt on the line Praga–Warsaw–Vistula–Jaslo. Stalin therefore began to plan subsequent offensives, the most crucial of which would be the one from the Vistula to the Oder carried out by the 1st Byelorussian Front. This would bring this group of armies to the

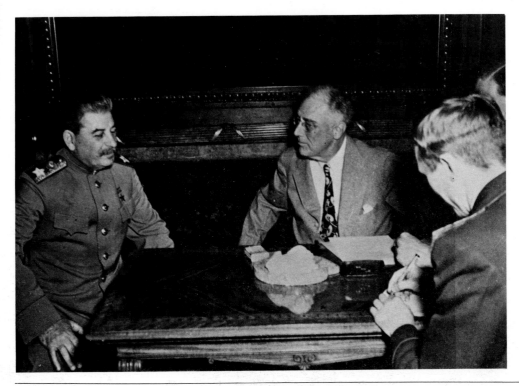

Top: Members of the Hitler Youth visit Hitler at his headquarters during March 1945. At the end of the war these youths were called upon to fight and defend Germany.

Left: Josef Stalin and President Roosevelt at the Yalta Conference in February 1945. At this conference the future of Europe was discussed.

Berlin strategic zone, to be ultimately responsible for the final operation of the war, the taking of the Nazi capital, Berlin. This was Stalin's idea in October 1944, when he appointed Zhukov Commander in Chief of the 1st Byelorussian Front, one of the most brilliant staff officers, Colonel General M S Malinin as his Chief of Staff and Lieutenant General K F Telegin, one of the most experienced political officers, as members of the War Council.

The thrust toward Berlin was to be prepared most thoroughly by Zhukov and Malinin during November 1944. Although Germany still had some 7,500,000 men engaged in the war, Hitler was draining the Eastern Front of its best units in preparation for a counteroffensive in the west, the Battle of the Bulge. Zhukov's strategic planning included a feint thrust in the south toward Vienna in order to draw German reserves from his front, which was approved by Stalin and GHQ (Stavka). However, once again Stalin forced on Zhukov several strategic limitations. First of all, Stalin neglected to reduce East Prussia and in particular Königsberg (Kaliningrad) during the summer of 1944, and though he had now charged General Ivan D Chernyakhovsky and his 3rd Byelorussian Front with this task, he still persisted in ignoring the danger to the offensive operations of the 1st Byelorussian Front, about to be launched. Next Stalin charged General Konstantin Rokossovsky and his 2nd Byelorussian Front to strike in the general Northwest axis, from north of Warsaw, and coordinate this advance with Zhukov's, running along the axis south of Warsaw to Poznan (Posen) and in the general direction of the Oder and Berlin. Even to a politician, Stalin, this joint, coordinated operation, must have appeared as two separate missions to be treated on their own, but once again Stalin insisted on coordination so that he could more easily control the actual operations. Finally, Stalin also arrogated the time factor: although the preparations for the offensive were completed early in December 1944 he refused to give it the go ahead, because he thought heavy mud and poor visibility would make it impossible to exploit Soviet armor and mechanized superiority and set the tentative D-Day for 15–20 January 1945. Zhukov and Malinin had therefore unexpectedly more time for the planning and rehearsing of the offensive, which for the first time in the war was taking place on unfamiliar territory. All supply routes were in Poland and the military intelligence seemed unfamiliar coming from the secret service and aerial reconnaissance rather than from guerrilla sources. In addition the Red Army soldiers badly needed political explanations and education, in order, as Zhukov put it, to prevent irresponsible acts by Soviet soldiers in the liberated territory. Thus Zhukov was able to hold staff maneuvers in which he was able to consider logistical support (only two comparatively small bridgeheads), and he was able to resolve more or less the problem of cooperation with Rokossovsky's armies by staging maneuvers on the army scale. In a sudden change of direction Stalin launched both armies against Germany on 12 January 1945, apparently in response to Churchill's requests.

For this last but one push forward the combined Soviet forces were staggering: some 164 infantry divisions; 32,143 guns and mortars (7:1 superiority); 6460 tanks and self-propelled guns (5:1); 4772 aircraft (17:1); and 2,200,000 men (5:1). On Zhukov's front there was one infantry division for each 1.3 mile. Artillery barrage on a depth of 2 miles lasted $2\frac{1}{2}$ hours, and after two days of hard fighting Zhukov's forces forced a wedge of over seven miles. After two or three days tank armies were used in support of the infantry and they swiftly developed the offensive pursuing the Germans through breakthroughs up to 62 miles every day. After six days of the offensive General Guderian had to contend with Soviet penetrations of up to 100 miles on a 310-mile wide front. Cities began to fall – Warsaw was finally liberated – or were besieged and all the objectives were reached ahead of the schedule by 25 January 1945. By this time Stalin wanted to stop Zhukov's offensive to wait for the final defeat of the Germans in

Right: General Koniev and Bokov in 1943. Koniev was in command of the 1st Ukrainian Front in 1945.

Left below, center and bottom: On 12 November 1944 a parade was held for members of the Volkssturm in Berlin. The Volkssturm units were made up of older men and younger boys who were to defend the fatherland during the last battle. In the bottom picture Goebbels takes the salute at a march past.

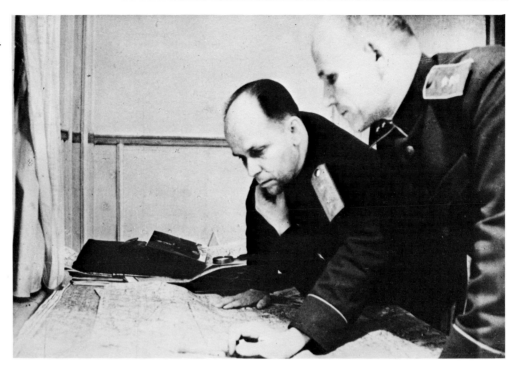

East Prussia, but Zhukov objected: instead he asked for one more army to strengthen his right flank and then ordered a forced advance into the fortified Meseritz zone. For he knew that once the line Bydgoszcz-Poznan was reached by his and Rokossovsky's armies, all future operations, which also meant the ultimate one against Berlin, would be decided on the spot.

However, Stalin's telephone calls slowed down Zhukov, especially since Stalin refused to send Zhukov reinforcements which he needed if he was to reach Küstrin on the Oder river, on the direct line to Berlin. As Rokossovsky's offensive north of Bydgoszcz got stuck Zhukov's right flank was now in real danger and though the Oder was reached on 3 February Zhukov was obliged to halt, even though he had issued a directive to his armies and staffs to get ready to resume the final offensive on Berlin by 9 February: after all Berlin was only some 50 miles from Küstrin, which his armies had by then reached. Perhaps rather optimistically Zhukov ordered that Berlin be taken seven days later. This was indeed strategy on the spot, but rather different from what Stalin had in mind.

Instead of letting him dash for Berlin he obliged Zhukov to remain on the defensive and wait for the other commanders, Rokossovsky and Koniev to complete their tasks. Above all he was apparently worried about Zhukov's right flank: Soviet intelligence indicated that the Germans had the Third Panzer Army in Western Pomerania and it could either reinforce the East Pomeranian forces or defend Berlin. In either case it presented a risk to Zhukov's further operations. Although Marshal Chuikov, who was Zhukov's subordinate, claimed subsequently that the 2nd Byelorussian Front could have dealt with any threat along the Berlin axis, Zhukov came to agree with Stalin. On 1 March 1945 assisted by Zhukov's troops Rokossovsky's 2nd Byelorussian Front had finally broken through and reached the Baltic Sea by cutting the German armies into two. However, the attacking Russians still had their supply bases on the Vistula and this fact also forced Zhukov to

slow down. Marshal Koniev in the south reached Breslau with his 1st Ukrainian Front, but failed to cross the river Neisse as envisaged. Delays were caused on this front by the erratic supplies of ammunition, by the slowness of aviation to afford him cover, and above all by the lagging of the pontoon bridge units. Still by the end of March 1945 all these tasks were accomplished and Stalin summoned Zhukov and Koniev to Moscow to discuss the final phase of the war and let them into a few political secrets.

It must have been an unpleasant surprise for Zhukov to find on arrival at the Stavka in Moscow his chief rival, Marshal Koniev (who had been exclusively a field commander) in on the final operation. He probably suspected that his warlord might trick him of the final war trophy, Berlin, or make him divide the laurels with that 'simple' Koniev. Indeed Stalin was already engaged trying to outmaneuver the Allies. Before the generals arrived he had received a telegram about an Allied attack on Berlin under Field Marshal Montgomery, so Stalin now decided to give the operation top priority. However, fooling the Allies was child's play compared to tricking his own generals. General Eisenhower, with his straightforward naivety, informed Stalin, against Churchill's advice, that his main thrust in Germany would aim at Erfurt, Leipzig and Dresden and not at Berlin as the British had desired. Stalin in turn told Eisenhower that Soviet main effort would also aim at Dresden and would be launched in the second half of May. After misleading Eisenhower he immediately turned round to his generals and urged them to take Berlin before the Western Allies. Thus Stalin trusted neither his Allies nor his generals: now he played one general against another as he had previously done with the American and British allies.

In Moscow both Zhukov and Koniev wanted to take Berlin now that they had been given the green light. With his tough soldier mentality, Zhukov wanted a frontal attack by his 1st Byelorussian Front while the 'politician' Koniev favored a coordinated attack. Other general staff leaders

Left: One of the last pictures taken of Hitler in March 1945 at his bunker headquarters in Berlin.

Left below: A Volksturm member demonstrates the use of a Panzerfaust antitank weapon.

Right: Some of the men and boys who defended Berlin in May 1945.

Right below: Russians shell the Reichstag and Reichschancellery on 24 April 1945.

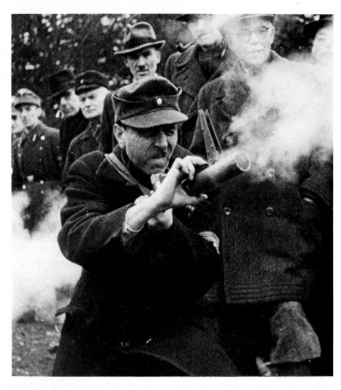

proposed pincer movements. Stalin had made up his mind long before and was just playing games with his generals. After all he had approved Zhukov's frontal proposal on 27 January 1945 and two days later Koniev's coordinated drive; the latter was a thrust from Silesia and river Neisse toward the river Elbe with the right flank of the 1st Ukrainian Front helping the 1st Byelorussians cut the German Army Group Center to ribbons, south of Berlin. However, both these proposals considered the reduction of the capital to be the business of the 1st Byelorussian Front, that is Marshal Zhukov. This would have been the climax of the Marshal's war career and might in a political sense overshadow even the real achievement of the Generalissimo. Cleverly Stalin pretended to consider all the proposals anew

and rather predictably approving the Zhukov-Koniev plans making them dependent on the demarcation line between the two army groups: the line ended at Lubben on the Spree river and Stalin added rather explicitly 'Whoever gets there first, will also take Berlin.' Thus he not only usurped all the prestige from the overall success of the operation, but made sure that he would control it throughout its stages up to the final point at Lubben, when he could decide which of the competing generals would be allotted the final trophy. As was usual with Stalin, once he had defined and safeguarded his own interests, he gave a completely free hand to Zhukov and Koniev to prepare and execute the operation on the spot.

As always Zhukov took the coming battle of Berlin most seriously. Immediately after his return from Moscow he invited all the commanders to his HQ and the conference lasted two days (5 to 7 April 1945). Commanders of support services also took part in these staff conferences and all the command aspects of the offensive were thoroughly thrashed out. Between 8 and 14 April Zhukov ordered more detailed war games to be conducted by the lower commanders. To Zhukov's mind the taking of Berlin whose defenses were well prepared and covered some 350 square miles was a formidable task and he ordered six aerial surveys by Soviet reconnaissance aircraft. Above all he was worried by the overextended lines of communications which made supplies difficult to move into operational zones. After all the 1st Ukrainian Front also had its supply problems, but it was the supplies of Rokossovsky's 2nd Byelorussian Front (which was to launch its offensive five days' later) which complicated Zhukov's supply situation. Up to the last moment Zhukov could not be sure that his supply requirements would be met in time.

Since 'never before in the experience of warfare had (Zhukov) been called upon to capture a city as large and as heavily fortified' he had his engineers construct an exact model of the city and its suburbs in planning the final assault: every street, square, alley, building, canal, bridge and the underground network were taken into consideration. Detailed assault maps compiled from aerial surveys, captured documents and interrogation reports of POWs, were supplied to all commands down to company level. Zhukov's next consideration was how his offensive would make the maximum impact on the enemy and he decided to launch it during the two hours before dawn. In order to avoid confusion among his own troops 140 powerful searchlights were to be used to illuminate the German positions. Thus Zhukov personally took care of every detail of the operation even allowing his politruks [political commissars] to take care of his men's morale, which they did without unduly disturbing the general, who was completely absorbed in military matters.

When Zhukov began to plan the Berlin operation, following his great victories between the Vistula and Oder rivers in January–March 1945, he knew practically nothing of Allied military plans. Stalin must have let him know that General Bradley had turned down the operation against Berlin on account of heavy casualties. However he did not add Bradley's rider 'that after all that the Americans would have to hand over Berlin to the Russians because of the zonal agreement.' Still Zhukov never cared much about casualties and this time he was prepared for any sacrifice, since Stalin himself urged the final operation for political reasons. In March 1945 Zhukov had to face new factors on the German side as soon as he had finished his own regrouping in his zone of operations between Schwedt and Gross Gastroze and particularly in the Küstrin sector, where

he had a beachhead on the other side of the Oder river. These new factors would make the Berlin operation even more costly. After the February breakthrough the German High Command reorganized its Berlin defenses into three zones: the first, main defense line and two other, rear ones. The first line ran along the left banks of the rivers Oder and Neisse and consisted of three fortified networks protected by minefields, in the depth of three to six miles. The second defense line was some 10–14 miles from the first defense line and was connected by means of strongpoints, up to the depth of two miles. The third line was seven to 14 miles from the second one, but was unfinished when Zhukov launched his attack.

On paper Zhukov, who had detailed intelligence reports, had to face a formidable enemy: for the defense of his capital Hitler concentrated round and in Berlin Third Panzer Army and Ninth Field Army from the Army Group Vistula and Fourth Panzer Army and Seventeenth Field Army from the Army Group Center. Thus only in regular troops Hitler, who assumed the defense of the capital himself, had some 48 infantry divisions, four Panzer divisions and 10 motorized divisions. In addition Berlin contained a garrison of some 200,000 men, of whom, however, 200 battalions were Volkssturm formations. Youths of 16–17 years of age were specially trained in Panzerfaust handling and were to perform miracles in the defense of the capital against the Russian tanks. Hitler also concentrated some 72 percent of his Luftwaffe in Berlin. Altogether Hitler amassed some 1 million men, 10,400 guns and mine-throwers, 1500 tanks and self-propelled guns, more than 3,000,000 antitank rockets (Panzerfaust) and 3300 aircraft. Thus he had one division per nine kilometers of the front; 17.3 guns per kilometer of the front; and in the Küstrin sector, where a frontal attack was rightly expected, he had one division per three kilometers and 66 guns and 17 tanks per kilometer of the front. (A greater density was achieved only at Kursk in 1943, where the Russians deployed 105 guns per kilometer in the expected sector of

Soviet sharpshooters pick off snipers in the streets of Berlin. The fighting for the inner city was bitter and lasted for five days.

attack.) In addition Hitler put in charge of the Küstrin defenses General Heinrici, an acknowledged Wehrmacht expert on defense fighting: once again Heinrici succeeded in withdrawing from the first line of defense under cover of darkness, so that the Russian artillery barrage hit empty trenches. While the German High Command was a little disorganized, because of Hitler's interference, German soldiers were in a desperate mood, ready to defend the capital to the last shot, largely because of the barbaric behavior of the Red Army in East Prussia.

To bring this impressive edifice of Hitler's power crashing down Zhukov was given a free hand in the actual offensive planning and execution and Zhukov could also alter the deployment of the Stavka's strategic reserves. Stalin, nevertheless, sent another of his watchdogs to check on his tough general in the shape of General Vasiliy Sokolovsky, whom he appointed as 1st deputy commander. In fact Sokolovsky, who was a finer soldier than Zhukov himself, strengthened Zhukov's forces rather than restricting him and Stalin never forgave him, giving him no appointment of distinction while alive.

Zhukov's front was narrowed from some 200 to 120 miles and for his frontal assault it was in fact some 28 miles. In this narrow zone Zhukov concentrated a group of shock armies consisting of Forty-seventh Army, Third and Fifth Shock Armies, Eighth Guard Army, Third Army and First and Second Tank Guard Armies. His artillery had some 250 guns and minethrowers per kilometer of the assault sector and some 1000 rocket guns (Katyushas) which were mobile. From the air Zhukov was supported by Colonel General S Rudenko's 16th Air Fleet and the Polish Air Corps. With the support from the 2nd Byelorussian front (Marshal Rokossovsky) and 1st Ukrainian front (Marshal Koniev) Zhukov had an overall control over some 2,500,000 men, 41,600 guns, 6250 tanks and 7500 aircraft.

According to Zhukov's plans, approved previously by Stalin, this formidable force was to be launched on 16 April 1945 to annihilate frontally the opponent in the Küstrin sector, break through toward Berlin which at first would be bypassed from the northwest and southeast and then stormed. The tank armies were made responsible for the exploitation of the breakthroughs: on the second day the Second Tank Guard Army would fight its way in the northwesterly direction while the First Tank Guard Army would do the same in the southeasterly. As a result the Fifth Shock, Eighth Guard and Sixty-ninth Armies would take the city on the sixth day of the operation. Zhukov was to achieve this straightforward success provided that Koniev's Twenty-eighth Army and Third Tank Guard Army succeeded in breaking through into Berlin from the south and Rokossovsky's armies covered his right flank, for they were not intended to launch their offensive attacks until two days later.

It was only on 15 April 1945 that Stalin informed the Supreme Allied Command of the Berlin operation; up to then he maintained that the Russian main thrust would be in the direction of Leipzig. Then at 0300 hours on 16 April Zhukov's barrage was started, but Heinrici had anticipated it and evacuated the first line at 2000 hours the previous evening. During the murky dawn, before 0500 hours, the barrage was shifted farther on, and the four armies (Third and Fifth Shock, Eighth Guard and Sixty-ninth) pulled out of their positions to attack the empty German line in the light of some 143 search lights (zenith projectors). However, the terrain was extremely difficult for tracked vehicles and the German Flak and antitank guns were hitting Russian tank formations with alarming accuracy. Men on both sides exhibited incredible heroism and in many sectors Russian attackers were beaten back. At 1430 hours, after some nine hours of fighting, Zhukov's armies hardly dented the German lines, advancing only some four miles, without achieving a breakthrough. Zhukov suitably depressed telephoned Stalin, who after listening to him quietly, just told him that Koniev's armies had already crossed the Neisse river. However, Zhukov was given permission to react to the circumstances of the battle as he deemed necessary.

Zhukov immediately changed his tactics ordering the 16th Air Fleet to make massive air strikes: enemy gun positions were to be blasted to smithereens; Soviet artillery was ordered to pulverize German strongpoints on the heights and tank armies were thrown into combat even before the important Seelow Heights had been reduced. Tough fighting continued – in the sector of the Third Shock Army the German 309th Infantry Division lost 60 percent of its men – and the Russians only succeeded in destroying the first line of German defense. That night Zhukov once

Soviet troops in the heart of Berlin. Thousands of civilians died in the intense house-to-house fighting.

Right below: Su 122 assault guns
move into Berlin April 1945.

MILES   0   40
KILOMETRES   0   60

BALTIC   SEA

Rügen

STRALSUND
• RIBNITZ
2SA
PEENEMÜNDE
GRIESWALD
Usedom
ROSTOCK
DEMMIN
SWINEMÜNDE
19A
65A
Stettiner Haff
WISMAR
British
Second
Army
GÜSTROW
ANKLAM
UECKERMÜNDE
70A
FRIEDLAND
Third Pz Army
2 Belorussian
Front (Rokossovsky)
attacks AM 20 April
SCHWERIN
NEUBRANDENBURG
PACEWALK
STETTIN
2SA
7 May
WAREN
Army Group Vistula
(Heinrici, then Tippelskirch
acting for Student)
65A
STARGARD
PARCHIM
Müritz
NEUSTRELITZ
PRENZLAU
70A
LUDWIGSLUST
49A
WITTSTOCK
TEMPLIN
49A
DÖMITZ
PRITZWALK
SCHWEDT
LENZEN
WITTENBERGE
ZEHDENICK
ANGERMÜNDE
61A
61A
NEURUPPIN
Operational
Group Steiner
Oder-Havel Canal
61A
US Ninth Army
Pol1A
Rhinkanal
EBERSWALDE
Pol1A
2 GTA
1 Belorussian
Front (Zhukov)
attacks 0500 hrs, 16 April
ORANIENBURG
47A
3SA
Warta
18 Apr
BERNAU
5SA
PRÖTZEL
STENDAL
47A
RATHENOW
47A
STRAUSBERG
3SA
8GA
KÜSTRIN
TANGERMÜNDE
KETZIN
BERLIN
SEELOW
1GTA
1 GTA
3A
Havel
POTSDAM
5SA
GENTHIN
3A
8GA
FÜRSTENWALDE
69A
3A
BRANDENBURG
FRANKFURT an der Oder
BURG
Twelfth Army
3A
BEELITZ
3GTA
29A
33A
MAGDEBURG
69A
BELZIG
4GTA
ZOSSEN
Ninth Army
& part
Fourth Pz
Army
BEESKOW
EISENHÜTTENSTADT
33A
LUCKENWALDE
MARKISCH
BUCHHOLZ
Oder
ZERBST
JÜTTEBOG
BARUTH
GUBEN
LÜBBEN
WITTENBERG
13A
Spree
1 Ukrainian
Front (Konev)
attacks 0615 hrs, 16 April
DESSAU
LUCKAU
3
GA
BERNBURG
US front
25 April
SCHLIEBEN
FINSTERWALDE
COTTBUS
22 Apr
FORST
Saale
HERZBERG
3GTA
18 Apr
Mulde
TORGAU
5GA
Army Group
Centre (Schörner)
SPREMBERG
Fourth Pz
Army
TRIEBEL
13A
4GTA
HALLE
5GA
Elbe
ELSTERWALDE
28A
EILENBURG
25 April 1945
US and Russian
forces make
contact
HOYERSWERDE
Pol2A
LEIPZIG
Neisse
NIESKY
52A
FRONT LINES
15 APRIL 1945
18 APRIL
25 APRIL
6 MAY
RIESA
GROSSENHAIN
KAMENZ
Pol2A
BAUTZEN
GÖRLITZ
GERMAN DEFENCE LINES
GERMAN POCKETS
GERMAN COUNTERATTACKS
ANGLO-AMERICAN ATTACKS
ANGLO-AMERICAN FRONTS AT DATES SHOWN
MEISSEN
RADEBERG
Seventeenth Army
COLDITZ
DRESDEN

US First Army

again telephoned Stalin who excitedly reprimanded him for throwing in the tanks prematurely, altering their axis of attack to a sector (Seelow Heights) where defenses were too strong. Zhukov defended himself with ability by pointing out that he was annihilating the enemy and drawing to his sector Berlin reinforcements. Stalin, however, ended the conversation on a sour note: if Zhukov got stuck, Rokossovsky would take Berlin from the north and Koniev from the south. Still Zhukov's progress on the 17th would decide the issue.

On the following day, albeit the Seelow Heights were taken, the Germans did manage to bring up reinforcements, especially antiaircraft artillery from Berlin, and their stubborn resistance slowed down the advance of Zhukov's armies. Zhukov personally inspected his armies before they lurched forward and used all sorts of gimmicks to boost up Soviet morale. Thus fighter pilots covering and supporting the Eighth Guard Army, threw down on the advancing guards, four parachutes with copies of the keys to Berlin captured by the Russian armies in the Seven Years' War, together with an unhelpful exhortation: 'Forward to Victory – here are the keys to the city.' However, the three reserve divisions and 50 tanks which the enemy threw into the battle slowed down the attacking Russians considerably. On this decisive day of the 17th Zhukov's armies failed to annihilate the second enemy line and Stalin told Koniev in the evening to direct his tanks to Berlin from the south and gave him a free hand to take it.

Zhukov later claimed that he had asked Stalin to shorten his attacking front even further concentrating thus the most formidable firing power to blot out the enemy, but Stalin refused. As it was Zhukov acted feverishly and in

despair, as he saw his competitor, the dullard Koniev, taking from him the final prize. He ordered night raids on enemy strongpoints by the 18th Air Fleet. At 1030 hours the Eighth Guards and First Tank Guards, went forward after an artillery barrage lasting half an hour. Colonel General V I Kazakov, one of the greatest artillerymen, personally directed fire and even he had to acknowledge defeat, when the two attacking armies were brought to a standstill. General M Ye Katukov's First Tank Guards performed all sorts of miracles with their armor, while Chuikov's Eighth Guards pressed on despite their losses. However, this was all a crawl reducing plans to nought and upsetting time schedules. Only early in the morning of the 18th did the right flank of the attacking armies (Forty-seventh and Third Shock Armies) break through the second line of defense: Zhukov's armies were two days behind the schedule. Stalin had to issue new directives to the supporting armies: on the 17th Koniev was ordered to advance on Berlin from the south; a day later Rokossovsky was ordered to drive in the southwestern direction instead of northwest. Thus during the operation itself the offensive was transformed into a tripartite one, instead of the envisaged frontal attack with subsidiary attacks on the right and left flanks.

Zhukov continued his inspections to resolve the problem of non-advancement. He realized that the Russians did not have a full picture of German defenses and above all failed to take into account the water obstacles which the Germans skillfully exploited against the advancing tanks. He also noticed that his armies wasted a lot of artillery fire and the air forces failed to penetrate enemy defenses and annihilate them. Thus on the 19th Zhukov decided on new tactical changes. He considered that his right flank, consisting of the

Forty-seventh and Third Shock armies, managed a great enough break to continue its drive in northerly and north-westerly directions in order to take Berlin from the western side. Colonel General P Belov's Sixty-first Army also changed the direction of its advance along the Hohenzollern canal, while the First Polish Army, Forty-seventh Army and Third and Fifth Shock Armies were ordered to strike in a southwesterly direction instead of westerly. Orders went out to continue the offensive night and day until modified objectives were achieved. Although this concentric attack did drive the Germans from their second defense line they swiftly reorganized and dug in in the unfinished third line. The Ninth German Army took the overall command in this sector, and was reinforced with three infantry divisions and the 11th motorized division, SS Nordland, withdrawn from the northern sector.

Thus on the 18th, when the Third Shock Army advanced to Bazlow where the SS reinforcements were concentrated, they were halted. Both Shock Armies waited until the night and then, after an artillery barrage, they fought all night in close hand-to-hand fighting to overcome this strongpoint. However further advance was checked by increased German air activity: in groups of 30 the Luftwaffe attacked Russian ground formation and kept them pinned down in this sector all day long. However, the right flank once again achieved a breakthrough of some 14 kilometers in the third line and Zhukov poured his tanks into this breach. This was taking his armies further away from Berlin rather than into the city. It was only on the 20th that the Forty-seventh and Third Shock Armies finally broke through the third line and Colonel General S Bogdanov's Second Tank Guards wheeled through to reach Ladeburg–Zepernik pass north of Berlin. The guns of the Third Shock Army closed on Berlin sufficiently to fire two symbolic shots at the city. However, it was only a day later that the Russian armies reached the northern fortifications of the city and the northern ring of the *autobahnen* and began systematic shelling. On that same day the Fifth Shock Army and XII Tank Guard Corps pushed their way into north eastern suburbs achieving the original objective of the whole 1st Byelorussian Front after considerable delay.

The toughest fighting had to be undertaken by the Eighth Tank Guards and First Tank Guards; even as late as 19 and 20 April both armies were bogged down on the third line of defense. Although their superiority was threefold the fanatical resistance of the 23rd Motorized Division, SS Niederland together with five Volkssturm battalions and a special antitank brigade, was able to halt these two elite tank armies. In the sector Fürstenwalde the Germans counterattacked several times; only on 21 April did the units of these two Russian armies reach the outer defense of Berlin at Petershagen and Erckner, while they were supposed to storm the inner city next day.

By 20 April Zhukov more or less acknowledged the failure of his frontal attack on Berlin and decided to wheel round the city and by joining with Koniev's and Rokossovsky's forces cut the capital off, encircle it and storm it afterward. Although Koniev's Third and Fourth Tank Guards were three times as distant from the city as Zhukov's tanks, they reached the outer defenses of the city, after some tough fighting, on the 19th. In this drive to northwest, far

from their original objective, the hardest nut to crack was the Zossen defense strongpoint, which among other things was GHQ Wehrmacht-Heer. On the approaches to Zossen at Barut the Third Tank Guards had to fight hard and once in the defense perimeter it took them two full days to reduce the strongpoint. The terrain was not ideal for tank maneuvers and when at night on the 22nd the strongpoint was taken the Germans blew up and flooded the underground GHQ. However, the Fourth Tank Guards commanded by Colonel General V Gordov, succeeded even better, for after their breakthrough at Kottbus, they drove on toward Potsdam, on the western side of Berlin, ripped a hole in the German defense round Zossen, forcing the German Ninth Army to give up its stand to avoid outflanking. On 21 April Koniev's tanks crossed the outer belt road, but further progress was slowed down by tough resistance especially round the Teltow Canal. It was only on 25 April that Koniev's forces finally made contact with Zhukov's and Berlin was encircled. Even before Lelyushenko's tanks made contact with Perkhorovich's soldiers their respective supporting air forces were strafing and bombing each other. On that day Stalin ruled that the city be divided between Koniev's and Zhukov's fronts along a line running 150 meters west of the Reichstag building. Also on that day Koniev's soldiers reached the river Elbe near Torgau and met for the first time American troops.

Zhukov was however completely absorbed in directing

the fighting. It became clear that Hitler had ordered General Steiner's Army Group and General Wenck's regrouped Twelfth Army to counterattack and relieve the city. While the former's attack never really got off the ground, the latter was joined by a hastily assembled group isolated in the south of the city, consisting of one motorized, three infantry and a tank division, and they managed to break through between Koniev's Twenty-eighth and Third Guards. Once again there was some tough fighting around the town Barut, but within a day the Third Tank Guards were let loose on these improvised and desperate formations and they broke them up. This was the final masterstroke that Hitler conjured up and sent Keitel to implement. Afterward the Germans acknowledged that they were surrounded in the capital, but rather than surrendering they were willing to go through the *Götterdammerung* while Hitler was alive and even after. Although their situation was hopeless they continued to form Volkssturm battalions and at the time that the capital was encircled they had some 200 battalions in position. Apart from the Volkssturm they had some 80,000 infantry in the city from the various armies defeated on the approaches. Hitler and the Nazis could feel quite safe from the security point of view, for there were some 32,000 police troops. Throughout Berlin at strategic crossroads, squares and parks the defenders had built block houses and pillboxes, tanks were dug in and mobility was assured by the underground railroad network. However, there was also the population to feed and no antiaircraft cover: the Russians now concentrated the 16th and 18th Air Fleets on heavy bombing. Thus in the night of 26 April 563 aircraft of the 18th Air Fleet dropped on Berlin some 569 tons of bombs.

Despite all this Zhukov found it quite a task to reduce and take the city fiercely defended by some 300,000 fanatical soldiers under the leadership of General Weidling. However, once the breakout efforts by the Germans had been contained, both Zhukov and Koniev, after Stalin had altered still further the respective front boundaries on the 29th, threw themselves onto the hapless city with great gusto. According to Stalin's ruling Zhukov's troops would take the central sector of Berlin and in compensation Koniev's armies were permitted to divert to Prague, which had risen against the Germans at this time, and liberate that capital. Zhukov ordered the Third Shock, Forty-seventh Armies and two tanks armies, First and Second Guards, to storm the inner city from the north. Zhukov said that he had thrown in the two tank armies, because they had no other operational tasks and their impact would further destroy the morale of the enemy. It seems, however, that the employment of the tank armies in storming a city was the result of political pressure. Stalin had been worried by the lack of progress and by delays, and was once again suspicious of his allies. He thought they just might make a dash for Berlin from Torgau, despite an agreement with him. He therefore ordered Zhukov to engage in this costly way of taking a city. The tanks undoubtedly demoralized the German defenders, but at a cost: in the street fighting they could not maneuver and were sitting ducks for the youthful defenders with their Panzerfausts. In all parts of the city hand-to-hand fighting continued from house to house, block to block, street to street.

The central sector of the city (9th district) was particularly well prepared for the defense. The river Spree formed a natural defense in the north, while in the south the Tiergarten and other parks and boulevards were transformed into fortresses. The Reichstag building in the very center, at which the two Russian armies were both aiming, was a veritable Festung which reinforced walls, railings all round, and windows covered with cement plates. All the streets leading to the Reichstag were barred with barricades and fierce fighting continued from one to another. The Third Shock Army forced its way into Moabit and reached the Spree and were poised near the Moltke bridge to fight its way to the Reichstag. The Fifth Shock Army and the Eighth Guards with the First Tank Guards were making their way into the center from the east and southeast. Koniev's Third Tank Guards and Twenty-eighth Army were making their way through the southern defenses. The Second Tank Guards, after taking Charlottenburg, began to make their way into the center from the northwest. In the west the Forty-seventh and Thirteenth Armies together with Fourth Tank Guards were protecting the rear of the storming armies.

To demonstrate how fierce the fighting was we must realize that on 29 April, when units of the Thirteenth Army stormed and captured the Moltke bridge they were some

By 1 May 1945 Soviet troops had reached the Reichstag. These troops are carrying a flag which they were to fix on top of the building.

300 meters from the Reichstag, which Stalin, for his own reasons, singled out as the ultimate objective. Still it took the Russians three days before they could hoist their flag over the ruined building. In the night of 1 May the Third Army command ordered Colonel Zinchenko with his 756th Regiment to get the flag on the building for symbolic reasons, even though the Reichstag block was still largely in German hands. Sergeants Yegorov and Kantariya, under heavy fire, scaled the ruins, and the Russian generals and soldiers in the center could see their flag flying. The Russians give enemy casualties in that sector (2500 dead and wounded, 2604 captured; 28 guns destroyed, 59 captured together with 15 tanks), but not theirs, for their symbolic gesture must have cost Zhukov and Stalin heaps of casualties.

Even after the Soviet flag had been unfurled on the Reichstag fierce fighting continued. The Russians had no idea what was happening in Hitler's bunker under the Reich Chancellery and on 1 May they thought the Germans would surrender, when at 1500 hours General Krebs, then Chief of Staff, appeared on the line of the Eighth Guards and asked for parley with the Soviet command. Zhukov refused to see him, but he sent his first deputy, General Sokolovsky to assist General Chuikov in negotiations. They all had Stalin's order to accept unconditional surrender only. Krebs, who was the last military attaché in Moscow before the war, told Chuikov that Hitler had committed suicide and handed over power to Admiral Karl Dönitz and Dr Josef Goebbels. The latter was interested in an armistice, but the Russians told Krebs that it would have to be unconditional surrender: if the garrison surrendered Chuikov guaranteed them their lives, personal belongings to the soldiers and small arms to the officers. At 1800 hours Krebs brought back a message from Goebbels that Russian conditions were unacceptable and the fighting was resumed.

Immediately after artillery barrages the Russians went on with street fighting; it was only now, 1 May, that the Third Shock Army effected junction with the Eighth Guards south of the Reichstag. Only early next day did the Second Tank Guards finally meet Eighth Guards and First Tank Guards in the area of the Tiergarten. Although they had met, not all Berlin was under their control; in fact counterattacks continued in all areas, even in the Tiergarten, where the Russians overran General Weidling's command post. Still the hapless general decided to throw the sponge in and sent Colonel von Duwing to negotiate surrender. For the German command it was all over at 0630 hours when they all trudged into Russian captivity; in the afternoon, at 1500 hours, the rest of the garrison, some 70,000 men, gave up. It was only now, on 2 May 1945, five days before the general surrender, that Zhukov could report to Stalin that he had successfully completed his mission and that the Nazi capital was in his power. At this stage Zhukov had no idea at what cost this had been accomplished. Only in 1963 were we given details: the Berlin operation was described as one of the biggest of the war. Some 3,500,000 men fought in it equipped with 50,000 guns, 8000 tanks, and over 9000

Above: The scene on the Kurfürstendamm, a street that was famous for its theaters and clubs.

Left: The final assault on the Reichstag.

Far left: Soviet troops charge down to the Reichstag.

aircraft. The Russians captured 480,000 Germans, 1500 tanks, 4500 aircraft and 10,917 guns. They lost 304,887 dead, 2156 tanks, 1220 guns and 527 aircraft. We can immediately see General Omar Bradley's point: overall Allied casualties for the whole of 1945 operations were 260,000 men.

Immediately after the unconditional surrender, 8 May 1945, Marshal Georgy Zhukov held a press conference at which he briefed the world about his part on the surrender of the German Reich. He emphasized that the German

armies were smashed on the river Oder and that the Berlin operation was really a mopping up. He did not mention any other generals who might have helped him with Berlin and generally seemed to play down 'this crowning achievement of World War II.' Still in 1965 when he finally published his memories of this battle, he acknowledged that the Berlin battle was his greatest. It is true that he had planned and executed the three decisive battles in Russia, at Moscow, Stalingrad and Kursk, but in all these battles his participation was overshadowed by that of his warlord, Stalin. It

Right: Jodl and von Friedeburg sign the instrument of surrender with Allied representatives.

Left bottom: Marshal Zhukov signs the four-power pact on the surrender of Germany.

Far left above: Soviet troops congregate in front of the Brandenburg Gate on 2 May 1945.

Far left center: Soviet troops raise the victory flag over the Brandenburg Gate.

Left: The view from the top of the Reichstag as a Soviet soldier raises the Red Flag on 2 May 1945.

was only at this last battle that the warlord singled Zhukov out for the 'crowning glory,' very much against the opposition of the other generals. Stalin not only accepted Zhukov's strategic plans, but gave him a completely free hand in tactical matters. Thus he foisted Zhukov on the 1st Byelorussian Front (and transferred Zhukov's rare friend, Rokossovsky, to command the 2nd Byelorrusian Front), and then determined, by means of demarcation lines that the 1st Byelorussian Front and not the 1st Ukrainian Front take the capital.

However, he also revised the time schedules and demarcation lines to suit his personal and political purposes. It is thought that he delayed Zhukov's dash for Berlin in February 1945 for political purposes – he had the Yalta conference to attend and Allied political pressures to consider. In the final phases of the operation he changed the demarcation lines between Zhukov's and Koniev's armies several times, probably not to give any of his generals total credit. So apart from these two basic considerations Zhukov, for the first time in the war, acted not as a representative of the Stavka, or coordinator, or '*Spasitel*' (Savior) as in the Battle of Moscow, but on his own with control over strategic reserves, changing both strategic and tactical plans as he went, with the Stavka (and Stalin) approving them subsequently.

Thus the battle of Berlin had all the characteristics of Zhukov's past battles. Each time he amassed and commanded huge armies; millions of men were involved on both sides; meticulous staff work, preparations and rehearsals were conducted before each battle; each time he expended artillery and air power lavishly; each time armor was massively deployed and used; each time infantry did the actual fighting on a gigantic scale inflicting irreplaceable losses on the enemy; each time his own casualties were enormous. The series of Zhukov's battles was started in 1939 against the Japanese Kwantung armies and even then it was described by the British expert, Professor John

Erickson, as brilliant but costly. This was a characteristic Zhukov had in common with Stalin and may be the key to their wartime close friendship: both believed military aims can only be achieved by sacrificing life on a massive scale.

In addition Zhukov's personal characteristics contributed to this 'crowning victory' of his military career. He was not a popular figure; he never put a human touch to his orders; he had no friends only subordinates and one superior. He had a will of iron, tempestuous temper and almost supernatural determination, all of which characteristics were those of his principal opponent, Hitler. While Hitler could let loose these terrible traits on the German nation and the Wehrmacht to a certain extent, Zhukov let them loose liberally. He spoke rough, acted rough: his terrible threats – obey orders or face the firing squad – were invariably backed up. By means of these unattractive qualities he achieved success everywhere, and though he was a lonely figure, he was respected even by his rough fellow soldiers. The Berlin battle reflected both his character and military genius, and Stalin recognized it by sharing the podium with him at the victory parade in Moscow in June 1945. In Berlin Zhukov proved to the world that he was the master of the twentieth-century mass warfare and had no equal either at home or abroad. However, in strictly military terms he cannot be ranked highly. All the strategic decisions concerning his battle were taken by a committee whose chairman was Stalin. Even his tactical decisions were controlled by the committee, and above all Stalin, who rectified some of the costly errors: the initial frontal assault was a failure, and the line of the armor attack had to be changed several times to achieve success. In the battle for the city Zhukov also made many costly tactical mistakes, which undoubtedly overshadowed the overall achievement. One judgment that can safely be made about his generalship was that he was infinitely ruthless about his men in order to achieve overall success: however, such generals of World War I, were termed butchers of their men, not great generals.

MACARTHUR AT INCHON 1950

The amphibious landing at Inchon, one of the most
successful operations of its kind in military history,
took place in mid-September 1950, early in the
Korean War. Men from 17 member countries of the
United Nations fought in that remote country. Yet no great
novels or poetry no major cinematic efforts (with the
possible exception of the comedy, M*A*S*H) have emerged
to make the war real to those who stayed at home.

This nonwar – this 'police action' – claimed some
100,000 American casualties alone in three years; at one
point US forces numbered 750,000 (the largest American
force ever fielded under one command). Quite apart from
the numbers of men committed, the technological advances
and the war's strategic implications in the Far East, its
unique place in military history – as the bridge between
traditional conflicts fought to achieve total victory and the
more recent 'limited' wars – must mark it as a major
military event.

By the same token Inchon – the latest and probably the
last great amphibious operation – has often been dismissed as a wild gamble that succeeded only by virtue of
incredible luck. In fact, it was much more. Admiral Halsey
called this dramatic switch from defense to offense 'the most
masterly and audacious strategic course in all history.'
David Rees, in Korea: The Limited War, has called it, 'a 20th-
Century Cannae, ever to be studied.' It stands as a monu-
ment to military professionalism – in the formulation of
complex plans under great pressure, in the execution of
those plans against tremendous odds, but most of all to the
strategic genius and iron will of one man – General Douglas
MacArthur.

Against all advice and despite all apparent disadvantages,
MacArthur decided to divide his Korean forces, using part
to hold the besieged Pusan Perimeter and the rest to mount
an intricate amphibious attack on the port of Inchon, far
behind enemy lines. It was a daring plan that turned out to
be the most brilliant stroke of a brilliant, if controversial,
career. It also foreshadowed – indeed, its very success
contributed to – the downfall of the commander, while the
war of which it was a part was to end in stalemate.

Douglas MacArthur was intelligent, courageous, professional, impressive and even attractive – but not loveable.
At least a partial explanation lies in the fact that MacArthur
himself was, as William Manchester notes in American
Caesar, 'a great, thundering paradox of a man.' For virtually
every strength in his character one must cite a corresponding weakness and for every military triumph a mistake,
often caused by overconfidence or an inability to look at
facts squarely and objectively.

MacArthur's background is well known. He came from a
family with a strong military tradition. His father, Arthur
MacArthur, was a popular hero during the Spanish-
American War. Following in his father's footsteps he went
to West Point Academy and graduated first of his class in
June 1902.

MacArthur saw his first action in World War I in
February 1918 and at the same time collected the first of his
many combat decorations – the American Silver Star and
the French Croix de Guerre – for leading a raiding party
through the barbed wire. During World War I he was to
receive two Distinguished Service Crosses (second only to

Above: MacArthur meets Emperor Hirohito after the Japanese surrender. Hirohito is supposed to have admired MacArthur.

Top: President Harry Truman with whom MacArthur was to have such a difficult relationship.

the Medal of Honor), another Croix de Guerre, six more Silver Stars, and an appointment as a Commander of the Legion of Honor. In this first intensive, practical experience of war he proved that he could operate bravely and effectively in combat. He also turned out to be a fine commander. His men were proud to serve under him, and after the war General Pershing wrote that he was 'the best leader of troops we have.'

In June 1919 he took over as Superintendent of West Point – at the age of 39, one of the youngest men ever to hold that position. A three-year tour of duty in the Philippines (1922–25) strengthened his commitment to that island country. His wholehearted support of Philippine independence made him many friends among the Filipinos – and a corresponding number of enemies among those who preferred the colonial system.

In November 1930 MacArthur returned from another posting to the Philippines to Washington as Chief of Staff with the rank of general. On his retirement from that post in 1935, MacArthur set off once more for the Philippines (this time as Military Adviser to the Commonwealth). This last sojourn in the Philippines proved unfortunate in several respects. It marked the final disappearance of the tough field commander beloved by the doughboys of the Rainbow Division and the emergence of the pompous, theatrical mini-dictator who caused World War II GIs so much amusement.

In July 1941, when the US, Britain, and Holland froze Japanese assets in their respective areas, MacArthur was named commander of the US Forces in the Far East. In the four months between his appointment and the Japanese attacks on Pearl Harbor and the Philippines in December, his relations with Roosevelt were strained – especially as the President resolved to put European affairs first. Even in the days just before the invasion MacArthur remained optimistic about his ability to repulse – or at least delay – a Japanese attack on the Philippines. His staff may have kept from him the knowledge of just how badly equipped his troops were. In addition, he seems to have convinced himself with his own rhetoric and believed that he was invincible.

MacArthur's role in World War II is well documented: the attack on the Philippines that destroyed most of his air force on the ground; the subsequent, badly organized retreat; and the comeback, in the brilliantly conceived New Guinea campaign and retaking of the islands. He soon became a hero to the American public. In part this adulation was based on real achievements. However, the general consistently issued communiques that were greatly exaggerated and gave all the credit to the commander and little or none to the men who did the actual staffwork or fighting. Ostensibly this was an attempt to build up morale at home. However, the practice continued long after there was any need for morale building, and the troops were less than impressed. The cynical, antiauthoritarian GIs did not appreciate 'Dugout Doug's' gold braid and turgid rhetoric. The more accessible Eisenhower ('Ike'), with his friendly smile and relaxed, unassuming manner, was more their style.

Throughout the war MacArthur demonstrated a complete inability to see his theater of operations as part of an overall tactical plan. He bitterly resented his low priority

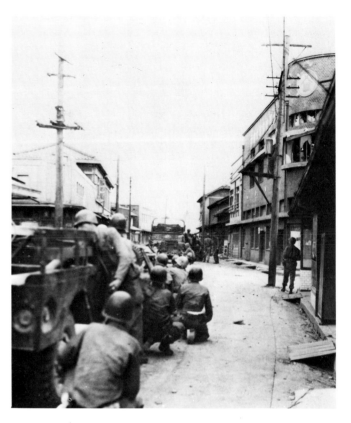

vis à vis Europe, and conducted a running battle with the President, the State Department, and the Pentagon – all of whom were credited by his staff with being in league with the British imperialists or, worse still, the Communists. Even before the end of the war this complaint had begun to creep into his news releases – and of course it was eagerly seized upon by disaffected Republicans at home.

MacArthur's appointment as viceroy of postwar Japan was one very much to his taste, and he turned out to be a compassionate and generous dictator. Surprisingly, the political reactionary introduced a wide range of liberal policies including civil rights for women, the organization of labor unions and a series of land reforms that completely restructured Japan's feudalistic rural society. Despite his model administration and many achievements, MacArthur on the whole had a bad press at home, mainly the result of his high-handed treatment of correspondents and his public quarrels with those who offended him in any way. The Republicans still hoped to field him as a serious presidential candidate, but his refusal to leave Japan spoiled their hopes. His reason for remaining was that he was absolutely convinced that if he 'returned for only a few weeks, the word would spread through the Pacific that the US had abandoned the Far East.' Though he was nominated at the 1948 Republican convention, he suffered a decisive defeat.

In 1950 the American defense establishment was in a sorry state. Wholesale demobilization after the war had severely reduced its numbers, and the recent unification of the Armed Forces had divided the remainder into hostile cliques, each striving to ensure the survival of its service. The two units under strongest attack were the Navy's air arm and the Marine Corps. In October of the previous year General Omar Bradley had informed the Armed Services Commission that 'large-scale amphibious operations . . . will never occur again.' In the next months of in-fighting a series of savage cutbacks reduced the number of Navy amphibious vessels from 362 (in 1947) to 91. Plans were also afoot to transform the Marines into a 'lightly armed,' largely ceremonial force.

In the Far East MacArthur, now 70, had long since passed retirement age. His military bearing as he paced vigorously through his Tokyo headquarters, his penetrating gaze and his unassailable self-confidence made observers forget his age. The forces under his command consisted of the Eighth Army (four undermanned and undertrained divisions commanded by General Walton H 'Johnny' Walker) and US Naval Forces Far East (one light cruiser and four destroyers). The Seventh Fleet, commanded by Vice Admiral Arthur D Struble in the Philippines, included one carrier, one cruiser, a squadron of destroyers and a division of submarines, and was not under MacArthur's control. As the only senior American commander who still believed in the value of amphibious operations, he requested, and in April 1950 received, a small Marine mobile training unit of 67 officers and men. They were augmented the following month by a tiny, naval amphibious force from San Diego headed by an enthusiastic, capable veteran, Rear Admiral James H Doyle.

Korea had also been occupied after World War II. The Soviet Union controlled the northern half, above the 38th Parallel, while the US occupied the south. MacArthur saw the danger clearly, but he had cried 'wolf' too often and his warnings about the 'Communist menace' went unheeded – as were CIA reports which as early as March 1950 described mammoth build ups north of the 38th Parallel and predicted an invasion for June. In Washington the re-unification of Korea was viewed as a political problem for the United Nations – not as a military or strategic one for the United States.

By June 1950 the only American personnel left in the Republic of Korea were a handful of diplomats and the 500-man Korean Military Advisory Group, which stayed to train and advise the Republic of Korea (ROK) Army. This South Korean army was seen as little more than a police force and was purposely kept underequipped to inhibit 75-year-old President Syngman Rhee's bloodthirsty plans for reunification. The 65,000 combat troops were equipped with cast off, American small arms and old Japanese Mausers, along with a few short-range M3 105mm howitzers and 2.36-inch bazookas. They had no medium artillery or combat aircraft.

In North Korea it was a different story. Beginning with a cadre of some 3000 North Korean veterans who had seen action in China and the Soviet Union during World War II, the Soviet Union had been laboring since 1945 to build up a tough, well-equipped, well-trained army. By 1950 the *In Min Gun*, or North Korean Peoples Army (NKPA), numbered 120,000 men equipped with almost 100 Yak and Sturmovik fighter planes, 150 T-34 tanks, and a vast array of modern artillery and infantry weapons.

At 0400 hours on 25 June eight NKPA divisions exploded over the 38th Parallel. The summer monsoons had just begun. Rain was falling heavily as the big guns opened up along the 40-mile front and the fighters headed toward the South Korean capital of Seoul, less than 50 miles away. The ROK Army – what was left of it – fell back in confusion before the disciplined NKPA columns. Within 72 hours Seoul had fallen and the South Koreans were in full retreat toward the south.

At MacArthur's headquarters the news of the invasion was soon followed by a message from Washington notifying

Far left above: Street fighting in southern Korea on 21 July 1950.

Left: Americans receive first aid during the first few chaotic months of the fighting in South Korea.

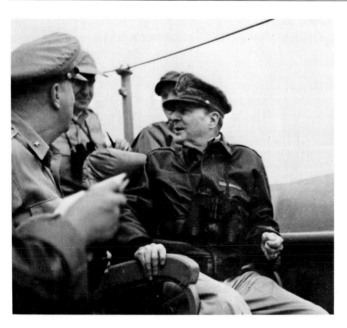

MacArthur watches the Inchon invasion from aboard the USS *Rochester* with Vice-Admiral Doyle and General Harris.

him that he would be in command of any US military operations. Immediately he flew out to Korea to assess the situation. He stayed eight hours and spent only 20 minutes watching a battle for the bridges over the Han outside Seoul, but it was enough to convince him that on their own the South Koreans were doomed. Hurrying back to Tokyo, he informed the Pentagon that he needed US ground combat troops and he needed them immediately. Truman received his message at 0300 on 30 June. The Security Council of the United Nations had already met in hasty session to censure North Korea and, in another, had voted to render South Korea 'every assistance.' At 0500 hours, therefore, Truman authorized MacArthur to send one regiment into combat. By lunchtime he had met with his war cabinet and approved not only the expansion of the expeditionary force, but the calling up of American reservists. The US was at war again, though no one had asked Congress for so much as an opinion.

One of MacArthur's first acts on receiving his orders from Washington had been to send a GHQ Advance Command Group to Korea under Major General John H Church, to collect supplies, information about the best places to use American troops and so on. On 1 July the first combat forces – 406 officers and men of the 24th Infantry Division – landed at Pusan, in the southeastern corner of the peninsula. On 7 July MacArthur was officially named Supreme Commander Allied Powers (SCAP) by the United Nations.

Most observers assumed that the tide would turn as soon as the Americans landed in Korea, but it was not to be. Less than 20 percent of the men in 24th and 25th Infantry Divisions had seen action in World War II and even the veterans were out of shape and yearning for their soft jobs back in Japan. They were outnumbered 20 to one, and their 10-year-old bazookas had no effect on the powerful T-34s. As US and ROK forces were driven relentlessly back toward the coast at Pusan, defeatism began to creep into the high command.

However, MacArthur remained confident. Tirelessly he paced and thought, studied maps and talked to himself. As the American defense finally stiffened and held in the small corner around Pusan, a plan began to take shape. Obviously, the NKPA supply lines were dangerously attenuated after their rapid advance. He planned to land in the rear, cut the supply lines and – in one great enveloping action – cut the army off and destroy it. Geographically Inchon, a Yellow Sea port just a few miles west of Seoul, was the perfect spot. The more he thought about it the more he liked it, and the doubts of his staff regarding its obvious unsuitability for an amphibious landing only reinforced his notion that it would be the perfect spot for a surprise attack.

On 3 July the Joint Chiefs of Staff received a message from MacArthur requesting the immediate dispatch of a Marine regimental combat team. JCS had not yet decided whether Marines would be sent to Korea at all but on 4 July, while they were discussing the matter, MacArthur was already outlining his plan to army, navy and air force staff in Tokyo.

The first scenario, code named Operation Bluehearts, called for landing the 1st Cavalry Division at Inchon on 22 July. It was too ambitious. Eighteen days were not enough to plan any amphibious operation, and the plan was finally scrapped when 1st Cavalry was needed to help defend Pusan. The basic idea was still alive. On 9 July MacArthur received a visit from Lieutenant General Lemuel C Shepherd, the new commander of Fleet Marine Force, Pacific in Hawaii. On his arrival Shepherd heard that General Collins (the Army Chief of Staff) had already told MacArthur that no Marines were available. Shepherd's response – an assurance that he could get 1st Marine Division together in three weeks and in Korea in another three – resulted in the first of a series of messages from MacArthur to the Pentagon. Under the bombardment, JCS finally gave way. On 20 July MacArthur was told that he could have his Marine division plus air support in November or December. Back shot another message from SCAP, 'Essential Marine Division arrive by 10 September 1950. There can be no demand for its potential use elsewhere that can equal the urgency of the immediate battle use contemplated for it.' This was enough to elicit a prompt request for more information, and the resulting outline of MacArthur's plan (now code named Operation Chromite) did little to ease minds in the Pentagon. On 25 July they gave in – but almost immediately began to have second thoughts.

One of MacArthur's major problems was an acute shortage of trained men. Truman was understandably reluctant to call back seasoned World War II veterans who were just settling down in civilian life, and raw recruits could be of only limited value against the North Koreans. The crack troops of 1st Marine Division gave MacArthur the edge he needed – men already familiar with the host of specialized techniques required for an amphibious operation who, as the long lines of reservists outside Marine offices showed, were anxious to employ them.

Doyle and his staff of Amphibious Group I (usually called Phib-1) were already at work on preliminary planning for the landing when news came that the Marine division had been approved. They continued work on the naval side of the operation while responsibility for the main coordination and planning was shifted to the Joint Strategic Plans and Operations Group (JSPOG) – MacArthur's 'staff within a staff' which contained representatives from all four services.

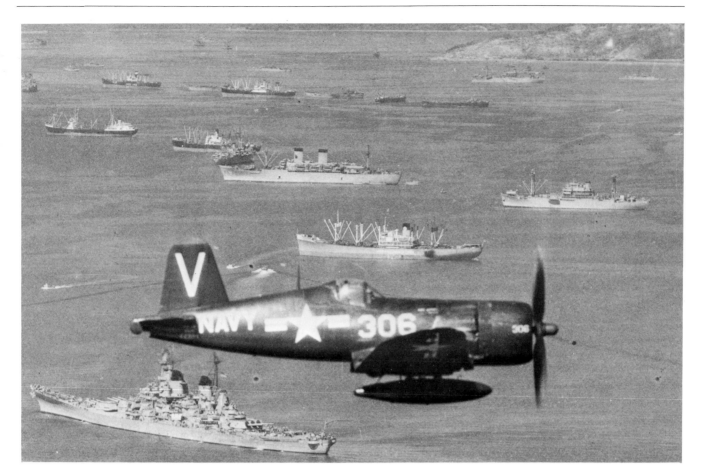

A Navy F4U-4 from the USS *Philippine Sea* flies over supply ships in the Inchon anchorage.

Though the planners considered other landing places, such as Kunsan, it was obvious that MacArthur was set on Inchon. Traditionally, landings take place on lonely beaches, not on city waterfronts that are strongly held by enemy forces. Add Inchon's other disadvantages and you have the oft-quoted remark by Lieutenant Commander Arlie G Capps: 'We drew up a list of every natural and geographic handicap – and Inchon had them all.' Or as Doyle's communications officer put it, 'Make up a list of amphibious "don'ts" and you have an exact description of the Inchon operation.'

In 1950 Inchon – the ancient gateway to the Korean capital of Seoul – was an ugly, dreary industrial port about the size of Jersey City. Its sheltered harbor is always ice-free, but that was its only asset. For the rest, it was a planner's nightmare. The only viable approach was through Flying Fish Channel – a tortuous and difficult passage studded with rocks, shoals and islands, where currents ran up to eight knots and which, moreover, was easily mined. It was so narrow in places that one disabled ship would block all others behind it. Once through the channel the landing force would be in a cul-de-sac, facing high seawalls (higher than the standard ladders) and piers, and overlooked by the hills on both the mainland and on the mile-long island of Wolmi Do, which dominated the harbor. The tidal range of 32 feet was second only to the Bay of Fundy, but the only time tides would be high enough to support a landing operation would be on 15 September and again on 11 October. Then, during short periods in the morning and evening, landing craft could get in, but between tides they

would be stranded on huge mud flats. On 15 September high tide would be reached at 0659 hours, only 45 minutes after sunrise. This meant that the landing force would have to negotiate Flying Fish Channel in the dark. In the evening the tide rose at 1919 hours – 37 minutes after sunset. On top of everything else, September was the middle of the typhoon season.

August came. In the small rectangle around Pusan 'Johnny' Walker worked frantically to avoid being overrun. In Tokyo JSPOG and the Navy planners continued to collect information for Chromite. Navy intelligence men scoured the country for anyone who knew about Inchon – tides and currents, the trafficability of the beaches and mud flats, the position and heights of the seawalls and so on. MacArthur was assaulted on all sides by demands from Walker for every available man, by worried messages from JCS, by the fears of the naval planners, the arguments of the Marines and even the concern of his own staff. Through it all he remained supremely confident and aloof, blandly refusing to contemplate the impossibility of the operation. As far as he was concerned, the benefits to be derived from retaking Seoul and the nearby Kimpo airfield, cutting the North Korean communication lines and beginning a two-front war outweighed every disadvantage his superiors or staff could present.

His attitude may have been infuriating, but he did ensure that plans for Chromite continued to move forward instead of getting bogged down by the sheer impossibility of the action. By this time almost everyone in GHQ had a hand in some part of the planning, much of which was carried out by word of mouth. Not surprisingly, news of the operation leaked out and soon every correspondent in Tokyo was aware of Operation Common Knowledge. All the planners could do was try to direct their attention to Kunsan and other sites. This task was made easier by the very disadvantages they were trying to conquer at Inchon.

On 20 August two members of JCS, General Collins and Admiral Sherman, came to Tokyo. Ostensibly they came to discuss MacArthur's plans but in reality they were there to dissuade him. The general realized that their conference, scheduled for 23 August, would be vital and that his most important job would be to convince Sherman, the highly respected Chief of Naval Operations, that Chromite was feasible.

After the introductions, the conferees heard nine officers from Phib-I give presentations on various technical details, summed up after 80 minutes by Doyle, 'Inchon is not impossible.' Then MacArthur took the stage, exerting every ounce of his reason, courage and histrionic ability to swing the chiefs. He pointed out that most of the top NKPA forces were concentrated around the Pusan Perimeter, and demonstrated the ineffectiveness of a short envelopment from Kunsan. He recalled Wolfe's surprise landing at Quebec in 1759 and countered the Navy's objections to Inchon by insisting that he had more confidence in them than they had in themselves. Finally, after an impressive 30-minute performance, he reached his closing lines, 'I realize,' he admitted, 'that Inchon is a 5000 to one gamble, but I am used to taking such odds . . .' Here he stared impressively into the faces before him and his voice dropped to a near whisper, 'We shall land at Inchon and I shall crush them.' After almost a full minute Sherman broke the silence, 'Thank you. A great voice in a great cause.' Completely won over, the shaken audience filed quietly out of the room.

Of course, once the spell had worn off, not everyone remained convinced of Chromite's viability. Collins complained that he had been 'mesmerized' and Doyle remarked, 'If MacArthur had gone on the stage you would never have heard of John Barrymore.' However, in the absence of any concrete alternative, and in view of MacArthur's obvious determination to carry on with the operation regardless, JCS finally gave him an unenthusiastic go-ahead on 28 August, only 17 days before the operation began.

The planners from 1st Marine Division, headed by Major General O P Smith, had arrived in Tokyo on 22 August and in their preliminary briefings had found that much of their spadework had already been done for them. Now they settled down to work out the details of the landing while the Navy concentrated on finding the ships to transport them. The usual assault vessels (attack transports, cargo ships and landing ship, tanks) could not negotiate Flying Fish Channel at night. The first force would be sent in on high-speed APDs (rebuilt destroyer escorts) and an LSD (Landing Ship Dock).

The Marines' task would be to take Inchon and establish a beachhead, seize Kimpo airport, cross the Han River and take Seoul, and occupy blocking positions to the north, northeast and east of the capital. They would have support from General Harris's 1st Marine Air Wing (temporarily named TAC X Corps), operating first from carriers and then from Kimpo, and from 7th Infantry, who would land behind them and advance along their southern (right) flank. Smith would be in charge of operations during the landing. Thereafter General Almond (MacArthur's Chief of Staff, who had been placed in charge of 'X Corps') would be in command.

Amphibious operations are enormously complex and usually take about six months to plan. The fact that Chromite was completed at all in the time available was an amazing feat. In addition, the Marine team had to work out many details normally handled by regimental commanders. The 5th Marine Regiment was still fighting with the Eighth Army in Pusan (so well that Walker claimed he would not be responsible for holding the front if they were pulled out), and the 1st Marine Regiment had not yet reached Japan. As Smith said later, more time would have allowed them to make the operation more precise but it would not have changed its essential character. As it was, the plans for the Inchon landing eventually came to 185 pounds of Secret and Top Secret documents.

As D-Day approached, the already hectic pace became frantic. There was no time for the usual rehearsals, and certainly none for mistakes. On 2 September, in one of dozens of maneuvers and operations, Navy Lieutenant Eugene Clark landed with a small team on a little island about 11 miles southwest of Inchon. Their mission, which they carried out with the help of friendly villagers (many of whom later paid with their lives for their assistance), was to collect first-hand, current information on the height of the

Landing craft head for the beach
at Inchon, 15 September 1950.

On the map:

US SHIPS AT 0520 HRS, 15 SEPT, 1950
US ATTACKS AT TIMES SHOWN
US POSITIONS, EVENING, 15 SEPTEMBER

MILES 0 — 2
KILOMETERS 0 — 3

© Richard Natkiel, 1981

BEACHHEAD, EVENING, 15 SEPTEMBER
MILES 0 — 10

YONGJONG DO
MANSFIELD
LSMR 403 (P.M.)
DE HAVEN
H.A. BASS
5 Mar Regt
SWENSON
North Pt
0633 hrs
1 Btn
2 Btn   1724 hrs
Red Beach
Cemetary Hill
Brewery
Observatory Hill
3 Btn
Green Beach
WOLMI DO
Causeway
British Consulate Hill
INCHON
Radio Hill
Inner Harbor
SU WOLMI DO
FLYING FISH CHANNEL
Tidal Basin
US 1 Marine Div (part) O P Smith
WON DO
Salt pans
Blue Beach
To Seoul
Pt 117
1 Btn
2 Btn   1800 hrs
3 Btn
1 Mar Regt
To Suwom
Mud flats at low tide
Tok Am
Pt 233

UIJONGBU
Han
US 187 Abn Regt
US 7 Mar Regt
US 5 Mar Regt
Korean Marine Regt
SEOUL
KIMPO AIRFIELD
YONGDUNGPO
US 5 Mar Regt
US 1 Mar Div
YELLOW SEA
ASCOM CITY
INCHON
16 Sept   17 Sept   18 Sept   19 Sept 20 Sept   21 Sept
US 7 Inf Div
US 32 Inf Regt

seawalls, numbers and positions of gun emplacements, and a host of other vital details. On 10 September Clark reconnoitered a lighthouse on the tiny island of Palmi Do, five miles north of his base, and found to his surprise that it was still in working order. Thus, on the 14th, he and his men were able to make their way to the islands and help guide the landing force to the rendezvous.

On the 3rd, as if fate was determined to make everything as difficult as possible, Typhoon Jane struck, with 100-knot winds and 40-foot waves. The resulting damage took 24 hours to repair. At the same time the Marines from the West Coast were being transshipped to their transports and LSTs; they would take part in the second, evening attack. The process was complicated by the need to transfer every Marine under the age of 18 (some 500 men) to non-

combatant status, to conform with a last-minute Navy decision.

On the evening of 5 September the men of 1st and 5th Battalions, 5th Marines were fighting in the pouring rain to hold down a section of the line at the perimeter. At the stroke of midnight they were silently replaced by infantrymen, marched four miles to the rear, and trucked back over the muddy roads to Pusan. They only knew they were being shipped out to fight another battle — but most had no idea what kind or where it would be.

That same day MacArthur received a request from Washington for details of his plan, which he had been consistently refusing to discuss with JCS. True to form, on this occasion he replied simply that his plans were unchanged. The Chiefs, understandably anxious for more

Arthur would be the first US commander of a unified force to take the field tactically. Doyle was not happy about participating in this historic occasion. Space was at a premium on his flagship and he did not have enough room for even one general – much less the crowd accompanying MacArthur. Doyle, MacArthur and Smith were the only ones with cabins to themselves. From there down, generals doubled up, you had to be a captain or a colonel to get a bunk, and no one with less than two stripes could even commandeer a cot. The flagship sailed out into the teeth of Typhoon Kezia. MacArthur was seasick during the storm, but by dinnertime he had recovered his form and during the meal delivered a long monologue – which some found 'illuminating' and others 'pompous.'

For some time, while the assault force ships had been performing the intricate maneuvers designed to get them all to the right places at the right times without getting in each other's way, softening-up operations had been going on at Inchon. Between the 5th and the 10th air operations had been stepped up on both coasts of the peninsula (to keep the North Koreans guessing), and British warships had begun shelling Inchon from the sea on the 7th. On Wednesday 7 September two American and two British cruisers entered the harbor along with a number of destroyers. As they had hoped, the defenders on Wolmi Do opened fire, exposing their positions; the ships began their own bombardment while from four carriers over the horizon a swarm of heavily armed ADs (single-engine

information, demanded an estimate as to Chromite's 'feasibility and chance of success.' This message, which he received on 7 September, chilled MacArthur to the core. Defiantly – and still without revealing any concrete details – he shot back a reply: 'There is no question in my mind as to the feasibility of the operation and I regard its chance of success as excellent.' The Chiefs knew when they were beaten; there was nothing left but to send a last, grudging cable, 'We approve your plan and the President has been so informed.'

On 10 September meteorologists spotted Typhoon Kezia, heading straight for Japan. They estimated that the storm would hit Kobe on the 12th. That was the day the assault force was due to sail, and there was no way Admiral Doyle could get them out a day early. Somehow he managed and his flagship, *Mt McKinley*, left the harbor at 1030 on the 11th.

The same day MacArthur flew in his official plane, *Scap*, from Tokyo to Kyushu. Behind him, in *Bataan*, came the press. The care and feeding of 86 news correspondents from the United States, Britain, France, Scandinavia and Taiwan was an important part of the operation. Press arrangements had been made on a mammoth scale, and there was practically one Public Information Officer available for every two reporters.

On the 12th, MacArthur and his entourage (five more generals, their aides, and several of his favorite correspondents) rendezvoused with Doyle at Kyushu. Mac-

Left: The day after the landings: the view across the harbor at Inchon.

Far left above: The scaling ladders are ready for the assault of the Inchon sea wall.

Far left center: Marines scale the walls at Inchon in what was one of the fastest amphibious operations ever.

Far left below: MacArthur goes ashore at Inchon on 16 September.

Below: A wounded Marine is evacuated from Seoul on 28 September 1950.

Bottom: An American jeep convoy stops by knocked out North Korean tanks during the advance from Inchon on 21 September 1950.

Douglas Skyraiders) blasted every position they could spot. By the night of 14 September, as 261 ships from seven nations prepared to negotiate Flying Fish channel, Wolmi Do was a pile of rubble or, as one Marine pilot reported, 'one worthless piece of real estate.'

The first 18 ships rendezvoused at the entrance to the channel just after midnight. First in line were three destroyers, followed by the advance assault group carrying 5th Marines (*Diachenko, Wantuck, H A Bass,* and *Fort Marion*). They were followed by three more destroyers, *Mt McKinley* with her load of top brass, and finally the four British and American cruisers. About two hours later, as they passed Palmi Do, a light flashed out; above them Lieutenant Clark, wrapped in a blanket, sat watching the ships slip by. His secret had been so well kept that neither MacArthur nor General Smith had even known of his role in the operation. Both assumed the light had been left burning by the North Koreans, by mistake.

As the ships picked their way through the darkness, MacArthur paced the deck, unable to sleep. He had faced many amphibious landings in his time, but never one like this, at such short notice and under such abnormal conditions. If anything happened to upset the all-important coordination and split-second timing the operation would fail – and he would certainly be held solely responsible. The light from Palmi Do seemed to be a good omen and finally, at about 0230, he managed to fall asleep.

When *Mt McKinley* dropped anchor at 0508 hours, Corsairs from five carriers were already blasting Wolmi Do. At 0520 hours the deliberate, traditional landing procedure began. Captain Sears of the Green Beach control vessel, *Fort Marion*, signalled to Doyle that all was ready, and the Admiral sent the old signal up the yardarm of the flagship, 'Land the Landing Party.' The Marines immediately began embarking, filing past the chaplain one by one to receive his blessings as the landing craft slipped into the water and the first streaks of dawn began to brighten the eastern sky. At 0540 hours the ships began their bombardment. First the destroyers, a few seconds later the cruisers, and finally a number of rocket ships began shelling the island.

While the terrific bombardment was going on, the men of G and H Companies of the 3rd Battalion, 5th Marines circled in their LCVPs, less than a mile off Wolmi Do. The 5th Regiment of 1st Marine Division was traditionally considered the elite unit of the corps. It had seen action in France, Nicaragua, Guadalcanal, Okinawa and the Pusan Perimeter. Even these tough, experienced veterans had a hollow feeling in their stomachs as they anxiously watched the red and white flag fluttering on *Fort Marion*'s yardarm. The flag was flying 'at the dip'. At 0615 hours it rose and the small ships got into line, then it was let down and the coxswains steered at top speed for Green Beach — a rocky, 200-yard strip on the northwest shore of the island. Almost all fire from the ships stopped, and at 0628 hours, through the sudden silence, roared 38 Corsairs, making one final run. Finally, at 0633 hours, the first ships hit the beach, bow ramps went down, and the green-clad, crouching men burst out with a shout.

As they waded in the Corsairs laid down a protective curtain of machine-gun fire 50 yards ahead of them. Once on the beach, they immediately turned toward their first objectives, which had been drummed into them all the way up the Yellow Sea from Pusan. G Company pivoted sharply to the right and up the northern slope of 351-foot Radio Hill, while two platoons moved along the western shore to seal off the causeway leading to So Wolmi Do (Little Wolmi Do). H Company, meanwhile, marched straight ahead to the opposite shore to secure the base of the causeway leading to the mainland. At 0646 hours the reserves (I Company) hit the beach with 10 tanks of the 1st Tank Battalion, and moved out to mop up North Point.

At 0650 hours 3rd Battalion's commander, Colonel Robert Taplett, landed. Within five minutes an American flag was flying on the summit of Radio Hill. By 0800 hours scattered resistance at North Point and in the industrial complex on the southern end of the island had been mopped up. The only area not cleared was So Wolmi Do, where the

NKPA was still putting up a stubborn defense.

MacArthur, who had been awakened by the noise of the bombardment, had been watching the operation from the bow of *Mt McKinley*. He was sitting in the Admiral's chair, wearing his old Bataan cap and a leather jacket, peering through binoculars and paying no attention to his staff as they jockeyed for position with the horde of press photographers. One of his first questions was about casualties. When he was told that about 12 Marines had been killed and perhaps 15–20 wounded, he remarked, 'More people than that get killed in traffic every day.' Then he turned to Doyle with the remark which was, if a bit pompous, still music to the ears of the men whose service had been threatened with extinction only a few short months before, 'Say to the Fleet, the Navy and the Marines have never shone more brightly than this morning.' With a broad grin, he invited his colleagues to join him for coffee. As it was being served he dispatched a jubilant message to JCS. He had been vindicated. His self-confidence increased still further when he heard that the landing force had found the beginnings of intensive fortifications being built on the island. If the attack had been delayed until October he would have been attacking a well-armed fortress. As it was, without the heavy preliminary bombardment his men could easily have been pinned down on Green Beach, just as the landing parties were at Anzio.

At 1115 hours So Wolmi Do was finally subdued. The defenders had been able to prevent anyone crossing the causeway from the larger island, but had been wiped out from the air by eight Corsairs armed with 20mm cannons

As they approached to within 1000 yards of Red Beach on the mainland, Shepherd reminded the general that the area had not yet been taken – and that he made a tempting target. At that Struble turned the boat around and the party returned to the command ship for lunch.

The North Koreans had shared the American planners' opinion of Inchon as a landing spot for a major amphibious assault, and now all the commander of the meager forces there could do was wait for the inevitable. In Seoul, the news of the invasion threw the 16,000-man NKPA garrison (many of whom were administrators or political types) into a state of panic. Reinforcements were hurredly called up and 'volunteers' collected from among the 2,000,000 civilian inhabitants.

The trickiest part of the operation – simultaneous twilight landings on two mainland 'beaches' – was still to come. At around noon the transports carrying the Red Beach assault force, 1st and 2nd Battalions of 5th Marines, arrived in the harbor while relays of Navy Skyraiders and Marine Corsairs bombed everything within 25 miles of the port and the ships began their preliminary bombardment. At 1430 hours the ships started the final bombardment which was to last three hours. Fifteen minutes later, Doyle again sent up the traditional signal and the Marines began filing into their landing craft.

At 1704 hours it began to rain. The first assault group was about a mile offshore, and all eyes were fixed on the flag waving above *H A Bass*, the Red Beach control vessel. At 1722 hours it went up; two minutes later it was down and the first wave was speeding toward the beach, disappearing

and napalm. As the tide receded the Marines solidified their positions while the 17 wounded men were transported back to the ships across a specially made pier. No Americans had, in fact, been killed; they had taken 136 prisoners and found 108 enemy bodies. It was assumed that another 150 lay buried in the shattered gun emplacements.

Admiral Struble invited MacArthur to come for a ride in his barge, to take a closer look at the beaches. The offer was accepted eagerly, and SCAP, along with Generals Shepherd, Almond, Whitney, Wright and Fox – and a crowd of newsmen – climbed aboard. As the boat stood off Green Beach, MacArthur struck a Napoleonic pose in the bow.

Top: Members of the 1st Marine Division mop up Communist positions on 18 September 1950.

Below: Navy Corpsmen evacuate a wounded man out of a helicopter to hospital.

into a thick cloud of smoke from the burning city. As in the morning, the naval fire stopped when the lead boats reached the halfway point, and the planes moved in. The covering fire from Wolmi Do, however, continued. Their position was such that they could keep on firing until the last minute without endangering their own men.

Behind the dense smoke screen the first boats crunched into the seawall; men scrambled up shaky, improvised scaling ladders and tumbled over, just as infantrymen had gone 'over the top' in World War I. Unexpectedly, there was one woman landing on Red Beach as well – Marguerite Higgins, correspondent for the *New York Herald Tribune*, the first woman reporter to advance with front-line troops since Martha Gellhorn covered the Spanish Civil War. At 1733 hours a Marine pilot flashed word back to *Mt McKinley*, 'Scaling ladders are in place and Marines are over the wall.'

On the left, Company A soon captured Cemetery Hill bypassing, for the time being, another vital objective – the gigantic Asaki Brewery. (1st Battalion had been promised an equally gigantic bender if the brewery and its contents were captured intact). By 1845 hours Company E, on the right, had easily taken British Consulate Hill and the lower slopes of Observatory Hill, while in the rear the rest of the 2nd Battalion had control of the area around the Nippon Flour Mill, at the foot of the Wolmi Do causeway.

At this point the Marines had a most unwelcome opportunity to gain first-hand experience of their own Navy's shooting ability. A number of LSTs were scheduled to land at 1830 – within an hour of the initial landing – and unload their supplies (including heavy equipment, fuel, ammunition and napalm) while the Marines secured the beachhead. This would have been a dangerous maneuver at the best of times, especially since the LSTs were expected to pull up side by side on the narrow beach like cars in a parking lot, in rapidly failing light. At Inchon, with rusty,

decrepit, unmaneuverable hulks (all the Navy could produce) manned by inexperienced officers and crews, it was daring. Accompanying the cargo vessels were eight other LSTs, whose job was to distract enemy fire. As they lumbered in, guns blazing, the NKPA fired back, exposing their position. The trigger-happy LSTs, carried away by the battle, returned the fire, and the Marines on the beach were caught in a murderous crossfire while 2nd Platoon, preferring enemy machine guns to the Navy's high-intensity fire, was blasted off Cemetery Hill.

Red Beach finally became quiet at 1900 hours. One Marine had been killed and 23 wounded by US bullets – more casualties than the battalion suffered at the hands of the North Koreans. Despite some confusion on its southern slope Observatory Hill had been cleared and defensive positions had been consolidated before midnight. The port of Inchon was in American hands. Only one objective had not been taken. The brewery caught fire that night and burned to the ground before the very eyes of the thirsty Marines.

While the 5th Marines were fighting at Red Beach for Inchon proper, the 1st Marines were landing on Blue Beach, four miles to the southeast, on the other side of the port. This regiment too had a long and valiant history, from the Boxer Rebellion through Okinawa. It had been disbanded, then hastily pulled together again in only 10 days and rushed to Japan from San Diego. Most of the men were World War II veterans, led by a fearless old warhorse, Colonel Lewis B 'Chesty' Puller – an iron-disciplined, archetypal Marine. Some said that a kind heart beat beneath his crusty exterior, but few among the staff officers, support units or lazier members of his squad, whom he terrorized

Marine tanks oversee operations as Communist troops are marched to a stockade, 26 September 1950.

ruthlessly, would ever believe it.

The approach to Blue Beach (actually, Blue Beaches 1 and 2) had to be made over two-and-one-half miles of mud flats, which have (according to Robert Heinl in *Victory at High Tide*) 'the crust and underlying gooey consistency of solidifying chocolate fudge – but the smell is different.' The run took 45 minutes in 172 tiny amphibious tractors (amtracs), and was carried out in an impenetrable fog composed of smoke from burning Inchon, mixed with rain. Going in blind and unrehearsed, with only four guide boats instead of the 32 they should have had, it is little wonder that the landing soon disintegrated into utter chaos. Amtracs milled around helplessly, landing on the wrong beaches, searching for their commanders, cursing each other, the Navy and life in general. Despite the confusion, the first three assault groups, which had landed on time, managed to secure the beachhead by themselves and by 0130 on 16 September, Puller was able to report that the beach was taken.

The commanders on *Mt McKinley* went to bed happy. Despite the inevitable confusion and disorganization, Doyle had put 13,000 Marines, with their weapons and heavy equipment, ashore on an 'impossible' coast. Both regiments had achieved their objectives on schedule at a cost of only 21 dead, one missing and 174 wounded. Before he turned in, General Smith noted in his journal, 'D-Day has gone about as planned.'

At daybreak on the 16th the Marines moved inland behind their tanks, leaving a detachment of Korean Marines to mop up the town of Inchon. 1st and 5th Marines were due to link up at the '0–3' line, where the Inchon peninsula narrows to a bottleneck. By evening the beach-head had been secured. The 5th Marines held the forward line overlooking Ascom City (a former US supply depot) and Puller, who had had to secure his southern flank, was about

a mile behind. At 1800 hours General Smith took his leave of MacArthur, who told him, 'Be sure to take good care of yourself and capture Kimpo as soon as you can.' Twenty-four hours from the beginning of the operation he took command of land operations, establishing his headquarters on Yellow Beach (Blue Beach 2).

MacArthur was up early the next morning. He set out for shore with his fellow generals and a gang of reporters. As Smith was greeting him the tension that had been building up during the previous weeks broke and, quickly excusing himself, MacArthur doubled over and threw up. A moment later he was himself again, inspecting enemy corpses and listening to Smith's briefing. The group set out toward the front line to find Colonel Puller. Suddenly, to Smith's dismay, MacArthur headed off to see some T-34s that the 5th Marines had just 'killed'. As he approached, a young lieutenant dashed up and tried to stop him. 'General, you can't come up here!' he panted, 'We've just knocked out six Red tanks over the top of this hill!' 'That was the proper thing to do,' MacArthur calmly replied, and continued his climb to the top of the hill. There he surveyed the smoking hulks, disdainfully ignoring the rattle of small arms fire around him. Then, having made his point, he descended and agreed to let Smith take him back. That evening he was able to send another triumphant cable to Washington. Kimpo airfield had been captured.

While the 1st and 5th Marines moved on toward the Han – the next formidable obstacle – Smith continued to work in Inchon, to get the harbor functioning again. There was much to be done. Hospitals had to be established for the wounded and burials arranged for the dead. Supplies were unloaded while the engineers repaired track and got the

The UN forces undertook another amphibious operation on 26 October 1950 against Wanson.

trains running. The civilian population had to be cared for; food distributed, housing found for the homeless, the sanitation system repaired. By the 19th Smith was able to reestablish civilian government in the city and move his headquarters up to Kimpo.

On Wednesday, 20 September, MacArthur came ashore for another tour of the command posts, reaching the front lines in time to watch the 5th Marines cross the Han after two abortive attempts. After a congratulatory word with their commander, Lieutenant Colonel Raymond Murray, and a visit to General Barr (commanding the 7th Infantry on the right flank, near Yongdongpo), he returned to *Mt McKinley*. He was getting anxious about General Walker and the Eighth Army, who were not surging northward according to plan. Instead, they were advancing at a painfully slow rate, against stiff resistance, and he began thinking about setting up another landing, at Kunsan. The North Koreans were bringing up reinforcements at Seoul as well, and it was starting to look as if the capital would become another Leningrad.

The next day General Almond went ashore and assumed command of the X Corps. He would have a difficult time during the next six days. The NKPA commander, General Wol, knew he had no hope of dislodging the American forces – but he could and did use his men wisely to fight a strong delaying action. Although his dual position was not unprecedented, Almond occasionally found himself torn between his responsibilities as corps commander and his duty to MacArthur as the latter's Chief of Staff. His troubles were not eased by the traditional antipathy that existed between the army and Marines, which made his relationship with Smith uneasy and often acrimonious.

By Saturday the 23rd, however, MacArthur decided that Seoul was within reach and ordered his entourage to pack for the return trip to Tokyo. The next morning he received an invitation from Admiral Struble to visit the *Missouri*. The general accepted gladly and as he stood on the quarterdeck for the first time since he had accepted the Japanese surrender there in 1945, his eyes filled with tears. Turning to Struble, he said feelingly, 'You have given me the happiest moment of my life.'

That afternoon MacArthur and his aides boarded *Scap* at Kimpo, the general's mind filled with memories of his triumph at Tokyo Bay and his vindication at Inchon harbor, along with prospects of an early victory in Seoul. As soon as the plane had taken off he leaned back, took a contented puff on his pipe, and asked for a briefing.

Events moved quickly during the next week. On Monday 25 September Puller and his Marines finally took Yongdungpo. On Tuesday the Eighth Army, who had finally broken out of their encirclement and raced north, made the first, tentative contact with the Seoul attackers. By Wednesday the NKPA was on the run and on Thursday Seoul officially fell to the X Corps. On Friday, 29 September, MacArthur, this time accompanied by his wife, landed again at Kimpo and drove into the city. At an impressive ceremony in what was left of the Capitol Building, he handed the reins of government back to Syngman Rhee. Operation Chromite had officially ended. MacArthur's 71,300 troops had defeated 30–40,000 North Koreans at a cost of just 536 dead, 2550 wounded and 65 missing in action.

In the short term, the victory at Inchon bred further triumphs. By 1 October, only 15 days after the landing, the NKPA had fled in disarray across the 38th Parallel. MacArthur's northward sweep to the Yalu River (ordered by Washington based on his opinion that the Chinese would not enter the war) soon had all of North Korea under UN control; on 28 October the general confidently predicted that American boys would be home by Christmas.

In fact, of course, it was only the beginning. A month

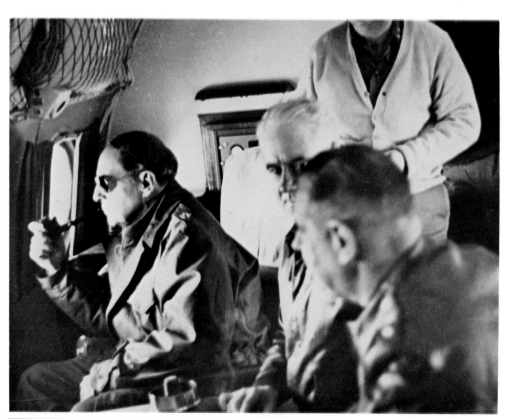

Left: MacArthur inspects territories along the Yalu River in Korea, 24 November 1950.

Right: In 1957 MacArthur's statue was unveiled at Inchon: a fitting tribute to a victor.

Right top: After bitter fighting at Chosin Reservoir, Marines of the 7th Regiment leave the shores of Hungnam.

the action he was truly invincible. As Ridgway put it, if he had suggested, 'that one battalion walk on water, there might have been someone ready to give it a try.'

The old soldier was already beginning to fade away. Not in large things (in his misreading of the Chinese reaction he was, for the most part, misled by faulty intelligence), but in smaller matters. For example, he would not take the elementary precaution of issuing winter clothing to the troops in the fall of 1950, just in case the campaign took a bit longer than he expected. More importantly, the success – as usual – went to his head, and he lost all perspective on his situation. An army man of the old school, he was unable at his age to make the switch from the concept of total victory to that of limited war. He began ignoring direct orders from JCS. When his insubordination extended to the President, his Commander in Chief, the situation became intolerable and he was recalled, to end his days as a private citizen.

No one man can ever be credited with the success or failure of a military operation. In the case of Inchon, the Herculean efforts of the men who devised the 'impossible' plan and the professionalism of the troops – especially the Marines – who executed it were ultimately responsible for the victory.

In this case we can give one man credit for the fact that the action took place at all. It is probably safe to say that, although envelopment is a standard tactic in any general's arsenal, only MacArthur had the imagination to conceive this one in the face of such adverse conditions. More important is the fact that, having hit upon the plan, only a man of MacArthur's overwhelming self-confidence and high-handedness could have stuck to his guns so stubbornly and – in effect – forced the entire US military establishment to undertake it against their will. History has not yet passed its verdict on Douglas MacArthur. But at Inchon, where he precluded certain defeat in Korea, he was – in Heinl's words – 'as he would wish to be remembered: bold, judicious, assured and unwavering.'

later, on the day after Thanksgiving, 300,000 Chinese Communists stormed the Yalu, sending the UN forces reeling southward once more. On 4 January 1951 Seoul changed hands again. The bitter conflict would not end in equally bitter compromise until July 1953. This unsatisfactory conclusion is probably one factor that has overshadowed the brilliance of the operation at Inchon.

For MacArthur personally, the success of Chromite had much the same effect. Coming at the age of 70, after more than half a century devoted to his country's military affairs, it was his finest hour. In the weeks immediately following

PICTURE CREDITS

Bildarchiv Preussischer Kulturbesitz
pp 16 (bottom), 18–19, 21 (top),
37, 38–39, 94, 97, 98–99 (main
pic), 99 (top), 100, 124 (bottom),
165, 175, 210 (both), 221
Bison pp 4–5, 44, 168 (both), 169
(both), 172 (both), 174 (bottom),
176, 178 (both), 179 (bottom),
182 (both), 183 (both), 186
(both), 190 (bottom), 239
(bottom), 240
Bundesarchiv pp 111 (top), 112
(both), 124 (top), 137, 138–39
(both), 154 (top), 167, 171 (all
three), 173 (all three), 174 (top
two), 179 (top), 180–81, 184
(both), 185, 188, 189, 190 (top),
191 (bottom), 196 (both), 197
(both), 199 (all three), 203
(bottom), 204, 205, 209 (top),
211 (top), 210–11 (center both),
211 (right), 217 (left, center and
bottom), 219 (top), 220 (both),
223 (top), 229 (all three), 226
(both)
Cooper-Bridgeman Library p 35
Mary Evans pp 10, 14 (bottom), 15,
24
Giraudon pp 13 (bottom), 31 (inset)
Robert Hunt Library pp 2–3, 12
(bottom), 13 (top), 21 (bottom),
23, 29, 30–31, 33, 34, 40, 41,
42–43, 49, 50, 51, 52–53, 54,
58–59 (top), 60, 61, 62, 63, 64
(top), 67, 69, 71, 82–83, 87
(both), 88, 89, 90 (both), 91
(both), 92 (top), 95, 96, 101,
105, 106 (bottom), 107 (top),
108 (top), 109 (top), 121, 122
(both), 126 (both), 127, 128
(bottom), 130 (all three), 131
(both), 132 (both), 133, 141,
142 (center and bottom), 143,
144–45 (main pic), 145 (top),
152 (top), 153 (top), 154 (far
left), 155 (top), 156 (both), 157
(top two), 160 (top), 161 (top),
162, 203 (top), 214, 218 (both),
219 (bottom), 225, 239, 247
(all three)
Imperial War Museum pp 1, 123,
128 (both), 149, 150–51 (both),
152 (main pic), 154–55 (main
pic), 157 (both), 159 (all three),
160–61 (main pic), 163, 166,
191 (top), 193, 195, 198, 201,
202, 236 (bottom)
Library of Congress pp 47, 66,
76–77 (main pic), 77 (top), 78,
81, 85
Mansell pp 72, 76 (top), 79
Musée de l'Armée p 12 (top)
National archives pp 57, 58, 64–65
(main pic), 74, 75, 84, 242, 243,
247, 248–49 (main pic), 251
National Army Museum pp 26–27
National Maritime Museum p 22
Novosti pp 107 (bottom), 108
(bottom), 113 (bottom), 119,
234, 236 (top)
Radio Times p 106 (top)
Ullstein pp 36, 92 (bottom), 98
(top), 102, 103, 109 (bottom),
110–111, 114 (both), 115,
116–17, 118 (both), 129, 135,
136 (both), 140 (both), 142 (top),
145 (top), 146, 147, 227 (both),
228, 229, 231, 232, 235
US Army pp 46, 70, 208, 209
(bottom), 212–13, 215, 216,
217 (right), 237, 241, 252, 253
(bottom)
US Marines pp 244–45, 246 (top
and center), 249 (top), 250, 253
(top)
US Navy pp 48, 56, 59 (bottom), 68
Roger Violet pp 3, 20 (top)
Peter Young p 14 (top)

Design: Laurence Bradbury
Captions: Catherine Bradley
Index: Penny Murphy

THE AUTHORS

Peter Young was one of the most
decorated soldiers in World War II,
and became the youngest brigadier
in the British army at the age of 25.
On his retirement from military
service he became head of the War
Studies Department of RMA
Sandhurst. He has written and
edited over 20 books on the subject
of military history.
Introduction

Richard Holmes was educated at
Cambridge, Northern Illinois and
Reading Universities. He is currently
senior lecturer in war studies at
Sandhurst and has written a number
of books on military topics.
Chapters 1 and 2

Ward Rutherford was brought up in
Jersey. He is a professional journalist
who has written over 10 books on
recent history. Among the many
titles he has worked on are *Hitler's
Propaganda Machine* and *Blitzkrieg
1940*
Chapters 6, 7, 8, 9 and 10

Douglas Welsh is one of America's
most highly decorated Veterans of
the Vietnam War. A contributor to
The Russian War Machine and *Great
Battles of the World on Land, Sea and
Air*, he has also written a book on
the American Civil War.
Chapters 3, 4 and 5

Patrick Jennings was born in
Chicago in 1937. Educated in both
the United States and Great Britain,
he is a journalist living in London.
Among his works is *A Pictorial
History of World War II*, a subject in
which he has specialized.
Chapters 11 and 15

Judith Steeh was educated at the
University of Michigan and then
became a journalist. She contributed
to the *Olympiad 1936* and co-
authored the *Directors' Guide to the
USA*. She has also written *The Rise
and Fall of Adolf Hitler*.
Chapters 12, 13, 14 and 16

INDEX